ELECTRIC CITY

Library of Congress Control Number: 2020944922

Paperback ISBN: 978-1-4197-5298-8
eISBN: 978-1-64700-044-8

Printed and bound in the United States
10 9 8 7 6 5 4 3 2 1

Abrams books are available at special discounts when purchased in quantity
for premiums and promotions as well as fundraising or educational use.
Special editions can also be created to specification. For details, contact
specialsales@abramsbooks.com or the address below.

Abrams Press® is a registered trademark of Harry N. Abrams, Inc.

ABRAMS The Art of Books
195 Broadway, New York, NY 10007
abramsbooks.com

ELECTRIC CITY

THE LOST HISTORY OF FORD AND EDISON'S AMERICAN UTOPIA

THOMAS HAGER

ABRAMS PRESS, NEW YORK

For the good friends who introduced me to the Shoals,

Amit Roy and Taylor Pursell

CONTENTS

Introduction   *1*

PART I   *Muscle Shoals*

CHAPTER 1   *Where the River Sings*   11
CHAPTER 2   *The Wonder City at War*   31
CHAPTER 3   *Uncle Henry*   47
CHAPTER 4   *$8 a Second*   65
CHAPTER 5   *Camping with the President*   77
CHAPTER 6   *Politics and Public Relations*   91
CHAPTER 7   *The Twin Wizards*   105
CHAPTER 8   *Roadblock*   121
CHAPTER 9   *President Henry Ford*   131

PART II   *Boomtown*

CHAPTER 10   *Swampland and Whiskey*   143
CHAPTER 11   *A Party of One*   149
CHAPTER 12   *The 75-Mile City*   167
CHAPTER 13   *Gutters of Political Filth*   177
CHAPTER 14   *The Last Meeting*   185
CHAPTER 15   *Scandal*   195

PART III   *TVA*

CHAPTER 16   *The Alabama Ghost*   209
CHAPTER 17   *A New Deal*   219
CHAPTER 18   *"I'm Goin' to Die for the Government"*   229
CHAPTER 19   *Electric Nation*   241
CHAPTER 20   *A Sign in the Sky*   251

Epilogue   267
Source Notes   273
Sources   283
Acknowledgments   289
Index   291

INTRODUCTION

IN DECEMBER 1921, THE richest man in the world and the greatest inventor in the world—the "Twin Wizards," as the press called them, Henry Ford and Thomas Edison—opened the door of Ford's private railcar, emerged onto a rear platform, and announced the future. They were on a side track at an old wooden station in what many Americans would have considered the approximate middle of nowhere: the small town of Florence, Alabama. They were surrounded by thousands of local people, the biggest crowd anyone had seen in the area for years, the area's merchant elite and government officials in their best suits and fedoras jostling shoulder to shoulder with sharecroppers and farm families. The throng murmured expectantly, and reporters from fourteen news-papers and wire services pulled out their notebooks. Ford, looking dapper and full of energy, beamed at the crowd. He was no public speaker—had a high voice and tended to get tongue-tied before any audience larger than a few people—and he did little more than introduce his traveling companions. There were cheers when he introduced Thomas Edison to the crowd. There were cheers when he introduced his wife, Clara, and Edison's wife, Mina, and his

The Twin Wizards: Ford and Edison in Florence, Alabama, 1921

son, Edsel, and Edsel's wife, Eleanor. The crowd would have likely cheered if he had introduced his private chef, who had just finished making them a light lunch.

He didn't need to tell the crowd much more, because they'd been reading about his ideas for weeks in the newspapers. Right here in their town, in this region along the Tennessee River, Ford and Edison were going to create jobs, bring in money, and build a new city unlike anything on earth.

Ford had given additional details to reporters during the trip down from Detroit. He was planning to build a city ten times the size of Manhattan at a spot next door to Florence called Muscle Shoals. This city of the future was going to combine the technological power of a city with the wholesome natural beauty of the country, marrying the best parts of urban and rural life. It was going to be a city without slums or tenements or smoke-spewing factories, no soul-destroying urban rot—a green ribbon city of small centers stretching for seventy-five miles along the river tied together by fast, smooth highways. The whole thing was going to run on clean, renewable energy in the form of electricity generated by the river itself. He was going to build dozens of small factories. He was going to create jobs for a million workers.

All the workers would have the chance to live on a few acres of land, in touch with nature and farming, growing much of their own food. Using modern machinery, there was no reason they couldn't get the necessary farmwork done in two or three months, he told the reporters. The rest of the time, they would switch to blue-collar jobs in small, electrically powered factories, earning cash wages they could spend on cars, farm equipment, radios, labor-saving devices, and their kids' educations.

And there was more. This new city—reporters were already calling it the "Detroit of the South"—would be built and financed in a new way that would help break the stranglehold that bankers and Wall Street fat cats had over America, and return economic power to people who actually worked for a living. The way Ford and Edison described it, the whole thing would be paid for with a new kind of currency they called "energy dollars." It wouldn't cost the American taxpayers a nickel. It was going to be an American utopia that would attract workers from all over the nation, stimulate the southern economy, and spur a new national prosperity. It would help feed the world. It would even, Ford said, help put an end to war.

Behind his brief speech was a deep drive to bring the benefits of new technology to one of the poorest, least-developed parts of the nation. The new city was going to be the summation of everything the Twin Wizards believed: Ford's passion for machines and efficiency and Edison's single-minded dedication to improving lives through new technology. This would bring their careers to a resounding finale. The great electric city was going to be their masterpiece.

The crowd cheered wildly.

THIS IS THE story of the rise and fall of the great electric city, how it became one of the biggest news events of the Roaring Twenties, was the cause of 138 bills and a decade of attention in Congress, spurred an investment frenzy bigger than anything since the Klondike Gold Rush, changed the direction of urban planning around the world, and helped fuel a movement that came close to electing Henry Ford president of the United States.

It also tells how, after years of feverish effort, the whole thing came crashing down. One man, Senator George Norris—a name little known today but vitally important in American history—was responsible for opposing and derailing Ford's plans, and this is his story, too. Finally, it describes what emerged from the ashes of Ford's idea for an American utopia. The area around Florence, Alabama, is today green and prosperous, its economic status vastly improved, its way of life transformed. The book describes how that happened.

This is a story that highlights American optimism and innovation, a peculiarly American eagerness to try new things, create new systems, experiment with new ways of doing business, and adopt new ways of living. Along the way, it includes stories of some vivid and little-known historical characters—an array of dreamers, hucksters, politicians, and business titans—who wrestled for control over the future of a kingdom-size chunk of the American South. Their battles over the river were forerunners of many of the issues that consume us today: achieving the proper balance between ambition and altruism, industry and environment, modern life and traditional ways.

Most of the action takes place in the 1920s, a pivotal time when, thanks to helping win World War I, the United States was taking a new role in the world, changing from a primarily rural, agrarian nation—the beloved, mythical American democracy of independent, free-thinking farmers, Jefferson's America—to an increasingly urbanized, industrial, global powerhouse of factory workers, mass immigration, corporate trusts, and big money.

Ford and Edison wanted to gift the nation they loved with a titanic, living example of how they thought America should work. They were going to take the best parts of the past—the independent and freeliving individualism of the early farmers, idyllic living close to nature—and revive them with the benefits that future technology could offer—cleaner industries, faster transportation, and labor-saving devices. The results would be new kinds of cities, new ways of making things, new approaches to labor and leisure, and improved lives for everyone.

Their proposals set off a firestorm of reaction on Wall Street and in Congress, igniting controversies we're still dealing with today. Now, as then, much of America's political dialogue can be boiled down to what seems like a simple question: Should our decisions be directed by private businesses to boost the economy, or by government officials for the public good? The simple answer we keep coming up with is: both. That leads to endless pushing and pulling over priorities, old arguments over which should come first, business interests or The People, broadly defined. You can see it played out in every public issue, every election cycle. The tension between these two poles is a good thing, too. The arguments over who knows best what's good for the nation help propel and energize our brash, rough history as a nation; the rhythm of political discourse is in many ways the beating heart of America. All this was highlighted in new ways by the Ford-Edison attempt to build their shining new city in Alabama.

UNLESS YOU LIVE around the Shoals, you've probably never heard of this story. I never had until I visited the area some years ago to deliver a speech to a fertilizer research group. (I wrote a book about fertilizer and how it changed the history of the world, and got invitations to speak about it.) I didn't know what to expect when I visited. I was raised in Oregon, and my fuzzy vision of the American South was pretty much based on reading Civil War histories and hearing about George Wallace and the battle for civil rights. The only thing I knew about the Tennessee River region specifically was rooted in reading James Agee's *Let Us Now Praise Famous Men*, with its dramatic descriptions of Depression-era shacks, poverty, and hunger. So I didn't have high expectations.

What I found was a series of pleasant surprises. I was put up in a large, elegant, brand-new hotel in a town I'd never heard of—Florence, Alabama—a charming and historic little city perched on bluffs over the Tennessee River. The land around there is green and rolling, with modern highways, tech firms, small factories, and housing developments built over old cotton farms. The town has put money into maintaining a truly outstanding local library next to a park; in that park is a statue honoring not a Southern Civil War hero but a Black native son, the Father of the Blues, W. C. Handy. The people there were uniformly friendly, helpful, and happy to chat.

I did know the name of one place in the area, Muscle Shoals. Those two words are probably familiar to anyone who tracks the history of American music, especially soul, country, and rock. A lot of big stars of the 1960s and 1970s, from Aretha Franklin and Willie Nelson to Bob Dylan and the Rolling Stones, made their way to Muscle Shoals's recording studios to make their hits. Some locals think the music's so good because the Tennessee River creates a kind of melodious magic; an early Native name for the river translated as "Singing River." So I looked at the gold records on the walls and the pictures of Keith Richards eating barbecue at a joint in town, and read some of the historical plaques, and saw a big dam at one end of town and a picturesque old steel railroad bridge at the other. I was surprised how much I liked the area.

When my fertilizer talk was over, I had a little extra time before getting to the airport, and the man driving me suggested side-tripping a mile or two off the highway so he could show me something interesting. He drove me to the remains of an old fertilizer factory. Parts of it had decayed away, parts had been turned to other uses, but the original section still standing was impressive, tall and gaunt against the sky, out of scale with everything else around it. It had clearly once been gigantic. Now it was an Ozymandian ruin from another age. Then he took me a little farther. We drove down an aging stretch of road into what looked like a deserted field of yellowing grass. It wasn't until we were rolling through it that I could see there was something hidden in the grass: a grid of cracked streets, weedy sidewalks, and a few antique-looking fire hydrants. He said that this was all that was left of a town from the 1920s that had been platted and planned, started but never finished, now slowly returning to nature. He said it was going to be called "Ford City." He said it was well-known around there because you could go down and shoot quail from the sidewalk.

When I got home, I started wondering. Giant ruins, a lost city? I felt like I'd stumbled across the remains of some ancient civilization in the fields of Alabama. I started reading more to see what I could find. The first things I found out led to others, and those led to others, until all the facts and stories began to form into something bigger than I'd imagined. I was hooked now, so I booked a plane back to Alabama and spent a week looking at old records and talking with local historians; then a week at the Ford Archives, reviewing thousands of documents; then another week at the National Archives in Washington, DC, poring through congressional and White House records; then months looking at old newspaper and magazine clippings, and reading biographies, histories, technical papers, letters, century-old brochures and advertisements, and anything else I could find.

The result is this book.

Thomas Hager
Eugene, Oregon, 2020

PART I

MUSCLE SHOALS

CHAPTER 1

WHERE THE RIVER SINGS

ON A MAP, the Tennessee River looks like a big crooked grin that starts in the upper right, in the Allegheny Mountains of eastern Tennessee, then flows west and south through the top of Alabama before it curves back north and west, completing the smile about seven hundred miles from where it started, when it flows into the Ohio. It drains an area the size of England.

For uncounted years it was a great wild river, coursing through ancient hills and forests, placidly winding through some stretches, roaring through others, its banks teeming with wildlife. It varied in volume, force, and unpredictability by the season, growing to a torrent with heavy winter rains, dwindling to a trickle in the hot summers. Few American rivers were more beautiful. Today much of it has been tamed, channeled, and dammed into a string of lakes, still beautiful but in a very different way.

Toward the bottom of the smile where the river heads due west before angling back north (this northern twist is odd: Just about all the area's rivers flow more or less south, to the Gulf) the river hits a shelf of hard rock that forces it to go through a series of rapids, whirlpools, and shoals—thirty miles of shallow, dangerous, unpredictable water. That's where the action in this book takes place.

The area attracted Native people for thousands of years because it was a good place to cross the river if you were trading goods or making war—in late summer the water could get low enough that people could jump rock to rock, hardly getting their feet wet—and because it was a good place to harvest freshwater mussels, a mainstay food for local tribes. When the first whites showed up in the seventeenth and eighteenth centuries, they found the area heavily populated by various splinters of the Cherokee nation, with some Creeks farther south. You can still find Native burial mounds. The early white explorers called that stretch of river Mussel Shoals, which morphed over the years into Muscle Shoals.

Well before the Revolutionary War, trappers, hunters, and adventurers like Daniel Boone were trickling over the Alleghenies, blazing trails, fighting Native people, and starting small settlements in what would become Tennessee and Kentucky. They followed Native trading and war-making paths through the forests, tramping them into "traces"—early roads—like the Natchez Trace and Cumberland Trace. Some traveled by water, heading west down the Cumberland and Tennessee Rivers.

In 1779, a well-to-do Virginia adventurer named John Donelson, one of the founders of the city of Nashville, heard there was rich land around the Shoals, and set off to claim it. He and a group of would-be settlers—a few score men, women, and children floating in a ragtag assortment of canoes, flatboats, and rafts—left just before Christmas from Fort Patrick Henry up in the Alleghenies, not far from the headwaters of the Tennessee.

They were in trouble from the start. The weather was cold and wet—so "bogged," as Donelson called it, that one enslaved man froze to death overnight, his hands and feet covered with frost. Not long after that a young hunter took off to shoot dinner and disappeared, and when the flotilla took off, his father stayed behind to search; in a day or two the hunter showed up at their next camp down the river, but his father was lost and never found.

For week after week they battled the river and, occasionally, Native people. The Natives would seem friendly one moment, waving Donelson's party into their villages and offering to share food and shelter, then hostile the next, chasing the flotilla down the river, making hit-and-run ambushes, killing stragglers.

As the weather warmed, insects started coming out. Mosquitoes were fierce. Then disease hit. Some of the party fell ill with what looked like smallpox, furiously contagious and deadly. To keep the disease from infecting the entire group, twenty-eight sick settlers and family members were quarantined, asked to keep a distance behind the main group. The Native people saw what was happening, attacked, and killed or captured all of the doomed, sick band, so close behind that "their cries were distinctly heard by those boats in the rear," Donelson wrote in his journal.

A baby was born along the way. A few weeks later, it was lost in a battle with the Natives.

By March they still hadn't reached the Shoals. They were getting into shallow water, however. At a place on the river sometimes called the Whirl or the Suck, one of their canoes overturned. When the main group stopped to help recover the scattered goods, they were attacked; four settlers were wounded before they could get back into their boats. Then another boat hit a rock and was partially submerged. The family was stranded on a rock in the middle of the river and there was no way to get them off. They were abandoned to the Native people.

It was a grinding, exhausting, seemingly endless disaster. Then they got to the Shoals. "When we approached them they had a dreadful appearance," Donelson wrote. "The water being high made a terrible roaring, which could be heard at some distance, among the driftwood heaped frightfully upon the points of the islands; the current running in every possible direction. Here we did not know how soon we should be dashed to pieces and all our troubles ended at once. Our boats frequently dragged on the bottom and appeared constantly in danger of striking."

But they somehow managed to thread their way through the long series of rapids, rocks, whirlpools, and chutes. When it was over, Donelson wrote, "By the hand of Providence we are now preserved from this danger. . . . I know not the length of this wonderful shoal; it had been represented to me to be 25 or 30 miles: If so, we must have descended very rapidly, as indeed we did, for we passed it in about three hours."

The land they saw when they reached deeper water almost made it worthwhile: It was rich, well watered, and heavily forested, with plenty of game. There were bluffs and hills along the river, which meant if you settled up there, you could get away from the mosquitoes and malaria along the water. It would make fine farmland.

They floated past a large Native village and then kept going, all the way to the end of the Tennessee. Donelson returned to claim several hundreds of thousands of acres around the Shoals, unsuccessfully. Others already had their eyes on the land.

The Donelson family ended up back in Nashville, where his wife took in boarders, including a handsome newly arrived young lawyer named Andrew Jackson.

He ended up eloping with one of Donelson's daughters, Rachel, then settled down to practice law, speculate in land, serve in the militia, run a plantation, and make connections. Jackson was in short order named attorney general, judge, and then senator from the new state of Tennessee.

That was just for starters. His star really ascended during the War of 1812 and the Creek War, when he raised thousands of volunteers and commanded them to victory after victory, helping whip the British at the Battle of New Orleans, then returning to drive the Native people out of the Tennessee Valley. When he was elected president in 1830, he finished the job of clearing the South for white settlers by signing the Indian Removal Act, forcing tens of thousands of Native inhabitants to leave their ancestral lands and move west of the Mississippi. It was the start of the Trail of Tears.

AMONG THE NATIVE people herded hundreds of miles west from the Tennessee River to the Indian Territory in what is today Oklahoma was a girl identified in the records only as "Alabama Female, 18 years old, Number 59"—the number on a tag she was forced to wear. The government didn't bother to record her actual name, Te-lah-nay. She walked the whole way. And once she got there, she found she could not bear the flat, hot, windswept plains where she was now told she had to live.

She dreamed of the river where she'd spent her childhood, the murmur of the water, the chuckling and rushing sound it made through the shallows, the cries of waterfowl, the sound of wings. It was Te-lah-nay's tribe, the Yuchi, that had named it "Singing River." None of the streams in Oklahoma sang to her.

So she started walking home. It took her years to make the journey, a young woman walking hundreds of miles alone, eastward, toward her river. There are no records of what she experienced.

When she finally made it, her tribe was gone and things had changed. She settled with a local white man and raised a family. Many of her descendants stayed in the area; one of her great-great-grandsons, Tom Hendrix, was raised in Florence close to Muscle Shoals. He grew up hearing family stories about the Trail of Tears. And something about those stories would not leave him alone. He felt he had to do something to memorialize his

15

great-great-grandmother's courage. But it wasn't until he was close to fifty years old that he figured out what it was.

A member of the old tribe came to visit once from Oklahoma, and the conversation turned to honoring the past. As Hendrix remembered it, the visitor told him, "We shall all pass this earth. Only the stones will remain. Honor your grandmother with stones." She told him to build two walls made of stones laid on top of each other without mortar, one stone for each step his great-great-grandmother took on her journey. Two walls like that, one for each direction she traveled.

That idea stayed with him, too. And in the mid-1980s, Hendrix found himself driving his truck to the banks of the Tennessee River, where he started looking for flat rocks. He found one, picked it up, carried it to his truck, and went back for another. He filled his truck, and the next day came back and filled it again. Months went by, and then years, with Hendrix choosing rocks and driving load after load back to some land he owned up in the forest, unloading the truck and placing them, one for each step. First one wall, then another.

Thirty years later, in 2016, he told a reporter, "I've wore out three trucks, 22 wheelbarrows, 2,700 pairs of gloves, three dogs, and one 87-year-old man." He figured that by then he'd hauled around 27 million pounds of stones and built 1.25 miles of walls. Those walls are still there, snaking through the trees, parts as high as six feet. Some people say it's the largest un-mortared rock wall in the United States. It is also the largest memorial ever built to a Native American woman.

ONCE ANDREW JACKSON cleared the land of Native people, he started speculating. He bought a good chunk around the Shoals for himself, and made a play to take control of two million acres more. (The ins and outs of this sometimes-shady dealing can be found in Steve Inskeep's book *Jacksonland*.) There was a scandal and much of the deal fell through, but when the dust settled, he still ended up with 45,000 acres for himself, his family members, and his business associates.

And the Muscle Shoals area began to develop. The river ran east–west here at the bottom of the smile, and a company founded in part by one of Jackson's top military officers, John Coffee, set up a town on the north side. The surveyor was Italian, and he thought it should be named Florence, after the beautiful city on a river in Italy. Everybody made money when the building lots were sold. Jackson himself owned several of them. That was around 1820.

All sorts of farmers, foresters, merchants, and craftsmen began to settle in the newly opened region. But in the early days just one product drove most of the economy: cotton. There were big plantations in the area around the Shoals. There was big money in cotton, but it took a certain kind of farming to make it. It was labor-intensive, for one thing, so slavery, with all its horrors, became the norm. Cotton also soaked up the nutrients in the soil, which had to be replaced to keep production high. Without significant regular applications of fertilizer, the fields played out quickly, yielding less and less profit every year.

Despite it all, cotton was the king of cash crops in the South. The Shoals area in northern Alabama was part of that, but at the same time different from the big plantation areas that dominated farther south. Up north the cotton-growing operations tended to be smaller, with fewer slaves, and were part of a more diverse economy, mixed with independent small farmers, traders, entrepreneurs, and small industrialists. They had more ties with northern businesses, too.

They tended to be independent-minded. When talk turned toward secession in the 1850s and 1860s, many of the folks along the Tennessee (some historians say most of them) wanted to stay in the Union. North and east of the Shoals especially, up in the hills where the Tennessee River comes out of the Alleghenies, the land and climate were not so good for cotton. The hill folk there tended not to own slaves, and they took care of themselves, and they didn't think much of the cotton-growing aristocracy farther south. They didn't want to go off to a war where poor folks were going to die so that rich folks could rule big plantations like they were feudal lords.

There was talk about carving their own pro-Union state out of parts of northern Alabama and southern Tennessee; they were going to call it Nickajack (from an old Cherokee village name). But in the end it didn't come to anything. When war broke out, the Shoals area became part of the Confederacy.

It was going to be a tragedy no matter which side they joined. The Shoals was a strategic necessity. Large gunships going up or down the Tennessee couldn't get past the shallows, and neither could most shipping. It was a place where railroads crossed the river—the major lines through the Shoals-area towns of Florence on the north side and Sheffield on the south ran all the way from New Orleans up to Chattanooga and Knoxville—which meant that armies could cross the river. The Tennessee was a lifeline for the Confederacy, and the Shoals controlled much of the river.

So blue and gray armies started fighting over it. A couple of young Union generals, Ulysses S. Grant and William Tecumseh Sherman, first proved their abilities by fighting their way up the Tennessee. The Shoals changed hands forty times during the war. Armies and raiding parties blazed in and got forced out, eating the crops, killing the stock, burning the mills, destroying the bridges, ripping up the rail lines, and occupying the towns. The valley became one long killing field; the Battle of Shiloh, about sixty miles away, left 23,000 men dead, a slaughter so massive that when it was over one paper said the South would never smile again.

When the war was finally over, the towns near the Shoals were shattered. It took a half century to recover.

A crushing wave of poverty hit after the war. Everything broken and burned had to be rebuilt, but there was no money to do it with. The cotton plantations were gone; new businesses hadn't been started yet to take their place. The residents in the Shoals area—most of them lived in what they started calling the "Tri-Cities" of Florence on the north side of the river and Sheffield and nearby Tuscumbia on the south—pulled together, investing what they could in their communities, rebuilding infrastructure, forming civic groups, and working to attract new industries.

If any one man typified this moment, with its desire to raise a new, prosperous South out of the ashes of the War of Secession, it was John W. Worthington. He was born in a small town in Alabama in 1856, a few years before his father was killed at Petersburg. His mother passed a few years later, leaving him and his four siblings in the care of a great-uncle. Worthington came of age in the 1870s penniless, watching his brothers and sisters flirt with starvation, struggling to support them by taking any job he could.

Luckily, he had a few things going for him: He was smart, he liked to talk to people, and he was persuasive, the usual recipe for a successful salesperson. But he was more ambitious than that. He realized that the future of the South was going to depend on building a new economy, and that this new economy had to be based on something other than cotton. The South was going to have to diversify and industrialize. Worthington worked his way through the University of Alabama and got a degree as a civil engineer, a builder of transportation and power systems. It was a profession where he could make a good income while building things to make life better for everybody. A picture from the time shows a handsome young man with short, dark hair, a long face, and a steady, penetrating gaze.

One thing Alabama had was a lot of coal and iron ore, and Worthington helped put the two together to make the iron and steel needed for the nation's fast-growing railroads. One company he worked for was backed by a New York banking family who believed that the ruined South was on the upswing, ready to take off, a great place for investment. The rich northerners needed somebody local to scout for opportunities, and Worthington became their eyes and ears.

Now that he had access to New York money, his career took off. He was eager and educated, had Alabama roots so he could talk to the folks there, but he also knew how to sweet-talk Yankees into deals. By the early 1890s he was living in Sheffield, which was trying to turn itself into a center for making iron and had hopes of greatness. When Worthington arrived in town, one associate recalled, "As the old saying goes, he hit the ground running." He was soon convincing his backers to buy up some companies and start others. He had his fingers in everything from banking and hotels to water systems, cast iron, real estate, and construction of a new streetcar system. He knew the importance of getting politicians behind projects, and he began courting them, too. His days and nights were spent in hotel meeting rooms and corporate offices, government agencies and private homes, wining and dining officials and the wealthy, smoothing the way for development.

Out of everything he was dealing with, one particular new industry especially caught his eye. It was the big thing, the new thing, the thing that promised the most significant change in society and the strongest return on investment. It was electricity. The 1880s and 1890s were the decades when Edison's incandescent light bulbs and Edison's generators and Edison's power systems were beginning to reshape American cities. Everybody was crazy for the things electricity promised to do.

The question was how to make it and profit from it. Edison was making a fortune generating his electricity with steam engines, using the power to spin magnets around coils of wire. The steam was

Thomas Edison, 1878
Courtesy Library of Congress

made with coal, which made Edison generators smoky, somewhat costly, and highly dependent on coal companies.

But there were other ways. Those magnets could be made to spin using water power, too, letting falling water turn the wheel of the electrical generator in pretty much the same way people had been using falling water to turn waterwheels for thousands of years—only improved for speed and power. Early experiments on small rivers showed that you could build a dam just a few feet high and get enough falling water to supply electricity for a few houses.

To do more than that, however, would require more water, falling faster and farther. Big electrical generators were being installed alongside the world's biggest waterfalls, like Niagara.

But there simply weren't enough natural waterfalls in the United States to power the nation. What was needed instead were higher, bigger dams.

And J. W. Worthington was one of the first men to realize that one of the world's best places to build one of the world's biggest dams was right in front of him, on the Tennessee River at Muscle Shoals.

But he wasn't the only one.

FRANK WASHBURN WAS about the same age as Worthington and was also educated as a civil engineer, but in all other ways the two men were very different: Worthington born destitute and parentless in the South, Washburn the wealthy son of an Illinois bank president; Worthington educated in small Alabama schools, Washburn a graduate of Cornell; Worthington focused on local politics and small-town business, Washburn building aqueducts in New York, designing stockyards in Chicago, surveying canals in Central America, and consulting on nitrate production in Chile.

Their paths crossed at the Shoals. Some of Washburn's in-laws were from Chattanooga, upriver on the Tennessee, and he started visiting the area in the 1890s. It was pretty country, all right, and he liked the friendly people and the genial climate. But he was the kind of man who looked at a beautiful landscape and saw places to build things. What he saw on the Tennessee River got him thinking. This was a big river that fell fast out of the hills around Chattanooga and all the way down through the Shoals. Lots of water falling fast meant the possibility of electricity. When he walked up in the hills around the Shoals and looked down at the river, he saw dam sites.

After 1900, when he and his wife moved to Nashville, he began studying the river more closely. He measured flow and drop. He examined the rock that created the bluffs on both sides of the river, and the harder rock that lay under the Shoals. He considered possible dam heights. He ran numbers. And once he saw what was possible, he started raising money.

If he was right, you could build big dams upriver from Florence. Really big dams. Dams that could produce electricity to rival Niagara Falls, enough electricity to light up not just the local Tri-Cities, but the whole region, from Birmingham in the south to Nashville in the north. There would be so much electricity they'd have trouble using it all. There would be enough to power new industries, create new jobs. As a side benefit, a big dam at Florence would also create a lake deep enough to drown the rapids and whirlpools of the Shoals, and with proper navigation locks make it easier for boats to get up and down the river.

He started talking up his ideas. And one of the local business-men who listened was Worthington. They spoke the same civil engineering language, they wanted the same sorts of development, and in 1906 they went into business together, forming the Muscle Shoals Hydro-Electric Company, with Frank Washburn, president, and J. W. Worthington, vice president. They announced a proposal to span the Tennessee River by two dams sixty feet high near the town of Florence at the Muscle Shoals. They started attracting investors.

But Washburn didn't stop there. He had another idea for soak-ing up some of the flood of electricity that was coming. One of his many projects involved looking at an odd South American industry that mined nitrogen-containing fertilizer out of the Atacama Desert. A lot of that fertilizer ended up on southern cotton fields.

Washburn knew of a new industrial method to make nitrogen fertilizer, a "cyanamide process" developed recently in Europe. It was promising, but its development had been slowed because it required so much costly electricity. Washburn realized that big dams would solve the problem. If he built a cyanamide factory near his dam, Washburn could turn cheap excess electricity into a profitable agri-cultural commodity.

A year after incorporating the Muscle Shoals Hydro-Electric Company, Washburn founded a new company he called American Cyanamid.

WORTHINGTON BEGAN SPENDING more and more of his time in Washington, DC, to lobby for their plans. Government support was critical: The huge dams they were proposing would cost so much money, they would need tax dollars to help build them. The US government traditionally, at the time, stayed out of such business dealings, but not always. Building the transcontinental railroads was one example of federal help going to private companies; arms-making during wartime was another. This kind of public/private dealing opened the door to graft and the corruption of government officials, but the risks of letting the government mix with private business were considered worth it if national well-being was at stake.

The thing that might interest Congress in the Shoals dam proposal was not electricity but improved river navigation. The federal government controlled navigable rivers to the extent of keeping them open for commerce (as the commerce clause of the Constitution allowed). The chance of greatly improving commerce on the Tennessee with big dams gave Worthington a foot in the door for talking with government officials. In 1907, he managed to get a local representative to introduce legislation to support his scheme. He was turning into a skilled lobbyist.

Then things got complicated. The government might be interested in helping with navigation improvements, but Washburn and Worthington's grand plan—a combination of private power production, public navigation improvements, flood control, and fertilizer production—was something different. The thought of getting the federal government to support a private electrical utility, for instance, was an entirely new idea.

If a town wanted electricity, why should the government get involved? It was pretty much the Wild West in the early days of electrification. In the beginning, electricity was a novelty, a rich person's indulgence, with those who could afford it putting in a small coal-powered electrical generator in their basement or an outbuilding, something just big enough to light up their homes. But after Thomas Edison began making headlines with his revolutionary new incandescent lights around 1880—a sensational advance that gave the public a good reason to think about bringing those dangerous electrical lines into their homes and businesses—there was a rush to electrify entire towns. Edison showed how to do it by building

Light Thrown on a Dark Subject, *Puck*, October 23, 1878
Courtesy Library of Congress

the world's first big electrical generating plant in lower Manhattan, the Pearl Street Station, with six dynamos big enough to provide power to hundreds of customers. As the company that would become known as Edison General Electric began building similar plants in more and more major cities, private companies sprang up to run competition. Soon town councils were able to pick and choose from various offers, looking for the best deals from sales forces trying to sell them on putting in efficient systems with generating plants, poles and wires, and the best rates for customers.

Electricity was a gold mine. Thomas Edison's endless inventions, Nikola Tesla's dazzling demonstrations, and George Westinghouse's long-distance system for transmission had everyone thinking about putting in a few lights and plugs. Everybody wanted it, but it took a lot of money to put an entire system in place. That led to questions about competition and rate-setting and safety and oversight. Local officials wanted to make sure that their people were getting the best possible deal and that rates weren't raised without reason. And while towns and cities were attractive places to electrify, there were questions about getting electricity to small towns and isolated farms, distant places where the costs of stringing wires was high and the number of potential users (and potential profits) were low. Would rural areas simply be ignored?

The growth of the new technology was outstripping regulation. There had never been anything like it: sales of a product (electricity) that had to be made in great quantities, delivered instantly, and used immediately, and was always available at the flip of a switch. There were questions about the costs of the systems, the charges to customers, and the relationships between the providers and the towns they were serving. There had to be new sorts of contracts and guarantees. Industrial behemoths like Edison General Electric were rising, and with them questions about private control of what was increasingly being seen as a public good. It made no sense for several companies to serve a single town, which meant that whoever got in first to set up the system would have what some experts were beginning to think of as a "natural monopoly." Would that lead to corporate abuse and ever-rising rates without any brake?

By the turn of the century various smaller competitors were joining into larger trusts that controlled the electricity in huge regions of the country, exacerbating concerns that consumers might be at their mercy. More government control was inevitable.

Washburn and Worthington had to move fast. They had good ideas, but they didn't have enough clout to move a project of the size they were dreaming. Their first stab at legislation ended up dying in committee. By 1913 they decided to sell their Muscle Shoals Hydro-Electric Company to a larger competitor, the Alabama Power Company, which was positioning itself to dominate electrical generation in the state. Washburn, seeing his dam—and the chance to power his fertilizer plant—delayed, gave up on Alabama and moved his dream to Niagara Falls, where he built his first big American Cyanamid plant on the Canadian side of the border. It would take a war to get him back to Muscle Shoals.

But Worthington kept the dream alive. For a short time he took an executive job at Alabama Power, and never stopped lobbying for the giant dams at the Shoals. "Mr. Worthington has been a leader in the waterpower development of this state for a number of years, and might fittingly be called the father of the movement," one Alabama paper enthused in 1913. Now in his early fifties, he was more connected and more active than ever, shuttling between the Tennessee River valley and Washington, DC; funneling pro-dam materials to newspaper reporters; getting local boosters together to form the Tennessee River Improvement Association (TRIA); making sure champagne flowed and cigars were lit in backroom meetings; showing movies of Niagara Falls and talking about how the Shoals were going to be even bigger. He made an especially persuasive case to Alabama's most powerful politician, then House Majority Leader (and, after 1914, US senator) Oscar Underwood, who saw the sense of it for economic development and promoted dams for the next two decades.

Worthington—who around this time started using the title "Colonel" in his public life (although there's no record of such advancement in his military service)—knew something good would eventually happen. He quit Alabama Power to put everything he had into his own lobbying efforts. He stayed in touch with Washburn, who took time from building his Canadian factory to support TRIA. The two engineers again put their heads together.

With the powerful Senator Underwood on their side, Worthington and TRIA began lobbying harder in Washington, starting small,

Senator Oscar Underwood
Courtesy Library of Congress

asking for government-backed low-interest loans for navigation improvements, asking for an appropriation for geological surveys, asking for anything they could think of to get the dams on paper as a real government project.

In the spring of 1915, Worthington and TRIA succeeded in getting a large delegation of senators and congressmen to come down and see the Shoals in person. Their arrival was the biggest thing to hit the area since the Civil War. Thousands turned out to cheer Underwood and other senators, congressmen from the South and Midwest, a member of the Federal Reserve Board, and the governor of Alabama. The Tri-Cities were draped in red, white, and blue bunting. The crowd carried signs reading "Dam Muscle Shoals and Dam It Now" and "Dam It, We Need It." Worthington was everywhere in the background, arranging a steamboat river tour, making sure the "antebellum" barbecue lunch that followed was flawless and authentic, and that the long string of stump speeches later in the day were applauded by a large and enthusiastic crowd. "I never saw so many people in my whole life," said one local. "I thought everybody in Washington had come. I believed that nearly everybody in the state of Alabama was there, too."

It couldn't have gone better. Worthington had not only impressed the visiting officials, but also cemented his position as a big deal at home. Before the visit, everybody around the Shoals figured that Worthington was something; now they were sure of it.

By the time the politicians went back north, bellies full of barbecue and minds alive with visions of a transfigured Tennessee River, Worthington's people were already hard at work designing a lavishly illustrated booklet called *America's Gibraltar, Muscle Shoals*. It was a public relations masterpiece highlighting northern Alabama's central location, power potential, mild climate, and "contented labor" from "a local population of purely native Americans." By that they meant not Native people, of course, but hardworking white people.

It had been ten years since Worthington and Washburn first started putting the pieces together for their innovative mix of regional hydroelectric power, factories, and improved navigation, funded in part by the government, in part by private interests. And for the first time it was beginning to look like their dream might come true.

CHAPTER 2

THE WONDER CITY AT WAR

TWO DAYS BEFORE J. W. Worthington fed barbecue to the senators and congressmen on the banks of the Tennessee, the *Lusitania*
went down. The torpedoing of the huge, luxurious passenger liner
by a German U-boat with the loss of almost 1,200 lives (128 of them
US citizens) marked a turning point in American public opinion.
There were cries that America had to get ready to go to war, none
louder than those of that bellicose old Rough Rider, former president
Theodore Roosevelt. T.R. was waving his fist before enthusiastic
crowds, whipping them up about German atrocities and American
effeminacy, waving the bloody shroud of the *Lusitania* and hammering home the need to get into this European dustup on the side of
our old friends the French and our cultural ancestors the British.

He pushed for a program of "preparedness" to get Americans
ready for a war he felt sure was coming. Preparedness made some
degree of sense anyway, whether we officially got into it or not,
because having a strong military would deter aggressors and give the
US a stronger hand to play in the post-war world. Woodrow Wilson
might've been running his reelection campaign as "The Man Who

Kept Us Out of War," but he was also politician enough to see that the public opinion was shifting against peace. As the 1916 election neared, the president reluctantly climbed aboard the preparedness bandwagon and backed legislation to expand the military.

The result was the National Defense Act of 1916, designed to increase the size of the army and the National Guard and modernize their training. Those simple goals were attached to a long list of local favors and pork-barrel projects including, deep in the act, buried among bits and pieces like "Procurement of Gauges, Dies, Jigs and So Forth," a few paragraphs called Section 124: Nitrate Supply. It was likely masterminded and inserted by some of the same political figures who had recently visited Muscle Shoals. Section 124 directed the president to pick a site and start the process for building an American nitrate factory so the nation could be more independent in the production of both fertilizer and explosives. It included the allocation of up to $20 million in government funding to do it.

Soon after Wilson won the 1916 election by a whisker and was inaugurated, the Germans announced they were going to return to unlimited submarine warfare in the waters around Great Britain. They would once again start sinking any ship from anywhere, civilian or military, suspected of helping their enemies in any way. It was a last-gasp attempt to strangle England and win the war before the US could get into it. American merchant ships would be among the victims.

That was too much. Wilson declared war on Germany in April 1917. And at that point Section 124 of the defense act of 1916 became very, very important.

WHAT RESULTED WAS America's most important scientific/technological project of World War I, something like the Manhattan

Project of its time. The US faced any number of problems in shifting to a wartime stance, but one of the biggest was figuring out how to make enough of its own gunpowder and explosives. For five decades it had depended on shipments of a critical raw material from South America, a mineral mined from the Atacama Desert called Chilean nitrate. In 1917 it was one of the most important substances on earth. Chilean nitrate was what most of the world used to make both fertilizer and explosives (it contained a form of reactive nitrogen necessary for both substances). It was shipped from Chile all over the world by fleets of nitrate clippers and freighters. And that presented a problem in wartime. If an enemy could send out military ships to cut the shipping routes, it could starve an enemy nation of a critical resource, crippling its military. That's exactly what the British did to the Germans as soon as the war started: They set up a naval blockade that forced Germany to find some new substitute for the Chilean nitrate it had been using to make explosives. The Germans did exactly that by developing a new, secret technology invented by a pair of scientists, Fritz Haber and Carl Bosch, who would both end up winning Nobel Prizes for their work.

The Haber-Bosch system was a secret weapon that only the Germans had. The Germans had made it work, but only because the Germans had two things the US did not: the mastermind of the process, Haber, and the chemical company that backed him up, BASF, with its brilliant industrial chemist, Bosch. Bosch had spent staggering sums turning Haber's ideas into giant factories, recruiting teams of engineers and metallurgists and chemists and catalyst experts to quickly solve the thousand problems that came up, working fast and improvising fixes. It had taken him four years to turn Haber's little tabletop demonstration unit into a factory, one capable of making enough product to keep Germany in the war. That was mind-blowingly fast, and it was done with the knowledge of the underlying chemistry. It would take other nations much longer.

Unfortunately, the US was getting into the synthetic nitrate-making game late. There was Washburn's cyanamide process, but that required enormous amounts of electricity. Several nations in Europe had been at work on the problem, too, like Norway, which had tapped into its abundance of natural waterfalls to make the electricity it needed to start its own significant nitrate industry. Italy and France were working on projects, but without much success. Germany, of course, was making nitrates using its secret Haber-Bosch process.

North America, by contrast, had exactly one major factory successfully making the chemicals it needed: the plant Washburn built in Canada near Niagara Falls for his American Cyanamid company. It was not as efficient as the Haber-Bosch system, but it was all there was. The fact that Washburn had constructed his factory in Canada was an issue; although Canada was an ally, the US preferred total control over its own nitrate production. Building a giant cyanamide plant in the US might be America's only hope.

In 1915 a high-ranking general, the US chief of ordnance, saw a picture of Washburn's Canadian plant in a magazine and wrote him a letter asking what it would take to do something like that in the US. Washburn wrote back at length outlining the latest German experiments and emphasizing the value of his cyanamide approach. A few months later he wrote the general again, telling him about the idea of damming the Tennessee River for electricity, and saying that he could quickly build a huge factory there if the government would come up with money to subsidize it.

There was a glitch, however: Section 124 of the National Defense Act dictated that only the government could build and operate nitrate plants for the military, "not in conjunction with any other individual or entity carried on by private capital." Washburn's company, American Cyanamid, was private, so some new arrangement would have to be made. Some new way of mixing public and private money. Something like what Washburn and Worthington had been talking about for years.

As the 1916 National Defense Act came into effect, several government committees were formed to figure out a solution to America's nitrate problem. Top minds were put on it. The secretary of war asked the National Academy of Sciences to assemble a blue-ribbon committee with the goal of figuring out the fastest, cheapest way for the US to produce its own nitrates. After some months they reported that the US was a long way from getting what it needed and that the government would have to invest as much as it could as quickly as possible to play catch-up with developments in Europe. They emphasized the importance of big electrical generation facilities, especially dams and hydropower. In the meantime, they recommended, the US should import and stockpile as much Chilean nitrate as it could. At least one year's worth. Finally, they recommended further study.

The military got into the act, too, hiring a highly respected expert named Charles Parsons, the chief chemist of the Bureau of Mines, to go to Europe on a fact-finding mission, reviewing every factory he could get into and talking to every expert he could locate. Parsons spent the last three months of 1916 dodging battles and touring nitrate plants, meeting with experts in England, Norway, Italy, Sweden, and France.

And then Parsons found what he was looking for—in Germany. It was the Haber-Bosch process. Parsons could not examine the German factories directly, of course, but everyone he talked to seemed to believe that the German system was the best out there: cheaper, more efficient, and more productive than any other.

The problem was that only the Germans knew how to do it, and they weren't telling anyone. The Haber-Bosch secret had not yet been cracked by anyone outside of Germany. Some rough outlines were being guessed at, but none of the details. And it looked like Haber-Bosch was all about details: complicated chemistry, high temperatures, enormous pressures, hundreds of new fittings and gauges and mechanical devices needed to make it work. In America, only one firm, the General Chemical Company of Long Island, was making a serious run at building a Haber plant. Progress was being made, but no one outside of Germany had seen success.

Parsons was sure of one thing, however: Cyanamide plants like Washburn's required far more electricity than a Haber-Bosch plant. That made them more expensive to operate, which meant that the explosives made from those nitrates would in turn be more expensive. When a cyanamide plant was compared, head to head, with a Haber-Bosch plant, Haber-Bosch won.

On the other hand, America knew how to build a functional cyanamide factory. While Parsons was dashing around Europe, Washburn wrote the head of the Ordnance Department, telling him that Haber-Bosch was "relatively worthless." If the US wanted to make its own nitrates quickly, Washburn's proven cyanamide process was clearly the way to go.

Parsons came home from the war zone with a recommendation to build both. The government couldn't afford to ignore the Haber-Bosch process; it was too potentially valuable, so he advised that the government build a relatively small, experimental Haber plant in hopes they could crack the secret. Once they did, it would be easy to expand.

At the same time, he said, the government should fund construction of a giant cyanamide plant, one that could be put up fast and start producing reliably. To power it, they should also start building a big dam. A dam the size Parsons thought would be needed for the power-hungry cyanamide plant would take years to build, too long for wartime needs. So he also recommended building two gigantic coal-fired steam electricity generating plants big enough to power the cyanamide and Haber factories while the dam was being built.

It was almost too much: two enormous, completely novel nitrate factories, plus two huge steam plants, plus a dam that would rival the largest on earth. It would, however, cover all the bases, ensuring fast nitrate production and long-term possibilities for the Haber-Bosch process. If this experimental plant failed, there would be a complete cyanamide plant running right next door, pumping out nitrates with proven technology.

The government went with Parsons's ambitious plan. The question turned from what to where. This was a military project, a top necessity, and the generals wanted something inland, far away from naval or air attacks, ideally behind some mountains, and close to rail or water transportation for shipping out the nitrates. Also, if they were going to use coal-powered plants for electricity, easy access to coal. And if the whole thing was eventually going to run on hydropower, well, the perfect site for a big nearby dam was absolutely critical.

All of Worthington's lobbying made sure that the Tennessee River was on everybody's short list. But Muscle Shoals wasn't the only possibility. Some scientists favored the hills of West Virginia. The US Army Corps of Engineers recommended a site on the Black Warrior River south of the Shoals, near Birmingham. And there were other spots on the Tennessee River that could work. The secretary of war favored a site upriver from the Shoals, around Chattanooga, a good place for a dam and rich with rail connections.

But the Muscle Shoals boosters had a friend in Alabama senator Underwood, who lobbied hard for Worthington's site. And that was enough to turn the tide. Yielding to what one historian called "tremendous pressure" from Underwood and his Senate allies, President Wilson made his decision: This enormous wartime project would be built at Muscle Shoals.

AND EVERYTHING STARTED happening fast.

Around the Shoals, people started rejoicing. Getting into the war was not great, maybe, but the promise of the dam, the factories, the jobs, the millions in government investment—"the song of machinery, the busy hum of industry," as one local booster put it—was cause for celebration.

The government took control of swaths of farm and woodland along the river. Plans were quickly sketched out: about 1,700 acres for Nitrate #1, the Haber plant, and 2,200 acres for Nitrate #2, the cyanamide plant. The dam would be built at the foot of the Shoals near Florence, and the steam electrical plants would be built nearby—a big one, to power the cyanamide plant and a smaller one for the Haber factory. Altogether it would be gigantic; the project would fill much of the land between the three towns of the Tri-Cities.

The day Wilson announced Muscle Shoals was the place, workers began trickling in. After war was formally declared in April 1917, the trickle turned into a flood. Trains to the area were stuffed with job seekers: pipe fitters, painters, electricians, carpenters, secretaries, engineers, draftsmen, ditch diggers, cement mixers, bricklayers, metalworkers, auto mechanics, water plant operators, power plant operators, heavy equipment operators.

They quickly overwhelmed the area's capacity. Altogether the Tri-Cities had fewer than twenty thousand residents in 1917; the Muscle Shoals project alone would soon employ more than that, doubling the area's population in a single year. The infrastructure wasn't there for it, with nowhere near enough housing or public services, so the government had to build its own towns to house them. Two neat, trim, small villages were constructed for the higher-ups, the military officers, managers, and their families, one for each nitrate plant, complete with its own sewage and water systems, electrical lines, parks, schools, and curving streets lined with handsome bungalows. One of them was laid out with a street plan designed to look like the Liberty Bell.

There was housing for blue-collar workers, too—the laborers and construction men, one area for Blacks and another for whites. Some were housed in wooden barracks, others in a sea of canvas tents pitched on wooden platforms to keep them out of the mud. The tent city was nicknamed Helltown. In an interview years later, one local said, "Any form of sin you can think of, Helltown had. A red-light district, gambling, whiskey manufactured close by, everything." They might have been living in tents, but the laborers also got ice delivered once a day, could run a kerosene stove for cooking and warmth, and "lived pretty well," one remembered later.

Workers ate in one of twenty-three dining halls, including a monster that held 4,000 diners at a time, employed almost a thousand cooks and support staff, and dished out 24,000 meals a day. They said it was the largest mess hall ever built. It was served by a bakery that made 13,000 steaming loaves of fresh bread every day, 1,000 pies, 1,200 cakes, and 150 gallons of pudding. The government worked with the local towns, too, expanding water and sewer systems, paying for more security, and hiring more doctors and nurses to accommodate the growth. These were boomtowns with their own social halls, churches, clinics, baseball teams, and orchestras.

Ten months after breaking ground, Muscle Shoals was Alabama's fourth-largest city. There was so much going on that one local newspaper created a special section to cover it in every issue, and a brand-new newspaper, the *Nitrate News*, was created for the workers, featuring eight pages of stories about the duties of chaperones at the women's dormitory, the opening of a billiard parlor, and how good the orchestra was at the new movie theater. Headlines like "Muscle Shoals Is Wonder City Built from Patriotism" helped keep spirits up.

For the locals, it was like Christmas every day. Government money and new customers were everywhere—buyers in the stores, diners in the restaurants, drinkers in the bars—with all the bills paid, directly or indirectly, by Uncle Sam. Locals started talking about the "givament." It was good times.

But it wasn't all good. Local rents went through the roof, pricing out some of the locals. When it rained the mud could be thick, flies and mosquitoes were everywhere, and cases of malaria started popping up. Race issues bubbled beneath the surface. It was the era of Jim Crow, and while Black workers were hired in large numbers, they were not paid as much as whites, and housing and schools were strictly segregated. This was an era when the Ku Klux Klan was making a resurgence in Alabama and across the nation.

But at the Shoals, all the problems were drowned in money. Thousands of laborers, white and Black, were suddenly earning wages higher than most of them had ever seen. Until they started building the dam and the factories, northern Alabama had been one of the poorest regions in the nation. Many of its people lived hand to mouth as tenant farmers or sharecroppers. Now there were plenty of good-paying jobs that offered side benefits: a place to live, a chance to go to classes to learn a trade. As one Black community leader told a newspaper reporter at the time, the dam and factory projects constituted "the best chance for advancement, in every way, that the American negro has ever had."

THE WINTER OF 1917–1918 was unusually cold, and the frozen riverbanks made footing dangerous, slowing the work. But the pace quickened as spring warmed the vast construction site. Then, in the spring of 1918, it began racing. The realization was growing that the Germans were weakening, that the war might be over soon, that this vast Alabama project had to get done now if it was going to make any difference. There was a frenzy of construction on the great dam at the foot of the Shoals, at Nitrate Plant #1 (the Haber factory), at Nitrate Plant #2 (the cyanamide plant), at the power plants, on warehouses, roads—endless improvements and expansions at the living areas. Films from the time show an anthill of activity up and down the river, concentrated at the dam site, where giant steam shovels belched smoke alongside newly installed rail systems with their locomotives hauling away dirt and pulling in giant loads of lumber, machinery, and tools. Roads were clogged with mule teams and Model Ts and horse-drawn wagons. The river crawled with barges and tugboats. A forest of cranes and wooden frames sprouted around the dam. Huge steam shovels (some of them originally built for the Panama Canal project) chewed out places to lay foundations; crews banged away with big early-model jackhammers; laborers hoisted telephone poles and electrical lines along newly constructed roads; workers hammered frames for laying cement, tried to avoid tripping over hoses and ropes, strained to hear orders shouted above the racket of sawing, chopping, crashing loads of rock, the roar of heavy machinery, and the scream of steam whistles.

Everyone rushed, and the rush made the work dangerous. Clinics built especially for the project were kept busy treating smashed fingers, broken limbs, burns, cuts, and dismemberment. Fifty-six men died during the dam's construction.

THE GOAL OF all this effort was not the great dam, however. The goal was making armaments. And here things were not looking good. Nitrate #1, the experimental Haber plant, was a gamble from the start. The US company that sold the idea to the government and was in charge of putting the plant into production, General Chemical, was finding out that the Haber process—with its balance

"A wonder city built from patriotism": Muscle Shoals under construction, 1918
Courtesy Library of Congress

Sawing, crashing, roaring: Wilson Dam under construction. In the great rush to build the dam, fifty-six workers died.
Courtesy Library of Congress

of temperatures hot enough to turn cast iron cherry red, pressures high enough to explode cannon barrels, and a special secret catalyst, all able to work together only with specially designed and built equipment—was far more difficult than they had imagined.

General Chemical had talented chemists, but none like Fritz Haber and Carl Bosch. Nothing was going as fast as they'd planned. Problems were cropping up at every step. It was beginning to look like they might never get it right.

Nitrate #2 was a different story. This was Washburn's and American Cyanamid's chance to scale up the plant they had successfully built and put into operation on the Canadian side of Niagara Falls, to show the world that they could create a cutting-edge factory for nitrates in the US, do it quickly, and make it work. It was a monster facility from the blueprints on up, the biggest of its kind in the world. It was going to be seven times larger than American Cyanamid's Canadian plant, with 113 buildings housing long rows of huge ovens, a dozen giant furnaces, the world's biggest air compression plant, a liquid air plant five times bigger than anything that had ever been built, and one of the world's biggest power plants to keep it running. Its construction required 10 million bricks, 19,000 tons of steel, 262,000 barrels of cement, and enough wood framing to replace every structure in the Tri-Cities. Somehow, it was all coming together. With extraordinary management and dedicated work, it was rising from the Alabama fields with lightning speed: At its peak, eighty-five trains a day were needed just to feed it construction supplies.

And they pulled it off. Construction work on Nitrate #2 started at the end of November 1917; one year later the plant was ready to start continuous production. "Record time. A building feat that has never before been equaled, and will never, perhaps, be surpassed," a local paper enthused. At full production, Nitrate #2 by itself could have produced more than 10 percent of the nitrates needed by all the Allied armies on all fronts combined. It was one of the greatest American achievements of the war.

But at the moment it was done, nobody needed it. Just as the plant was ready to go into full operation, the news came: Germany had surrendered.

There were many conjectures about why the Germans gave up with the war half-won, without a single foreign troop ever setting foot in their country: the slow strangle of the British blockade, the danger of the Bolsheviks exporting their Russian Revolution to Germany, sheer war weariness.

Then there's this point, raised by a few historians: When the German leaders learned that Nitrate #2 was ready to start production, they simply gave up.

CHAPTER 3

UNCLE HENRY

A FEW MONTHS after World War I was over, the richest man in the world, Henry Ford, was sitting in a witness box in a small-town courtroom, fidgeting and sweating. He had been testifying now for a week while a team of high-priced lawyers badgered him on every conceivable subject, from what he read as a child to his views on the War of 1812. As their confusing and detailed questions ground on, Ford became flummoxed and tongue-tied. He couldn't remember facts. He started making mistakes.

Ford was a trim figure, spare, full of energy, with piercing blue eyes that could pin a person down. He had built the world's largest automobile company from nothing, revolutionizing it by speeding production on an assembly line and bringing costs down to where he could make a reliable car cheap enough for the mass of Americans to buy. He did it by making just one kind of car—a Ford—available in just one model—the T—and in any color you wanted, "as long as it's black," as Ford would say. Ford's genius was born of ruthless efficiency. He did one thing, did it less wastefully and more productively than anyone else, and drove down the price of his car to a point where no one else could compete.

And it paid off. As writer Bill Bryson put it: "When Henry Ford built his first Model T, Americans had some 2,200 makes of cars to choose from. Every one of those cars was in some sense a toy, a plaything for the well-to-do. Ford changed the automobile into a universal appliance, an affordable device practical for all, and that difference in philosophy made him unimaginably successful . . . he wholly transformed the course and rhythm of modern life."

Ford was the model of a self-made American, raising himself out of rural drudgery and into the stratosphere of the rich entirely through his own efforts. And for what? So he could spend another day squirming in the heat of this small-town courtroom?

Henry Ford at the peak of his power
Courtesy Library of Congress

It was all his own fault. It was his sense of pride that was getting him raked over the coals. It was his belief in world peace. He had been too much the innocent. And now it had come to this.

As America got ready to enter the war, Ford was in his early fifties, in the flush of his record-breaking success, full of energy, and making more money than he knew what to do with. He had started mass-producing his first Model T in 1909, less than a decade before, and now its phenomenal success had changed his life.

Ford was no artist, no deep thinker, nothing like what most people might call a "genius." He was just a Michigan farm boy who had shown a precocious talent for tinkering with machinery, raised in the country near Dearborn, just outside of Detroit, one of eight children born to a father who had emigrated from Ireland and a mother whose parents were Belgian. He spent most of his life within twenty miles of where he was born.

But he was no farmer. He hated agricultural work, the grinding daily labor, the endless cycles of clearing and digging, weeding and fencing, planting and harvesting, the dirt and smell, the repetition, the boredom. Farmers were at the mercy of too many things they couldn't control: weather, pests, the price of equipment, the market for their crops.

Ford was too quick, too keen for that. He was drawn away from the soil and toward anything that had gears and engines. He fixed tools and took apart watches, finished his chores as fast as he could and ran off to look at any sort of engine powering any sort of work. He especially loved the "road locomotives," big self-propelled steam engines that clanked and bellowed slowly from farm to farm before settling down in some field to help power the harvest. Ford understood those engines. He had an almost intuitive ability to see how they worked and where things went wrong. When he was twelve, he set up his first little machine shop; when he was fifteen, he built his first steam engine and started repairing watches. Soon after, he quit school, left the farm, and went to Detroit to become an apprentice machinist.

He had found his real home. He loved working in a machine shop. He was out of the mud and out of the weather, indoors every day, dry and warm, cocooned with the smell of grease and the throb of machinery. He was working with his mind more than his back. And the best thing was that every day there was something new: mechanical puzzles to solve, parts to piece together, problems to fix.

He had found his calling, making his living in ways he could control, designing and putting together gadgets and engineering systems. Part of him was still back on the farm—he never lost a kind of fuzzy nostalgia, a misty love of barn dances and fiddle music, one-room schoolhouses and country inns. Ford thought farmers were the salt of the earth and the cornerstone of American democracy. But he didn't want to *be* a farmer.

Soon he was working for Detroit Edison as a mechanic, keeping electrical dynamos humming. In his spare time he pursued a pet project, an idea he had about making a gasoline-powered horseless carriage. Here again he was going to give a nod to his farm roots. His machine was not going to be a rich man's plaything. It was going to be a workingman's car—cheap, rugged, and easy to fix, something rural families could depend on to travel over rutted dirt roads. He spent years figuring out how to get the engine right, then more time making the car stronger, more reliable, and easier to manufacture than anything else on the road.

That was the Model T. But he didn't stop with the car design alone. Ford, it turned out, was brilliant in another way. He could, it seems, sense the inner workings of a business the same way he could sense the guts of a machine. He could see where to cut waste and increase efficiency, how to increase speed and reliability. To keep the costs of his cars down, Ford brainstormed a system for moving each chassis and engine along an "assembly line," hauling the metal in front of workers who did just one or two things to it before it moved to the next workers. This allowed Ford laborers to stay in one place and become expert at one thing, reducing wasted movement. He made only one model of car so he could buy parts in large consignments, reducing costs. He started making his own parts to reduce costs even more. He pioneered new ideas in distribution, sales, and service. His Model T began selling in phenomenal numbers. It was the first car many Americans had ever owned, and it meant more than convenience and widening horizons. People felt fondly about their "Tin Lizzies," as they were nicknamed. And they felt fondly about the Michigan farm boy who built them.

In the years just before World War I Ford himself became a celebrity. The combination of his beloved affordable Tin Lizzies, the

Model Ts on the assembly line
Courtesy Library of Congress

growing renown of the Ford Motor Company, plus his all-American personal story of humble beginnings leading to phenomenal success, kept his name in the newspapers.

But he was more than a simple bumpkin who made good. He was a mechanical genius, a business genius, and, it turned out, a genius at publicity. He realized early that getting his name into the news columns of a paper rather than paying for advertising was an inexpensive and very effective way to break through to the public. Even before the Model T he had made race cars and hired the leading driver of the day, Barney Oldfield, to drive them, making news and welding the name "Ford" to images of speed and power. Later, he cultivated reporters, said things designed to get attention, and put together an effective public relations operation for the company.

The Ford communications office kept up a steady stream of press releases, tips, and, later, motion pictures that fed a growing public appetite to know everything Ford was doing or thinking. The papers couldn't get enough of him. Ford was something new, something fresh—a powerful capitalist who was also a common man, somebody who was super-rich but whom you could picture living down the street, the small-town guy who ran one of history's greatest industrial empires. He talked like small-town people talked, complaining about bankers and the wealthy elites back east, advocating good old American values. A public image emerged: a simple straight shooter who didn't abide rich phonies. He paid a fair wage and asked for fair labor in return. He was everybody's "Uncle Henry."

He was at his peak in the years around World War I—in constant motion, always announcing something big, like a new factory, a new labor plan, a new view of society. If a reporter was lucky enough to sit down with him, Ford was likely to say something interesting on just about any subject, whether he knew much about it or not. He gave great quotes, when he spoke informally, on just about any subject.

Part of Ford's appeal was that he spoke plain English. He hadn't gone to any fancy universities and didn't get distracted by complicated ideas, didn't pay attention to what most politicians said (and didn't believe most of them anyway), and did his best to ignore the big-money boys in New York. Ford was his own man, thought his own thoughts, and spoke his mind, just like any good American should. Instead of being swayed by others, Ford gave full play to a seemingly endless store of good country common sense. He respected the working people of America, and the working people of America loved him back.

ONE OF THE many ways Ford reflected his place and time was that, like most Americans, he was against getting mixed up in that war between the kings and emperors in Europe. That mess, he thought, was none of America's business. Ford was all about giving the common man a break, and (despite his mounting personal fortune) against greed; he saw this war as rooted in the lust for gold. People were being tricked into it because of the avarice of financiers and munitions makers, industrial and banking profiteers who pushed nations into conflict so they could make money off of it. It was a nasty business. Ford wanted no part of it.

In late 1915 he chartered a ship, filled it with peace activists, and took off for Europe to try to talk sense into the folks over there. It was an idealistic gesture, and it was doomed. Ford's "Peace Ship" was slated to sail to Norway, where he planned to hold a global conference and convince everyone to call off the war. But he had no official backing from the US government, and so had no standing to do much of anything. When he tried to talk his friends into coming along, he got polite refusals. His friend Thomas Edison came to the dock to see him off, and the automaker reportedly pulled the old inventor aside, leaned in close, and shouted into Edison's good ear, "I'll give you a million dollars." But Edison acted like he didn't hear him—a trick he often used to avoid unpleasant conversations—smiled benignly, and went home.

As soon as they left the dock, arguments broke out among the peace activists, and got worse the farther they steamed toward Europe. Ford got disgusted with his shipmates, and the press started calling the whole thing "The Ship of Fools." Shortly after they landed in Norway, Ford gave up and rushed back to America. The planned conference fizzled.

And the Ford critics came out in force, making fun of his naivete and his amateur peacemaking. Chief among them was

Ship of Fools: Ford's Peace Boat lampooned
New York Herald, November 27, 1915. Courtesy Library of Congress

Colonel Robert R. McCormick, publisher of the *Chicago Tribune*. McCormick saw Ford as more a country-fried con man than a role model, more adept at getting good press than actually doing anything good for America. This was especially true when it came to matters of international politics. Ford's antiwar statements might make him seem like a messiah of peace, but in reality, McCormick believed, Ford's words and actions were undermining American preparedness. His paper ran a number of articles taking Ford to task, including, notably, an editorial that ran on June 23, 1916, under the title "Ford Is an Anarchist."

He was no such thing, and the editorial didn't really say he was. But Ford was certainly against getting into the Great War, and McCormick was for it. The new National Defense Act had just been signed, and in response many companies were telling workers that if they had to take time off to train with the armed forces, they'd have jobs waiting for them when they returned. It was the sort of patriotic move that made for good feelings all around. But Ford had refused to make a similar guarantee to his workers. The *Tribune* editorial writers teed off on him for that, calling him "ignorant," "incapable of thought," and "deluded" for not climbing aboard the preparedness bandwagon.

Ford got stuck on the editorial's provocative title. He might be all for peace, but he was no anarchist. Nowhere in the body of the editorial did anyone accuse him of being an anarchist, a word with links to bomb-throwing leftists and terror killings. It was a gratuitous and unnecessary insult. Ford sued the *Tribune* for libel.

Then America got into the war, everything was sidelined, and it wasn't until 1919 that Ford got his day in court. Or, as it turned out, many days. McCormick decided to fight, and hired the best lawyers he could find. Ford did the same. They started by arguing over where the trial should be held: Ford's side said Chicago was the wrong place because the newspaper was too influential there, McCormick that

Detroit was unsuitable because everyone there was overwhelmingly pro-Ford. The baby was split and the trial held about twenty miles north of Detroit in a little resort town called Mount Clemens, known until then primarily for its mineral baths.

And McCormick's lawyers quickly earned their fees. They argued that in order to find out if Ford was an anarchist, broadly defined, rather than simply an ignorant idealist, they would have to plumb the sources of his idealism and the depth of his general knowledge about politics. Thus, they argued, they had to be permitted to question Ford's "knowledge of history, his ability to read, his knowledge of the Revolutionary War . . . his views on the Constitution of the United States, etc. etc."

The judge allowed it all. It was going to be open season on Henry Ford.

The trial dragged on for three months. Scores of witnesses were called. The marquee event took place in the Michigan heat of July 1919, when Ford himself was called to the stand and grilled for eight days. Taken out of his offices and his factories—places where he was in total command, where he was admired and focused and determined—and subjected to the relentless questioning of skilled attorneys, Henry Ford became anything but a commanding figure.

When quizzed on his understanding of word definitions and details of history and culture, he "floundered helplessly," a reporter noted. The journalists crowding the courthouse, recognizing the news value of seeing an American icon smashed, eagerly reported every mistake.

When asked to define "idealist," Ford said that he thought it meant "a person that can help to make other people prosperous." He said he thought that the War of 1812 was part of the Revolutionary War. And then came the bit that made it into just about every newspaper in America:

LAWYER: "Did you ever hear of Benedict Arnold?"

FORD: "I have heard the name."

LAWYER: "Who was he?"

FORD: "I have forgotten just who he is. He is a writer, I think."

Americans groaned, or laughed, or shrugged it off, depending on how they felt about Ford. The nation's intellectuals, the intelligentsia that ran the thought magazines and big papers, decided Ford had been shown to be a simpleton, a rube who knew a lot about cars and not much about anything else. By the end the great automaker was angry and embarrassed, or, as one reporter wrote, "an unhappy spectacle."

In fact, Ford was no simpleton. He was brilliant at what he did. But he was not book smart. He was a typical nineteenth-century farm boy with a formal education that totaled eight years in a one-room Dearborn, Michigan, schoolhouse, the same as most kids in the area got before leaving to work their family land. He kept a copy of the Bible handy, but other than that books meant little to him. He had famously been quoted as saying something to the effect of "History is bunk," a one-syllable dismissal of all previous human experience that encapsulated a lot about Ford. He didn't need to study the past. His bet was on the future.

In the end, the legal result was something of a draw, with the jury finding in favor of Ford, but the judge minimizing the verdict by fining the *Chicago Tribune* a total of six cents in damages. Both sides claimed victory.

And Ford emerged from the Mount Clemens courtroom a changed man. He was no longer the innocent idealist who had sailed off to make peace. He was bruised and wary. He would never again trust the press. He would never trust lawyers. He would no longer put his faith in courts. He already knew he couldn't trust most politicians, or Wall Street types. In the end, he could only trust himself.

AS FORD GOT back to work making the Model T, folks down at the Shoals were wondering what was going to happen with the giant construction project that nobody seemed to need any more. With the war over, what was the government going to do with its huge investment in the nitrate factories and dam, the jobs and unfinished projects, the towns housing thousands of workers?

Only one thing was clear: If the nation didn't need to make explosives, it didn't need the nitrate plants. And if it didn't need the nitrate plants, it didn't need the dam—which would make far too much electricity for the backward area around it to use. So the inevitable happened. As soon as peace broke out, the federal government first slowed funding for the Muscle Shoals project, then pulled the plug.

The great dam was about two-thirds done. Nitrate Plant #1, the Haber-Bosch experiment, had never worked and probably never would. Plant #2, the giant cyanamide factory Washburn had built for the government, had barely gotten started producing. It was mothballed. All construction work on the dam was halted. The military officers who had overseen the project were reassigned, and they packed up and took their families with them; the two villages built to house them were sold to local residents. Construction workers disappeared as quickly as they had materialized, along with the thousands of support workers who had run the mess halls, hospitals, and offices. Employee numbers dropped from 20,000 in November 1918 to 8,000 in March 1919. By mid-1920 there were just a few hundred workers left, mostly making sure the empty factories and idle dam site didn't fall completely to ruin.

Nitrate #2 in 1919: huge, expensive, and empty
Courtesy Library of Congress

They left behind echoing buildings and warehouses, phalanxes of gleaming, silent machines, fields full of abandoned equipment, and offices stacked with dusty blueprints, unfilled contracts, and old employment records.

It happened fast, and it happened at the worst possible time for the river towns around the Shoals. The years right after the war were tough. Food and cotton prices, driven high during wartime, collapsed in 1920. Unemployment shot up, deflation set in, stocks lost nearly half their value, and business failures tripled. Part of it was because the "givamint" stopped giving, as almost every wartime government project in the US was quickly pared down or shut down. Part of it was because the demand for American products lessened as Europe began to get back on its feet. And part of it was because tens of thousands of returning veterans were looking for work and there were few jobs for them. The economy began to cool, then freeze. Some people called it a recession, others a depression, but everyone agreed that for almost two years after 1919, America went through a sharp, deep, painful economic contraction.

At the same time, the nation (and the world) was being ravaged by one of the worst epidemic diseases in history, the Spanish Influenza. It hit just as the war was ending, a mysterious killer that tore through weakened, war-weary populations, killing more than half a million people in the US alone.

To make things worse, in the fall of 1919 President Wilson was felled by a stroke. It didn't kill him, but his energy was gone; he lingered on as a semi-invalid for the rest of his term. The debilitated president—thin, sick, sitting in a chair covered with a blanket—seemed to reflect the state of the whole country.

As bad as things were nationally, they were worse in the South. Without the government projects, the Shoals area fell back into its old economy, based heavily on cotton. But nobody could make any money on cotton in 1920 or 1921; when European demand went down, the price per pound plummeted to where farmers couldn't make back the money they put into growing it. Farm income in 1921 was only about half what it had been just before the war. It was not enough to survive.

But the folks around the Shoals were tough and resilient, and they knew how to get along without much money. When the dam jobs evaporated, the farmers went back to their old lives, trying to make a few dollars off of cotton, slaughtering their own meat, eating bread made from corn they grew themselves, patching their clothes, scratching by on what they could. Folks in town tightened their belts and looked for ways to help others. They'd been through bad times before.

The economic freefall had political effects, too. The country turned away from Wilson's League of Nations idealism and high-flown rhetoric. People were ready to put the war behind them and start making some money. So they started voting for candidates who promised fiscal responsibility, fewer foreign entanglements, and an emphasis on helping private businesses. Power shifted from Democrats to Republicans, who took back Congress in the 1918 election.

In 1920, when the votes for president were counted, only the South voted Democratic. A conservative Republican from Ohio, War-ren G. Harding, was swept into office in a landslide. He looked the part of president: sleek, silver haired, well-fed, and well-dressed, a genial, pro-business, and otherwise undistinguished career politi-cian. The Harding years would be advertised as a return to nor-malcy. Harding was backed by historic Republican majorities in both houses of Congress. The South's political power evaporated, and along with it, it seemed, the chances of getting any more money to finish the Muscle Shoals project.

All attempts to get tax money to finish the dam or get the nitrate plants up and running were tabled, delayed, or voted down from that point on. Instead, the Republican Congress opened a set of hearings into alleged waste and mismanagement during the hurried wartime construction. The hearings went on for a year and a half, keeping Democrats on the defensive (and in the end finding no evidence of major mismanagement).

The Republican hearings did bring some budget numbers to light, and the sums were staggering: the government had spent $167,163,296—about $3 billion in 2020 dollars—to construct two idle factories, some abandoned housing, and an unfinished dam. Not only were the nitrate factories idle, they were likely to stay that way forever, as they were already outdated. Once the war was over, inspectors from France, England, and the United States had finally been allowed to examine Germany's Haber-Bosch plants, and what they discovered astonished them. The technology was so efficient, so advanced, and so productive that it rendered all older techniques, like Washburn's cyanamide plants, obsolete. The plants at Muscle Shoals were junk. The whole enormous project was beginning to look like a very large, very expensive white elephant.

The Harding administration started looking for a buyer. Yes, a lot of public money had gone into the Shoals, but there was no need to continue throwing good money after bad. Even if the government had to swallow a huge loss, taking pennies on the dollar for its investment, at least the people would get a little of their money back.

The problem was finding a buyer. Or a leaser. Or anyone interested in taking it over. The fertilizer folks saw the mothballed plants as outdated. You might as well tear down the experimental Nitrate #1 for all the good it would ever do. And it would cost a fortune to update Nitrate #2 to the point where it could compete with plants that benefited from newer technologies. The dam? An even bigger pile of money would have to be found to finish the giant hulk over the river, and even if it was, who would buy all that power? The whole thing was a money sinkhole.

The project was still part of the War Department, so Secretary of War John W. Weeks was put in charge of finding somebody, anybody, to take it off the government's hands. When no buyers appeared quickly, some members of Congress started talking about the possibility of running the Shoals as a government operation, getting something out of the investment by making cheap fertilizers for farmers. But Harding wanted no part of it. There was no reason to put the US government into the business of making fertilizers. Or anything else, for that matter, that would compete with private businesses. The government running what should be a private business was un-American. That way lay socialism—or worse, bolshevism, of the bloody, radical type that Russia seemed eager to export to the rest of the world.

So, through 1920 and into 1921, Muscle Shoals became a political football kicked from one committee to the next, the factories and dam slowly decaying, the great wartime effort going to waste, the whole thing relegated to a series of endless wrangles in Congress. There it seemed to be stuck as the first months of the Harding administration went by. Two years of wasted time since the end of the war began to turn into three. And then, finally, a buyer showed up.

CHAPTER 4

$8 A SECOND

AFTER THE EMBARRASSMENT of the Mount Clemens courtroom, after successfully guiding his car company through the post-
war economic downturn, after the Spanish Flu pandemic eased and
Warren Harding was settled in the White House, Henry Ford began
looking for new worlds to conquer.

It was springtime, 1921. The business of America was once
again business; Harding was making good on his promises to bring
back good old-fashioned moneymaking. The economy started to
gather steam. Everything seemed to be speeding up; by summer
memories of the economic downturn were fading and there were
parties and jokes and the sounds of that new jazz music. The nation's
first radio broadcast of a baseball game went over the air, usher-
ing in a new era of sports heroes. The world's first fast-food chain,
White Castle, opened its first hamburger joint. Everyone was going
to the movies.

Farm kids moved to the cities to get in on the excitement,
and for the first time in US history, the number of urban residents
topped the rural population. Streets were filling with young women

with bobbed hair and slim silhouettes and scandalously high skirts, and young men with world-weary attitudes, snappy comebacks, and cigarettes dangling from their lips. F. Scott Fitzgerald called it "the Jazz Age." But the phrase that eventually caught on to describe what was happening was "the Roaring Twenties."

Ford roared along with it. The mini-depression sank a number of his competitors—about half the automakers in the country closed their doors because of slumping sales—but Ford thrived, chopping his workforce, shutting down his Model T assembly line for six weeks so he could clear inventory, using short-term loans to keep creditors off his back, and then, when sales picked up, buying out every major stockholder who wasn't a family member. He came out of it stronger than ever.

In 1921, as Ford's five millionth car rolled off his assembly line, half the cars on earth were Model Ts. By one estimate his company

Ford with his first and ten millionth car, June 4, 1924
Courtesy Library of Congress

was making eight dollars in profit every second. His personal fortune was growing so fast, he couldn't put a definite figure on it, but he was certainly the richest man in the US, and maybe the world. He didn't owe any major debts, he didn't have to answer to any bankers or moneymen, and he was able to make decisions quickly, decisively, and personally. That suited him. He couldn't bear anybody second-guessing him or looking over his shoulder. He reveled in his absolute control of the world's leading auto company—which, one reporter noted, was beginning to look more like a cult of personality than a modern corporation.

HIS ENERGY SEEMED endless. Once he'd made it through the hard times around 1920, he threw himself into his next great project: building the world's biggest car-making factory from the ground up, about eight miles from his house in Dearborn, on the River Rouge.

He had made the assembly line famous in 1910 when he finished his first Model T factory at Highland Park in Detroit. That was where he proved he could pump out cars faster and cheaper than any competitor could match, squeezing maximum work from his employees by making sure that they didn't have to do anything but focus on what was directly in front of them. Any wasted movement—turning to find a tool, bending to pick up a part—was analyzed and minimized.

Getting the most efficient work out of each employee meant higher productivity, which meant Ford could hire fewer workers to make more cars, which meant he could pay each of them more. He shocked the manufacturing world before the war by doubling his workers' average salaries to an unheard-of five dollars per day (about $130 per day in 2020 dollars), a move that endeared him to his men and also helped stave off any efforts toward labor organizing. Ford's high wages inspired worker loyalty. Once someone started working at Ford, they tended to stay, dropping turnover to next to nothing. That meant Ford needed to spend less money on breaking in new employees. His factories were full of well-paid, experienced, and generally satisfied workers.

There was a downside, too. Ford's actions could be seen as patronizing: He was the strong father who would take care of his workers. They didn't need unions. They only needed him. He was concerned not only with the efficiency of his workers, but their physical and moral well-being, so he started a sociology department to check up on them. Ford inspectors would visit employees' homes to see how they were doing and interview them about their marriages, religion, health, and hobbies. Immigrant laborers were required to take English lessons. Problems with drinking, drugs, or money were noted. Labor agitators and Communists were weeded out.

He wanted everything perfect, as clean and efficient as humanly possible, so that he could keep the prices on his cars low and make their benefits available to everyone.

A low price was critical. He wanted everyone to be able to buy a Model T without taking out a bank loan. Ford didn't like banks. Interest paid to banks, he thought, was money lost, money that could be used for better things. He'd seen too many farmers go under because they were paying interest on debts instead of putting the money back into their land.

To keep prices down, efficiency was everything. Early on, it had taken twelve hours to put together one Model T. With the assembly line at Highland Park, Ford cut the time to an hour and a half. The regularity of the assembly line also allowed the tightening and fine-tuning of parts supply, cutting down on unnecessary purchases and eliminating waste. The increased production made Ford the big dog when it came to negotiating with suppliers, allowing him to cut deals that kept manufacturing cost per unit to a minimum, which again allowed Ford to lower prices and expand the number of buyers.

Highland Park had been a dazzling achievement. But the industrial wonder of 1910 was already becoming outdated by 1920. In a way, it was a victim of its own efficiency. The plant pushed out cars so fast that it needed endless shipments of raw materials at the other end to feed the line: steel by the trainload, wiring by the mile, cloth by the ton, glass, rubber, parts, lacquer, and a thousand other things all had to be shipped to the plant. At any given moment Ford had a fortune's worth of materials in transit, which meant that any delay in delivery, from a railroad strike or a coal shortage to a storm at sea, could cripple production and lead to millions in lost income. It also put him in a position he didn't like, at the mercy of parts makers and mine owners and railroad magnates who could pressure him.

Ford decided to take the next step. He would control everything, up and down the line, including the supply of every raw material that went into his cars. He started buying up coal mines so he could power his own plants, and forests so he could grow the wood and make the paper used in the Model T chassis and transmission. Why should he pay a premium to iron smelters and steelmakers when he could build his own steel plants? And why not buy his own iron mines, and railroads to transport the ore? If he owned every part of the process, he could control his own fate.

The new River Rouge plant would be the crowning piece of the puzzle. He started buying land for it in 1915. When he had two thousand acres, he started digging, dredging a port on the river, putting in a sawmill, firing up a huge power plant, building blast furnaces and coke ovens for making metal, then a gigantic foundry to turn that metal into finished parts. The finished parts could then be used on-site or fed into the assembly line at Highland Park to

River Rouge, the biggest factory on earth
Courtesy Library of Congress

make the Model T, essentially tying the two big factories into a single integrated unit. He bought his own railroad and ran it to the plant. He put in a complete docking and warehousing system for shipping.

He started construction in 1917, and after it was finished in stages over the next decade, River Rouge would become the largest factory the world had ever seen: a mile long and a mile and a half wide, a complex that contained almost one hundred buildings and employed one hundred thousand workers. It was Ford's "do-everything" plant, where he not only made his Ford parts and processed raw materials, but manufactured new items like the Fordson tractor his teams had designed, a small, agile farm machine that made it possible for farmers to complete in hours jobs that just a few years earlier had taken days or weeks. The Fordson was his way of giving back something to agriculture, and it was a good business

Fordson Tractor
Courtesy Library of Congress

niche for Ford: By the 1920s he was selling hundreds of thousands of tractors per year. The combination of the Model T and the Fordson had made him a hero in the Farm Belt.

River Rouge would become another Ford marvel. But it still wasn't enough.

FORD HAD GENERALLY benefited from endless news coverage. But his battle with the *Chicago Tribune* demonstrated to him the need to get information out directly, unfiltered by editors and reporters. He built up his communications structure, hiring more PR writers to trumpet the Ford Motor Company's triumphs. He started a moviemaking department to produce and distribute a stream of short informational films to feed America's growing appetite for movies. They were well shot, they were entertaining, and they all created goodwill for Ford.

Then he went into the newspaper business, buying a sleepy hometown weekly, the *Dearborn Independent*, and trying to turn it into a national media player. Each issue of the *Independent* featured Ford's own opinion column (usually ghostwritten by his publicity team), with the rest hopscotching around a miscellany of topics Ford found interesting, from farming techniques to foreign policy. "I have definite ideas and ideals that I believe are practical for the good of all, and intend giving them to the public without having them garbled, distorted or misquoted," he said. "I am going to tell the people what they need to know. . . . I am going to tell them who makes war, and how the game of rotten politics is worked. I am going to tell them how to get the idle land into use. . . ."

One snarky competitor called the *Independent* "the best weekly ever turned out by a tractor plant." But Ford kept at it, growing the paper, distributing it through his dealerships and advertising and direct mail, and slowly building a subscriber base.

The *Independent* would find its readers, but it took a while to find its editorial voice. It started out as a mild general interest paper with a wandering focus. But then Ford began to target articles around one major theme, a pet idea of his, a sort of obsession. He thought that a global Jewish conspiracy was trying to take over the world.

A low-key form of anti-Semitism was as commonplace as it was accepted in America during the early 1900s. It was simply taken for granted in many levels of society that Jews were different, more clannish, inclined toward deception, often leftist, and generally greedy. They were discriminated against in ways large and small, from college admissions to golf club memberships. Still, America generally offered them broad opportunities for advancement, especially in professions like law, medicine, finance, and the sciences. The US was, broadly speaking, a better place to be a Jew than most nations in Europe.

Henry Ford took this mild, widespread American prejudice and heated it, focused it, and pushed it to a new level in the pages of his weekly. In 1920 the *Independent* started running a long series of cover articles, in issue after issue, blaming the Jews for just about everything that was wrong with America, from the cultural degeneration of jazz music and racy movies to the corruption of sports gambling and political graft. In Ford's mind America was in decline, and the Jews, organized in semisecret international cabals, were behind it all, beneath it all, undermining and weakening the nation's moral and economic foundations.

Financiers, bankers, lawyers, and leftist labor organizers—groups that Ford despised—all included high proportions of Jews. Jews, in his uneducated, distorted view, were big-city parasites sucking money from the honest labor of industrious Americans. He came to believe in a grand conspiracy he called "the international Jew." Much of his thinking came from a forged piece of propaganda first published in Czarist Russia during the time of the pogroms there, an anti-Semitic screed called *The Protocols of the Elders of Zion*, which outlined an international Jewish conspiracy to take over nations by controlling the world's money.

"The international financiers are behind all war," Ford told a reporter in 1920. "They are what is called the International Jew—German Jews, French Jews, English Jews, American Jews. I believe that in all these countries except our own the Jewish financier is supreme." There was still time to save America, where, he said, the Jew was still no more than "a threat." It was his job to wake the nation up before it was too late.

The *Independent*'s sensational series also tapped into a strain of nativist xenophobia, a fear of foreigners that had been heightened by the enormous influx of immigrants around the turn of the century—shiploads of millions of new arrivals, many from Eastern Europe, mostly poor, who settled first in the slums of America's largest cities. There were concerns about disease, dirt, foreign religions, and Communist agitation among the newcomers. These anti-immigrant fears melded with racist and anti-Catholic sentiments to fuel a resurgence of the Ku Klux Klan just after World War I. There were other factors, too: Everyone was worried about the Bolsheviks and their takeover of Russia; there was anxiety about changing mores, the loss of rural values, a world moving too fast, sweeping away the old Puritan spirit that had, in Ford's mind, built the country. Jews offered a single convenient enemy on whom to blame everything.

LIKE MANY WEALTHY and powerful people, Ford seemed to think that success in one area conferred upon him an authority in all. As he was conquering the automobile world and earning his fortune, his sights began turning to broader issues in society, from the "Peace Ship" to his musings on the national soul in the *Dearborn Independent*.

And in general, when it came to American society, he did not like what he saw happening. It seemed as if everywhere he looked he found lies, greed, and inefficiency. The mass exodus that was underway from rural areas to the cities, with families leaving their farms and getting jobs in factories, was creating an America he didn't like. "Every social ailment from which we today suffer originated and centers in the city," he said. Big cities were hotbeds of crime, disease, drugs, and lost lives. Ford was for temperance; cities were thick with speakeasies and gin joints. Ford was thrifty; cities were all about spending money. Ford believed in quiet, sober, country life. In the city, everything was phony, overhyped, and oversexed. In the city, he wrote in the early 1920s, "conditions of work and living are so artificial that instincts sometimes rebel against their unnaturalness."

Even worse, crime of all sorts, from individual transgressions to organized crime, was on the rise. The old morality that had built America was disappearing, and the loose morals of big cities were a major reason.

He believed that cities were doomed and saw no way to save them. "The modern city has been prodigal," he wrote. "It is today bankrupt, and tomorrow it will cease to be." If he had an alternative to offer, it was based in part on his own youth, in part on a nostalgia for a vanishing way of life. He thought Americans would be best off in a sort of early American village, in comfortable individual homes, surrounded by farms and forests. He couldn't see why people didn't simply do what he did: work hard, lead a clean life, and prosper. He was happy; he had prospered. Why couldn't everyone do the same?

CHAPTER 5

CAMPING WITH THE PRESIDENT

THE MUSCLE SHOALS problem now belonged to the big, bullet-headed, walrus-mustached secretary of war, John Wingate Weeks.

With the Great War over, Weeks had been spending much of his time paring down the military and shutting down wartime projects. A lot of what he was doing was more or less financial work, closing contracts and recouping investments, which was fine: Weeks had made a fortune in banking, and knew more about making money than he did about making war.

On most issues Weeks got along well with Harding. But they disagreed on Muscle Shoals. Harding wanted the whole thing off his desk. Muscle Shoals was a political headache he didn't need; finishing it would cost him money he didn't want to spend. He told Weeks to sell it, scrap it, lease it—he didn't much care. Get rid of it. But the banker in Weeks was loath to write off such an enormous government investment at fire sale prices.

Still, he did as he was told, and handed off the sales assignment to his head of the Corps of Engineers, General Lansing Beach. Soon after Harding settled into the White House, Beach started fishing for buyers.

He got no bites. The fertilizer companies didn't want to sink money into rebuilding outdated nitrate plants when they could build more efficient new ones. Power companies didn't want to pay the huge cost of finishing the unfinished dam. Nobody seemed to be interested.

As the process dragged out, Weeks himself took an interest in Muscle Shoals. It seemed to him that there were two parts to the problem. He was willing to sell the nitrate plants for scrap, if it came to that; they were old technology. But the dam was something else. It was a great example of American prowess, a giant gem among dams, by some measures the most ambitious construction project ever initiated in the country. The finished dam would be nearly a mile long and ten stories high, and wide enough at the top to run a highway across it. It was going to be the largest concrete dam in the world, "a great wall separating two periods of the world's history," a promotional booklet enthused. "On one side is the dark age, the stone age, the iron age, on the other is the age of electrical science and all its mighty possibilities. . . . Its usefulness to the human race outweighs the usefulness of all other structures in the world."

The only problem, Weeks's engineers told him, was that finishing it would cost at least another $30 million.

But there was more to it than electrical power and national pride. Weeks grew to appreciate that finishing the dam would be a very good thing for the region in other ways as well: The water behind it would open the river to ship commerce, the dam would help control the floods that had occasionally ravaged the valley, and the whole package would certainly boost the southern regional economy. Those were public benefits. Why would a private buyer pay to make them happen? So gradually Weeks came to believe that when it came to the dam, the government should complete what it had started. If the government paid to finish the dam, the project would be far more likely to attract a private buyer. He announced that he would be willing to recommend a $30 million appropriation from Congress to finish it as part of the package.

And still there were still no takers.

A last attempt by J. W. Worthington to get a stopgap $10 million dam construction appropriation—just enough to keep the construction crews from melting away—was killed in Congress. Its defeat was a disaster for the Shoals. The once-bustling dam site became a ghost town.

The only man still on the job full-time, it seemed, was Worthington. "Fight is not our middle name," he told the press, "it's the only name we've got." He intended to fight for the completion of the dam no matter how long it took. It meant too much to his state, his friends, and his career to stop. After Congress turned down his stopgap appropriation, Worthington shifted his attention to the cabinet, haunting the commerce, war, and treasury offices across the street from the White House, including the office of the man Secretary Weeks had put in charge of marketing the Shoals project, Corps of Engineers head General Lansing Beach.

The two men started talking, and found they spoke the same language. Beach had built dams for the Corps for decades; they were both engineers; and they were both bright, Beach graduating third in his class at West Point, Worthington a walking library of everything in the world there was to know about the Shoals area. They both strongly believed that dams were about a lot more than making electricity. They were the way you tamed rivers for economic development. Both men wanted to finish that dam.

Beach and Worthington chewed it over, looking for a way to get the project finished. They ran through the possibilities. And during

Lansing Beach, the government's chief dam
builder
Courtesy Library of Congress

their discussions an idea came up. Some accounts said Worthington
came up with it first; others said Beach brought it up. It doesn't matter much. What matters is that after some time together they began
to think about inviting Henry Ford to bid on Muscle Shoals.

FORD, AS IT turns out, was already thinking the same thing.
His many friends in the farm world had been talking to him about
the possibilities Muscle Shoals held for making cheap fertilizer.
Why leave that giant nitrate plant idle when it could help farmers?
Couldn't Ford do something to get those plants running?

Beach sent out feelers to Detroit. And in early April he was delighted to get a call back from Ford's personal secretary, inviting the general to meet with Ford to talk it over personally. Beach shared the news with his new friend Worthington, and the two of them quickly roughed out an outline of a deal they thought might interest both Ford and the president. Beach was too busy to make the trip, but he suggested sending another man in his place, one "familiar with all the details in the matter, and as thoroughly acquainted with every feature of the case as anybody in the country": J. W. Worthington. Yes, came the reply, that would be acceptable.

So Worthington packed up his charts, photos, and maps, boarded a train, and on June 6, 1921, was ushered into Henry Ford's private office at the Ford Motor Company. He was armed with letters of introduction from both Beach and Alabama senator Oscar Underwood, who wrote Ford, "I have known Mr. Worthington for more than a quarter of a century and wish to assure you that you can rely completely on his statement of facts. I don't know of any man in the United States who is better versed on the entire situation."

Ford called in some of his engineers. The men started talking. Worthington answered as many questions as he could, and then was asked to stay several more days to go over the details. They met again and again. Ford, Worthington knew, was interested in doing big things, so he helped him envision just how tremendous this project could be, sketching out the grand scope of what was possible along the Tennessee. Fertilizer was part of it, of course, and shipping, too, but the heart of it, the part Ford needed to hear, was about electricity—stupendous, dazzling, almost unlimited opportunities for making and using electricity. He told Ford that when the dam was finished, it would produce almost as much electricity as Niagara Falls, far more than the nitrate plants could soak up, enough to run endless industries. They talked about water flow and dam heights. They talked about construction estimates and the nature of the local labor force. They talked about the climate and the culture, and the natural resources within a hundred-mile radius, or two hundred miles, including metal ores and forests and water. What was local transportation like? Railroad service? Roads? The Alabama booster worked his magic. Worthington's Tennessee River Improvement Association had been gathering details about all that for years, and he answered every question frankly, courteously, sometimes humorously, in his soft southern drawl. Ford got more excited about the possibilities every time he talked with Worthington.

One Ford biographer wrote that when they were finally done reviewing the project, Ford turned to Worthington and said, "'I want to go down and look at it. When can we go?"

"Whenever you wish," Worthington replied.

"Well, we'll go tomorrow!" Ford answered.

It was mid-June when a private train pulled into the station at Sheffield, Alabama, and, without any fanfare, Henry Ford, J. W. Worthington, and a handful of engineers and officials stepped out. They got into hired cars, headed toward the dam site, and spent the day looking, asking questions, and dodging local reporters who'd gotten wind of their visit. Then, without offering any interviews, they got on another train and headed back north.

Ford was accustomed to massive projects, but after laying eyes on this one he was still stunned by the scale and the possibilities. He made his decision.

THREE WEEKS AFTER returning to Detroit, Ford presented Secretary Weeks with a brief formal bid for Muscle Shoals. It was very close in scope and wording to the brief draft Worthington and Beach had put together before meeting Ford.

The broad outline was this: Ford would buy the nitrate factories outright for $5 million. He would then pay to bring Nitrate #2—the cyanamide plant—into operation, powering it with electricity from the giant steam plant built for that purpose during the war. The fertilizer he made would be sold at an unspecified low price to farmers, but whatever it was, he would limit his own fertilizer profits to 8 percent. If there was a war, he would make the plant available to the government for making explosives. He would decide later what to do with Nitrate #1, the failed Haber plant.

Then the dam: The government would have to pay to finish it—a task Ford's engineers estimated would cost $28 million—but once it was done, Ford would pay back that sum through a one-hundred-year lease, paying the government 6 percent per year. That would come to about $1.7 million per year income for the government for a century.

The bid was welcome, but it was also puzzling. Ford packed it all into just a few paragraphs, a remarkably condensed bid for a project of this complexity and cost. The result was what one historian called "a certain vagueness of detail" that opened the door to endless debates over what exactly it was that Ford was offering. It seemed hastily written, lacking details—almost cavalier, full of holes and imprecision. Legally, the bid appeared to bind Ford to very little. Right off the bat there were eyebrows raised at the thought of selling the nitrate plants—which had cost the government close to $80 million to build—for $5 million. There was grumbling about the estimate of the costs to finish the dam, the $28 million on which Ford's lease payments would be set. The government engineers thought it would cost significantly more. There were potential legal problems, too: Asking for a hundred-year lease on the dam appeared to violate a fifty-year limit on dam leases set by the Federal Water Power Act.

But Beach was happy to have any bid at all. He wrote Secretary Weeks with a more or less positive response, stressing that the thing had to be figured not in terms of immediate money, but over the long term. At the end of one hundred years, Ford would have paid the government a total of something like $200 million. And the US would have a navigable river and a huge hydroelectric installation. He recommended that Weeks accept it.

News of the bid set off rejoicing throughout the South. Everybody down there seemed to think kindly about Uncle Henry, knew that he was richer than Croesus, that his ability to manage huge manufacturing projects was unmatched, his pockets were deep, and his name attached to anything was like a guarantee of success. The nitpicking about payments and details didn't matter to them. What mattered was that Ford was going to save the region. Newspaper editors ran banner headlines about the bid. In their eyes it was practically a done deal. The dam was going to go up. The factories were going to hum. There were going to be jobs again.

Within a short time, eleven sitting senators and forty-six congressional representatives endorsed Ford's bid, joined quickly by the Farmers Union, the American Federation of Labor, the Grange, state legislatures in Oklahoma and Alabama, and scores of chambers of commerce across the country.

Public support was fueled by Ford's publicity people, who kept a steady flow of positive facts and figures streaming to reporters, writers, and editors. One Muscle Shoals story in a magazine called the *Youth's Companion* was typical of the coverage that resulted: "It is a most promising opportunity to change a frightful waste of money into a moderately good investment," the article read. "There was a great danger that the enormous sum would be quite thrown away. No one believed that the government should go into the business of making fertilizers and selling power, or that it could do so without losing money through waste, incompetence, and graft." The answer, clearly, was to take the government out of it and give the Shoals project to that honest industrialist, that northerner who showed so much faith in the South, that man of the people, Henry Ford.

The Ford bid became a national cause célèbre during the summer of 1921. "The Ford offer for Muscle Shoals is being given more publicity in the press of the United States than any other one subject," one editor noted.

FORD WANTED QUICK action. He was a businessman, and he knew that delay meant lost opportunities and foregone profits, so he put everything he had into pushing the bid along. He became his own best salesman. Two weeks after submitting his offer, he took off on a well-publicized camping trip with his friends Thomas Edison and Harvey Firestone, the tire magnate. They'd been going camping together for years, but this time they invited a new friend to join them: Warren Harding. The president tented with them and an attending phalanx of journalists, photographers, and security men for two days in the woods of Maryland, where at various times they were reported to be taking naps, eating Irish stew, chopping wood, listening to sermons from visiting speakers, swatting mosquitoes, and riding horses. It gave Ford time to get to know the new president who would, more than any other, make the final decision about his offer. They all seemed to get along well enough, although Edison seemed relatively unimpressed with Harding. There were no reports of the men talking about Muscle Shoals. But it's likely they did.

The camping trip went on after Harding returned to Washington. Ford worked the press for the rest of the trip, telling them about the "stupendous" possibilities at Muscle Shoals and the "great wave of prosperity" that would follow a national investment in dams and hydropower, when "labor questions would settle themselves, factories would spring up in every section, and the country blossom like a rose."

Ford figured Harding was going to back his bid. Sure, $5 million for $80 million of nitrate plants wasn't much, but the long-term lease would bring in a lot more, and the development Ford would

Ford, Edison, Harding, Firestone: the Vagabonds on another well-publicized
camping trip
Courtesy Library of Congress

spur would generate a lot of tax money. Anyway, what else was
the president going to do with the mothballed factories, rusting
machinery, skeleton dam, and complete waste of money that was
Muscle Shoals?

Once the trip was over there was wild optimism around
the South that the Ford offer would, with Harding's backing, get
rubber-stamped by Weeks and the rest of the cabinet, forwarded
quickly to Congress, and passed there by a vast majority. By the fall,
they'd be ready to break ground. Worthington, now Ford's main man
in Washington, spent all day, every day, making sure that happened,
shepherding the bid through the federal approval process. Everything seemed to be falling into place.

Then an anti-Ford reaction set in. The main problem was Secretary of War Weeks, who began dragging his feet, concerned both

about Ford's miserly offer for the nitrate plants the military had spent so much time and effort building, and about Ford's lowball estimate of what it would cost to finish the dam. Weeks's people were now telling him that it would cost closer to $40 million than the $28 million Ford was talking about.

The more he looked at the Ford bid, the more Weeks realized that the numbers weren't adding up. As a former banker, he knew all about loans and leases. And, as a banker, he was not particularly happy that Ford, with his anti-banking sentiments, had been insulting the eastern finance scene for years. He didn't like Ford's idea of amortizing what amounted to a loan over a century. He didn't buy Ford's estimate for finishing the dam. And he certainly didn't like the vagueness of Ford's dashed-off bid. It was almost insulting to get a bid like that for a project this big. Weeks began raising some of

BUMP FOR BUMP
—Sykes in the Philadelphia *Evening Public Ledger.*

Weeks vs. Ford

his questions publicly. He slowed the approval process by asking for more detailed reviews. He put on the brakes.

Weeks wasn't the only one. Conservationists began lining up against the offer, too, led by Gifford Pinchot, Teddy Roosevelt's former head of the US Forest Service, an early conservationist and a strong voice for managing public resources for the public good. Pinchot thought that Ford's bid ran counter to the idea of proper public management of major rivers. Yes, private companies could build dams to make electricity, but only with government approval, careful oversight, and a lease deal that topped out at fifty years. The hundred-year Ford deal would run counter to federal law, essentially ceding one-man control over a critical stretch of a major American waterway for a century. Who knew what he would do with it?

With Weeks slowing approval, criticism began to build in the northern press. Ford's old nemesis the *Chicago Tribune*, the newspaper that had made him a national laughingstock at Mount Clemens, hit him hard again, running a front-page bombshell on July 26. It looked big—"LIGHT ON HENRY FORD'S BIG LOBBY. Pulling Wires to Put Shoals Offer Across. Big Men Involved in Amazing Scheme," blared the headline—but the story didn't deliver. Instead of detailing what the paper called "the most formidable and insidious lobby ever organized in Washington," the long article (and a couple of follow-ups) basically boiled down to this: There was a mysterious "directing genius" behind the Ford push, a shady Tennessee River promoter whose schemes already had been turned down multiple times by Congress, and who was calling in favors from old friends, buying people meals, and directing strategy to get the offer approved. The name of this Machiavellian genius was J. W. Worthington.

The real scandal turned out to be how the paper got the story. A few days before it appeared, somebody had broken into Worthington's hotel room during one of his visits to Detroit, rifled through his briefcase, and stole his private correspondence. The purloined letters showed up a few days later in the offices of the *Chicago Tribune*. Worthington thought that the paper had arranged the robbery; the paper's editors claimed that the stolen documents had been leaked to them by the actual thief, whose name they refused to divulge.

Once the robbery was revealed, Worthington looked more like an injured party than a mysterious mastermind. The content of his letters totaled little more than standard lobbying efforts, the meals and meetings that are the basics of the craft. The *Tribune*'s big exposé fizzled. In the end it did little more than link Ford's name to questionable Washington maneuvering and stir up some regional animosity. The Alabama papers responded by praising Worthington as an honest, courtly, suave, and intelligent southern hero, and lambasting the *Tribune* as "Receiver of Stolen Goods and Defamer of the South Always," bemoaning "the unpleasant spectacle of a great newspaper trading and trafficking with a thief who has robbed a hotel room."

WORTHINGTON HAD INDEED been very busy in Washington. With Weeks stalling, he switched his attention to the Commerce Department, using one of his old friends from the Tennessee River Improvement Association, now one of Commerce Secretary Herbert Hoover's top aides, to get that department's backing for the Ford bid. He tried Treasury, too, but ran into a wall there: Harding's treasury secretary, the fabulously wealthy banker and financier Andrew Mellon, counted among his many investments significant sums in the production of aluminum, a lightweight metal being used increasingly to make planes and automobiles. The thing about aluminum was that it required a lot of electricity to turn the ore into finished metal. There was aluminum ore near the Shoals. There was going to be a lot of electricity once the dam was done. To Mellon, it looked like Henry Ford was planning to get into the aluminum business.

Mellon had put a lot of money into the Aluminum Company of America (Alcoa), a company that would be greatly disadvantaged if Ford started competing in the field. Some of Worthington's stolen letters had touched on the issue: He had advised his friends to keep the whole aluminum subject quiet in order to keep Mellon from opposing the bid. What they should do instead, Worthington suggested, was to stress fertilizer. Everybody wanted fertilizer, and making it would win Ford the support of the Farm Bloc.

People were beginning to take sides.

CHAPTER 6

POLITICS AND PUBLIC RELATIONS

FORD WANTED TO get started at Muscle Shoals before the winter of 1921–22 set in. There was no reason he shouldn't, he thought, except for the government getting in his way.

John Weeks was still slow-walking the bid, digging into all sorts of niggling little details. Ford, for instance, had mentioned in his offer the amount of power that the finished dam would be expected to produce, asking for a guarantee of 60,000 horsepower. But Weeks's engineers told him that the flow of the Tennessee varied so much from season to season—flood high in early spring, a trickle by late summer—that no year-round steady horsepower guarantee was possible unless other "holding dams" were built upstream, making lakes that could fill with water in the winter, then be drained in a controlled flow when water was needed in summer. That raised the larger issue about how many dams were going to be built, and where, and how soon.

Ford fumed about the delays through the summer. But he also stuck with the project because he was beginning to appreciate more clearly how grand Muscle Shoals could be. He sent people down to scout out coal possibilities in the area, and iron ore deposits, and timber, and, yes, aluminum ore, too. He began to think about the whole region, one hundred miles up and down the river, the way he thought about designing a car—conceiving of it as an integrated unit, a giant manufacturing center as big as a small state, that would allow him to run his process from raw materials to finished products. It would be River Rouge, only many times bigger.

The key was the dam. With the dam in his hands, Ford would control more electric power than any other single person in the world.

Electricity had started out thirty years earlier being about little things—small generators lighting up Edison's incandescent bulbs. But in 1921 *everything* was going electric. The business and science journals were full of stories about it. Before Edison's light bulb, there were very few ways for the public to use this new power. But now, forty years later, there were electric telephones and electric vacuum cleaners, electric washing machines and electric refrigerators. The hottest new product on the horizon was an electric vacuum-tube radio that would bring music and entertainment into the home.

But from Ford's perspective, the big thing was going to be industrial use. Thanks to the innovation and promotion of alternating current by Nikola Tesla and George Westinghouse, electricity could now be transmitted over wires much farther and at higher power levels than with Edison's old direct current systems. Longer transmission lines meant it was possible to share the electricity produced at a central point—say a great dam on a river—over a much larger area, and in amounts large enough to power small factories. You could use electricity now to power motors powerful enough do just about anything the old steam engines could do.

Ford had been playing with dams and electricity, first putting in some small dams and turbine generators on his property in Michigan and using the power to electrify his house, then damming rivers near some small factories to power production. He was pleased with the results. Electricity made from falling water—the hydroelectric system—was clean and quiet. Once the dam was built, it didn't cost much, because nature provided the water for free. It allowed people to turn the untapped water in a river into pure, usable power. And it made another kind of economic sense for Ford: By generating his own electricity, he didn't have to make deals with or be subjected to the whims of whatever local power utility controlled the lines. Ford intended to make more of his own electricity to power his own factories, in the same way he wanted to mine his own metals to make his own parts. It was about controlling the entire production chain. And that, above all, was what Henry Ford wanted: control.

Ford and The Land of Opportunity (which looks a lot like Muscle Shoals)
Courtesy of the Benson Ford Research Center

He wanted control so he could benefit society. He wasn't in it to get rich. As he told reporters over and over, he had more money than he would ever need. What he wanted to do now was build a system that would be good for everyone, from the well-paid workers in his clean factories to the buyers of his cars. Using electricity on a huge scale, he would be able to piece together a new sort of industrial center the size of a city. It would be his gift to America.

Why stop at industries? Muscle Shoals had started as an idea for turning an unfinished dam into a way to power local factories. But now Ford was beginning to see a bigger vision. What he could do at Muscle Shoals could be a model for an entire future society.

IN ALL OF his dreaming and scheming about Muscle Shoals, Ford was assisted by two top men The first was his chief engineer, William B. Mayo, who analyzed all the construction and production numbers. The second, even more important in many ways, was Ford's personal secretary, Ernest Liebold.

Liebold was one of those "power-behind-the-throne" types who propel history without ever becoming famous. You had to go through Liebold to get to Ford. He was the man behind the desk that guarded Ford's office door. And he was much more. He was the man Ford turned to when he had anything that needed to get done quickly and efficiently—especially if that thing was unpleasant. Liebold spoke to Ford more every day than anybody else. Ford told him his wishes and listened to his advice. By 1921, Ford had grown to depend on Liebold absolutely.

That gave Liebold an unusual kind of power, which he had been cultivating and expanding for years. He looked like a mild-mannered bookkeeper, with a clean-shaven round face, thinning hair, and rimless spectacles. But in 1921 he was, next to Ford, arguably the most important man in the company. Liebold first came to Ford's attention around 1911, just as the motor company was about to take off. A story was told before the war that Model T money was coming in so fast that one day Ford, feeling around in a coat pocket, found a $70,000 check he had stuffed in there and forgotten. The amount was not trivial: In today's dollars it would be close to $2 million. When a business associate heard about the misplaced check, he gently suggested that Ford might want to hire a secretary to help keep track of things.

Liebold was given the job while still in his twenties. He had some bank experience, was clean and sober, appeared scrupulously honest, and had a mind like a calculator. He quickly earned Ford's trust. After he straightened out the boss's accounts, Ford praised him as having "the best financial mind in the country." As the years went by, Liebold was given more and more responsibility, first and foremost handling Ford's money, but soon many other things as well, from screening visitors and correcting his boss's notoriously bad spelling, to signing Ford's name on routine letters and acting as his legal representative.

Liebold spoke softly and precisely. But beneath the soft exterior was a demanding personality wrapped around a hard core of ambition. He came out of Detroit's German-American community (during the first World War, US military intelligence had taken his German ties seriously enough to investigate him as a potential spy, although the war was over before any conclusions were reached) and reflected some stereotypically German traits: a love of order and hard work, discipline and obedience, everything in its place and expected to stay there. He was exactly the right man to corral Ford's many activities and oversee his personal fortune.

But there was another side to Liebold as well. If he had to repeat himself, he could erupt into anger. Other executives grumbled about him being "a Prussian type," with that famous German humorlessness; writers later commented on his "cold, ruthless intensity" and labeled him "an ambitious martinet." One story that made the rounds told of Liebold making his children march around the dinner table until they were commanded, in German, to sit.

German-American he certainly was, and he encouraged Ford's own growing respect for Germany. Several historians have posited that Liebold was really behind Ford's anti-Semitism. One editor of Ford's paper, the *Dearborn Independent*, later wrote, "I am sure that if Mr. Ford were put on the witness stand, he could not tell to save his life just when and how he started against the Jews. I am sure that Liebold could tell."

But more than anything, Liebold was simply Ford's faithful servant, the keeper of the keys, the ear at the door, now elevated to a position of enormous influence. He gave his patron unquestioning, wholehearted loyalty. And this was what Ford wanted most of all: someone who would do as he was asked, immediately, efficiently, and without criticism or question.

Liebold made sure that getting Ford on the phone was about as easy as ringing up the pope. He also spent a lot of his time looking over and sorting all of Ford's mail before the boss got it. By 1921 Ford was getting deluged with correspondence. Mail came from "every man with a crank's turn of mind, promoters of every description; social and political dreamers of all kinds; inventors of hairpins, market baskets, and perpetual motion; of accessories for the Ford car," one of Ford's executives later wrote, "big men seeking millions and little men wanting enough money to pay for rent"—fine artists and con artists, journalists and professors, industrialists, housewives, and congressmen. Liebold passed along only the few letters he felt Ford needed to see personally and took care of the rest himself.

Liebold was also the tough messenger Ford sent when he needed to fire people or cut budgets, the bad cop who allowed Ford to play good cop. He helped make Ford's positive public image possible. And he praised Ford constantly. One reporter for a major magazine remembered that she could not get in to interview the great man until Liebold sat her down and made her listen for an hour as he explained what a great person Ford was.

Liebold was nearing the peak of his power in 1921. Which explains why, perhaps, Ford put him in charge of handling the Muscle Shoals bid. Ford had many other things to do, and the bid was tied to unfortunate amounts of politicking, glad-handing, and arm-twisting, all things the Ford hated. So Ford decided to put Liebold together with J. W. Worthington and let the two of them take care of it. It was a signature mark of favor. After 1921, one of Ford's former business managers recalled, Liebold was "riding high, wide, and handsome."

WORTHINGTON AND LIEBOLD began a lively correspondence in the summer of 1921, starting with an eight-page, single-spaced opus from Worthington that outlined for Liebold the entire history of the project and players.

Worthington then listed the project's most important opponents. It included an all-star roster of America's rich and powerful, starting with James Duke, the cigarette king (Duke University is named after the family). Duke was a major player among the East Coast elites that Ford hated; among his holdings was a major chunk of American Cyanamid, Washburn's company that built Nitrate #2. Apparently the idea of Henry Ford buying the plant for pennies on the dollar offended Duke. After hearing about Ford's bid, Duke "insisted that they would never have a chance again to get the Muscle Shoals power and nitrate plants, that if Mr. Ford got the power he would ruin the power business in the Southeast, and that he would put his crazy ideas into the fertilizer business and ruin that," Worthington wrote Liebold. He alerted Liebold that Duke had convened a meeting of powerful business associates, including the leaders of Alabama Power and a who's who of big-money interests in the East, among them chemical companies and fertilizer companies financed by the House of Morgan and a Jewish investment bank. According to Worthington, this shadowy cabal of power interests were putting their heads together to create a competing bid that might sink Ford's.

Worthington's mention of J. P. Morgan, his name synonymous with Wall Street and banking, and Kuhn, Loeb & Company, a leading multinational investment bank, was purposeful. He was playing to his audience. It had been well-known for years that Ford generally hated both Wall Street and investment banks. And Worthington knew, too, that Kuhn, Loeb had been founded by Jews. He was not above playing on that prejudice. "If the Jews had the chance to award the Muscle Shoals projects under any bid for them, Mr. Ford wouldn't get a look-in, but with the farmers for Mr. Ford, and as there are more farmers in this country than Jews, thank God! Mr. Ford will have a good chance, I think," Worthington wrote Liebold in August 1921. A few weeks later he warned of "New York Jew Merchants" banding together to oppose Ford, and how "Wall Street is not entirely made up of the Tribe of Israel, but even the Gentiles in the tribe are quite Jewish."

SUMMER TURNED TO fall, and still the Ford bid was stuck in the Department of War. The more Secretary of War Weeks looked at it, the less he liked it. Even General Beach walked back his initial recommendation as more was learned about the real costs of finishing the dam. Weeks's friends in the banking world were criticizing Ford's idea of amortizing his investment. Ford might add up the total payments and say he was paying for the dam and then some, but in fact most of the money he would pay was going to be interest on what was essentially a low-cost government loan stretched out over one hundred years. Meanwhile, he would keep all the money made off the electricity the dam produced plus make money on the fertilizer—if any—he made at Nitrate #2. It was a hell of a deal. It looked like Ford was trying to pull a fast one. Rumors kept flying that Duke and his rich friends were working with American Cyanamid to build a competing offer.

Alabama Power was circling around, too. Up to now, Alabama Power had controlled just about all the electricity generation and transmission in the state and was well-connected politically. If it jumped in with a counterbid, Ford was in for serious competition. There was talk of other wild-card investors diving in as well. Things were heating up.

FORD COUNTERED WITH politics and public relations. Worthington was assigned the task of firming up political support, getting people to go on the record supporting the Ford bid. Formal letters began streaming in from senators and representatives enthusiastically backing it. Ford deepened his relationship with pro-agriculture lobbies to help whip up support in rural areas, touting the Ford promise of cheap fertilizer. Pro-Ford rallies began to pop up in farm states, complete with buttons that read, "I want Ford to Get Muscle Shoals."

Ford himself played it low-key in public—mostly saying that he didn't really need Muscle Shoals, had plenty to do otherwise, could do fine without it—and let others make his points for him.

But he occasionally let his enthusiasm slip. In August he told a United Press reporter that he was thinking about building a cotton mill near the Shoals to make upholstery for his cars, and another factory for casting metal, and "many other and bigger opportunities." He had sent down investigators to take a look at raw materials in the area, he said, and they had told him there were all kinds he could use.

The more he talked, the bigger his ideas got. The fertilizer plants would only use a third of the energy from the dam; with the rest he could do things like build enormous electric furnaces to melt down old railway cars and make them into new ones, every old car turned into three lighter, stronger, new ones, thanks to a new alloy he was developing. He said that he had been on a trip down the Potomac with Thomas Edison where they saw a barge loaded with coal. "Why, coal ought not to be burned at all!" Ford said. Houses and factories should be powered with clean electricity from dams. Once that big dam at Muscle Shoals was running, he saw no reason why a city of 100,000 people shouldn't spring up around it.

The grander the plans, the more press he got. And he had his own people stoke the fire. In September the *Dearborn Independent* ran a cover story, "Muscle Shoals Foreshadows New Industrial Era," a lavishly illustrated two-page spread foretelling the "Dawn of a New Industrial and Economic Era." Anything, it seemed, was possible.

Weeks had to respond in some way. He asked Ford to come to Washington and talk things out, but Ford declined to make the trip, sending his engineer, William Mayo, instead. It was a mild, calculated insult, a way of showing the secretary of war how little Ford thought of him. Mayo and Worthington sat down with Weeks in mid-September but left with little to show for it. The major sticking point was a difference in how the two sides saw the costs of finishing the dam. Ford and his people wouldn't budge from their $28 million estimate for completion, but the military engineers were now thinking that $42 to $55 million was more like it. The gap was too big to paper over.

At the end of October, Weeks made his own headlines by going down to inspect the Shoals, a rare visit by a cabinet member. He was greeted by thousands of enthusiastic locals at the train station, reviewed the moribund project, and delivered a speech to local businessmen. Seeing the dam and the nitrate plants left him, he told a reporter, "amazed at the possibilities."

After returning to Washington, he again invited Ford to come chat. The Ford offer was still, for the moment, the only one on the table, and Weeks hinted that a quick decision might be made. Ford responded that he'd be there as soon as he could.

And Weeks responded by showing Ford that he was no longer the only player in the game. A few days after inviting Ford to Washington, he suddenly announced that emergency conditions down south—unusually low river levels, which crippled power production and electricity rationing for some industrial buyers—had led to a decision to lease the giant steam-powered electricity plant at Muscle Shoals (the one that had been built during the war to power Nitrate #2 until the dam was done). Until further notice, the plant was going to be run by one of Ford's potential rivals, Alabama Power.

Ford was somewhere between annoyed and incensed. He needed that plant to make the fertilizer he'd promised the farmers. It didn't matter to him that Weeks had included a cancellation clause that would allow the government to break Alabama Power's lease within a month if the Ford offer was accepted. What mattered was that the power plant was part of his bid. And now Weeks was going to let a competitor run it? The whole thing seemed fishy. Why this monkey business just as Ford was coming to Washington to ink the deal? Wouldn't this give Alabama Power Company an inside track for making its own bid? It was certainly a sign that the Ford offer was not as close to being accepted as it seemed. As one former Alabama governor said, the lease looked like "another excuse to block Henry Ford's acquisition of the Muscle Shoals project."

The game of chess Ford and Weeks were playing came to a climax on November 18, 1921, when Ford himself finally appeared in Washington to close the deal. He was in full press mode. Before arriving, he gave an interview on the train, telling the wire services, "I will put the South on the map," and expanding his promises: He was now talking about manufacturing aluminum as well as cloth, making enough fertilizer to feed the whole Cotton Belt, and building a string of a dozen hydroelectric dams at other spots on the river, in addition to the giant dam under construction. With all that clean power, he said, he could create a million jobs

The extent to which he had been thinking about the project became clear as he kept talking. He would transform the whole region with electricity. The workers he hired would be able to work a small farm for thirty days a year—enough, Ford figured, to do all the planting and harvesting required, if they used a Ford tractor—then load the crops on a Ford truck "and whirl them over good roads" to market. His companies would give employees enough time off to work the land, then bring them back in for comfortable factory jobs when they were done. This was going to be a new way of life, a new combination of city and country, with the old, backbreaking, isolated farm life transformed by part-time industrial jobs, by appliances, by electrical conveniences, by cars, trucks, and tractors. "The farmer's day is just about to dawn," Ford enthused.

He was making sure that Weeks would be under maximum pressure to okay such a sweeping, positive deal. Rumors flew that the Harding administration was ready to sign off. "Detroit Man Is Near Goal," read the hopeful headline in the Birmingham newspaper.

When he arrived in Washington, DC, Ford and his team, including Liebold, were given dinner and a briefing by Worthington. Afterward, they pored over maps of the area's mineral deposits. Everything looked like it was lining up.

But the chess game wasn't over. The next day Ford was told that Secretary Weeks had fallen ill and could not meet as planned. Commerce Secretary Hoover was offered as a substitute. But Ford's patience was growing thin. He had not traveled to Washington to talk with somebody who couldn't make a final decision. He quickly made it clear that his bid as originally written months ago was still his bid, and he was not going to change much if anything about it. He then paid a call on President Harding, slipping in a side entrance to avoid the front-door cadre of cameras and reporters, making his way to the president and talking for fifteen minutes. On the way out he once again avoided the press, exiting the White House by going through the telephone switching room, down a narrow flight of stairs to the cellar, through the Secret Service dressing room, and then through a side door onto the grounds. He sprinted across the street to Commerce, had a short courtesy meeting with Hoover, and went back to his private train to go home.

He was fuming. But just before his train was to depart, around nine that night, Ford got a last-minute call asking him to come to Weeks's home. Despite his illness, he wanted to meet after all.

Ford, along with Liebold and some engineers, was driven to the quiet residential neighborhood where Weeks lived and was taken in to see the ailing secretary, who was dressed in a bathrobe. He told Ford that, yes, he was feeling poorly, but would feel worse if he did not have a talk. Then they got down to it, wrangling over the costs of finishing the dam. Weeks told Ford that he had been down there, had seen the work, and stood by his people's higher numbers. His team had seen it, too, Ford said, and they stood by their lower esti-mate. Neither side would budge.

They didn't trust each other. They didn't like each other. There wasn't going to be any deal made that night. Ford stood up to go.

Before he left, Weeks tried one last thing. "If you and Edison will go to Muscle Shoals and make an estimate as to the cost of the completion of the work, we can settle the details in two minutes," he said. Edison's word, it seemed, was that good.

Ford thought, *Edison? Would that turn the trick?* It might not be a bad idea. It sounded like Weeks was saying that a stamp of approval from America's beloved inventor would move his decision along. And Edison and Ford were good friends.

As Ford boarded his train back to Detroit, a reporter asked him if his offer was going to be accepted. "You bet it's going to go through," Ford snapped.

Then he wired Thomas Edison.

CHAPTER 7

THE TWIN WIZARDS

THOMAS EDISON WAS Henry Ford's hero, as he had been for many young men and women in the last decades of the nineteenth century. The string of inventions by "the Wizard of Menlo Park"—the light bulb, the phonograph, electrical systems, motion pictures, improved batteries, improved telegraph, improved telephone, and on and on—inspired a generation of American scientists, engineers, and garage tinkerers.

They had met once prior to Ford's success with the Model T, when Edison was on top of the world and Ford was a fresh employee at one of Edison's companies. One of Ford's first jobs after knocking around the machine shops of Detroit had been as a night engineer at an Edison power substation, where he proved himself a mechanical genius at fixing problems with dynamos. He was quickly promoted to chief engineer at the main powerhouse of the Edison Illuminating Company of Detroit.

Shortly after that, in 1896, Edison came to town to see how his subsidiary was doing. At a large meeting one of Edison's executives pointed across the room to a slight, thin young man and said, "Over there's a young fellow who made a gas car." He was gesturing at Ford. Edison certainly was interested; he had been playing around with cars, specifically the idea of powering them with improved batteries.

Ford was thirty-three years old and utterly starstruck. Edison, then close to fifty years old, was everything Ford wanted to be: a brilliant inventor who made life better for everyone, a business tycoon, and a very rich man. They were introduced, made a bit of small talk, then started talking about gas engines. Soon Ford was making sketches. The two men lowered their heads over a table and talked about designs, and Ford's life changed.

"Mr. Edison listened to me very patiently," Ford remembered. "Then he banged a fist on the table and said, 'Young man, that's the thing. Your car is self-contained—no boiler, no heavy battery, no smoke or steam. Keep at it."

"You can imagine how excited I was," Ford said.

The improved gas engine was Ford's obsession at the time, the thing he spent every spare moment on. He intended to design one that could be used in a gasoline-powered motor carriage (the French were calling such machines "automobiles"). He had taken the job at Edison in part so he could have more money for tools and experiments. Being named chief engineer also gave him access to the Detroit Edison workshops, where he spent his spare time fashioning the bits and pieces he needed.

There was nothing new about gas engines. They had been in use in a small way for decades. And there was nothing particularly new about automobiles, either, which by the early 1890s were being produced in a number of shops. In Germany, for instance, a mechanical engineer named Carl Benz and a pair of business partners named Gottlieb Daimler and Wilhelm Maybach had been making gasoline-powered engines and cars since the 1880s. Americans made their entry into the field in 1889.

But these early engines were handmade, complex, finicky, and expensive. It was difficult to feed in just the right amount of gasoline to a small chamber in just the right way, ignite it precisely, contain and control the little explosion that resulted, and tame the resulting power to turn wheels. Then the whole thing had to be cooled and oiled continuously. Ford wanted to make a cheap car, a relatively simple car, an automobile that farmers could afford. He started with the ideas of others but then improved on them, making his engines tougher and more reliable. His first breakthrough came just before he met Edison. In 1896 he successfully tested his first Quadricycle, a rickety-looking wagon mounted on four bicycle tires and powered with a small Ford engine.

He was making good money working at Detroit Edison, but his heart wasn't in it. Three years after his introduction to Edison, Ford quit his job and went full-time into car making. It took him almost ten years to create and sell the first Model T (in 1908), then ten more to turn it into a global sales phenomenon.

As Ford's star rose over those two decades, Edison's sank. His peak had been in 1870s and 1880s, when his inventive genius seemed endless. But by the time he and Ford first met, Edison was becoming mired in business details, lawsuits, and patent questions, and the flow of inventions slowed. The Edison business empire—much of it based around wiring major cities for his particular brand of direct-current electrical system—was in decline as more customers turned to George Westinghouse's alternating current. Edison, unmatched as an inventor, was outmatched as a businessman. The Edison Illuminating Company's board and major stockholders ended up booting Edison out, putting new management in his place, and stripping his name from the company. They renamed it General Electric.

Edison came out of it with enough money to build a large new research laboratory where he could pursue any question that caught his fancy. But he never again achieved anything comparable to what he'd done back in his prime.

It didn't matter to Ford. He still idolized Edison. Soon after he formed the Ford Motor Company, Ford wrote his hero asking for an autographed picture. But Edison had no memory of the young man he'd once talked with in Detroit and treated Ford's note "the same as the dozens of similar requests he got every day," wrote historians Peter Collier and David Horowitz, "scrawling 'No Ans' on the letter and handing it back to his secretary to dispose of."

It wasn't until 1912 that Ford finally got the great man's attention, when he visited Edison in person, bearing the gift of a new Model T, a request for Edison to design a better electrical system for his cars, and the offer of a million-dollar loan to tide the inventor through a financial shortfall. It was the start of a beautiful friendship.

They were much alike. They had a shared background—farm boys who loved machines—were both innovative, and both made it big despite a lack of formal education. Edison once described himself as a "freak" because he had been such a success in technology without ever taking a college class. "Ford is another freak," he told an interviewer after their acquaintance had been rekindled. "I doubt if America will ever produce another man like him."

They were alike in another way, too. Considering how prominent they were in the business world at various times, they were both uncomfortable in groups, preferring the isolation of the laboratory and shop to the small talk of social occasions. They were both better with machines than with people.

Edison recalled Ford again showing up at his door in 1914, after his Menlo Park laboratory burned down, this time with a check for $750,000, offered as an interest-free loan. The next year they went to the world's fair (the Panama-Pacific International Exposition) in San Francisco together. Then they started going on a series of summer camping trips with Harvey Firestone and others, calling themselves "the Vagabonds."

Their friendship was a dream come true for Ford. "His knowledge is almost universal," he said of Edison. "He is interested in every conceivable subject, and he recognizes no limitations. He believes that all things are possible. At the same time he keeps his feet on the ground."

Ford could well have been describing himself.

AFTER HIS ABORTIVE meeting in Weeks's home in November 1921, Ford turned to his old friend and asked for a favor: Would Edison come along on a trip down to Alabama with him? They could bring their wives, make a brief vacation of it, and see some interesting engineering. It might be fun. And Ford could really use Edison's support.

Edison quickly said yes and they began planning the trip.

When word got out that Ford and Edison together were going to visit the Shoals, the South went wild. "Henry Ford may not build the eighth wonder of the world at Muscle Shoals," a local news story said, "but he will build things worth seven times seventy times what the old seven wonders were." The Ford bid was alive, and this visit would undoubtedly seal the deal.

They took off soon after Thanksgiving. Ford arranged to bring them down in his private railcar, the Fair Lane, a sort of luxury hotel room on wheels, with its own private chef, fine crystal, and private rooms for guests. Ford and his wife, Clara, brought along their son (and his heir apparent), Edsel, and his wife, Eleanor, as well as the Edisons.

The train also included a car full of reporters, and Ford and Edison took advantage of the trip to give easy access and long interviews designed to build excitement. Their every comment spurred national headlines: Ford promises to build "river fleet" of self-propelled barges; Edison predicts a new age of water-powered electricity; Ford promises to cut the price of fertilizer in half and give away a ton of it with each new Model T he sells; Ford will employ the whole work-force of Alabama. "Acceptance Ford Offer Is Assured," headlines read. "Ford Will Work Wonders in Shoals."

Along the way, countless meal and meeting invitations were extended to Ford and Edison from every mayor and chamber of commerce on their route. In Nashville, the train stopped to pick up twenty local business leaders and politicians, including the city's mayor, a former US senator, the state's commissioner of agriculture, and the governor of the state of Tennessee. At every town and crossroads people were waiting for them, waving and cheering as the train sped by. One reporter noted, "Mr. Ford remarked to Mr. Edison, 'We ought to be in politics.'"

Or perhaps real estate. The promise of an economic boom accompanying the Ford development was already starting to raise property values. Newly arrived real estate agents were gathering in the Tri-Cities around the Shoals, "not taking options on Sheffield property, they are buying outright," reported a local paper the day before Ford and Edison arrived. Their visit would supercharge the market.

It looked like momentum was once again on Ford's side. Was there any doubt his bid would be accepted? Ford had one. "Do you expect any trouble getting the approval of Congress?" a reporter asked him on the train down. "Yes, I do," Ford said. "The trusts and the international Jews will oppose me."

Given all the hoopla, it came as something of a surprise when they reached the station in Florence and found the place almost empty.

There was a crowd waiting for them, but it was at the wrong station, across the river in Sheffield. People had been milling around there for hours with "exactly the same thrill feeling of expectancy that usually comes on Christmas morning," a reporter noted, because they thought the Twin Wizards were coming in from the east, which would make Sheffield the logical stopping point. When word finally came, just as they were pulling in, that the great men had come from the north and were at the Florence station, the crowd had to hightail it over the bridge.

It took less than an hour to regather. Once the train was surrounded by the crowd, Ford emerged onto the train's back platform to thunderous cheers. He looked every inch the tycoon, his trim form highlighted by an elegantly tailored dark suit with a black derby. Women in the crowd commented admiringly. He was energized, electrified, full of vim, "miraculously young," the reporters scribbled, "keenly interested in everything, and moving about with great rapidity." Another roar went up when he introduced the seventy-four-year-old Edison, looking slightly rumpled and elderly by comparison. Then the Twin Wizards' wives were introduced (more cheering), and Ford's son, Edsel, and his wife (another ovation).

They all thanked the crowd briefly, then took off on J. W. Worthington's carefully planned tour of the area. The men and their wives were ushered into cars and driven through the broad streets of Florence—recently paved for the first time—to see the dam. All along the route crowds cheered them. At the construction site they were joined by uniformed military engineers who served as guides, and boarded a steel observation car for a tour. Edison, looking tired but in good spirits, made a joke of saluting one of them.

And the little observation train jolted forward. They came to the dam construction site, where the size and scale of the unfinished mile-long concrete barrier across the river astonished everyone. One of their military guides pointed out a giant rock crusher, which he

Second from left to right: Edison, Ford, and the levitating J. W. Worthington, who "can't keep his feet on the ground"
Sheffield Standard, December 16, 1921

said was the largest in the world. Edison asked them to stop, got out, climbed up on the machine, and announced, "It is out of date. I have a machine that will crush a solid rock as big as that water tank." They continued to a small wooden observation platform built to offer a panoramic view of the site, and everyone got out to take a look. The image of Ford and Edison standing there, gazing over miles of river, was captured by a movie cameraman who posed them at an angle to catch the setting sun. In great spirits, Ford shouted into Edison's one good ear, "See, Mr. Edison, we have broken into the movies again." Edison, a wisp of his hair tousled by the breeze, smiled and took a small bow.

Then it was on to the nitrate plants. Even though it was late in the day, Ford and Edison wanted to take a quick look before dark at the factories in which, it was hoped, they would make cheap fertilizer. Ford was as excited as a child, constantly joking, animated, and active as they drove the few miles to the factory sites. They ended up having to light their way with flashlights.

Back at the train, Ford was too excited to sit down. He went out to hold court with reporters at the station, talking about a giant steam shovel he was going to use that would cut costs in half, talking about benefits to farmers—"Say to the farmers that anything I do will be for them. My proposal is a farmer's proposal"—and confirming that while he didn't know a thing about nitrates, it didn't matter, because he'd brought the world's greatest chemist, Mr. Edison, with him. Edison was "here to take care of that." When asked about Weeks's recent decision to lease the steam plant, he replied, "I don't want any steam plants. I am down here in Alabama looking for water power and its developments. I have two steam plants in Detroit, and I would like to get rid of both of them. Water power is the great agency of the industrial development of the future."

Ford seemed exhilarated by the enthusiasm of the adoring crowds that gathered wherever he went. When a reporter suggested that he was the first of the big northern capitalists to talk of coming south, Ford said, "I know no limits. I never have known any. The only fault I find with the people of the south is that they are too darned hospitable."

Then he added something that made headlines everywhere. Muscle Shoals, he told the reporters, was not just about hiring a million men or building new industries. It was really about ending war. "This fostering, starting, and fighting of a war is nothing more or less than creating an active market for money—a business transaction," he told the reporters. Gold, the root of all evil, was behind it all.

And Muscle Shoals offered a way out. Instead of financing his enormous construction plans in the usual ways, going to the banks for a loan, or asking the government to float bonds, Ford was going to create a new kind of currency. Not US dollars, because those were based on gold. Ford felt the use of the gold standard in the US was a mistake. There was so little gold in the world that "its total supply can be controlled, can be got under the dominance of one interest or group of interests and thus the currency and capital of the whole world controlled," Ford said. "And just exactly that thing has happened. There's a group of international bankers—Jewish bankers—who today control the bulk of the world's gold supply. Break that control," he said, banging his hand for emphasis, "and you stop war."

Instead, Ford was going to build Muscle Shoals with his own currency, a new kind of dollar backed not by gold, but by the enormous value of the dam and the energy that it would produce. Print the money—he called it "energy dollars"—and use it to buy what was needed for construction, then buy it back with income from the completed project. "If the government will accept my suggestion of paying for the cost of the completion of the dam with money issued against the value of the structure itself, the people of this country can have this wonderful project completed and it will not cost them one cent," he said.

The alternative was for the government to float bonds to pay for the project, which would then be paid back with interest. Both Ford and Edison distrusted bankers, both hated being in debt, and both were against moneylenders who made interest off of loans. The energy dollar scheme offered a way to get around paying the useless, extra cost of interest. Anti–gold standard activism had been around a long time, and had been especially popular among farmers Ford and Edison had grown up around—voters who had backed

William Jennings Bryan with his thunderous speech about crucify-
ing mankind upon a cross of gold. Neither Ford nor Edison had a
deep knowledge of economics, but both were excited about their
new brainstorm. They thought they'd put together a revolutionary
advance in financing: "Gold is a relic of Julius Caesar and interest is
the invention of Satan," Edison said. It was time to get rid of it. And,
he added, "Ford's idea is flawless."

But their scheme had not been well-thought-out, and it didn't
take more than a few weeks for economists and editorial writers to
pick their arguments apart. "Ford's Energy Dollar Useless, Treasury
View," ran a headline in the *New-York Tribune*. Every expert the paper
talked to said it was economically unsound. If you could issue currency based on the future earnings of Muscle Shoals, why couldn't
you issue money based on any sort of future speculation? "Why not
issue as many dollars of the civilized people's paper money as the
remotest star is distant in miles," asked a *New York Times* editorial,
"or as the thoughts of these distinguished inventors are from the
teachings of experience?" The value of energy dollars would be based
on guesses, not real worth.

And the Ford-Edison attack on making interest from loans was
also misplaced, critics said. A person or institution loaning money
was taking a risk that it might not be paid back. Interest on the loan
was a reward for taking the risk. But floating currency in the form
of energy dollars assumed there was no risk.

Okay, but what if Ford promised to pay it back no matter what?
It would be risk-free. If that happened, money experts countered,
allowing the printing of energy dollars would simply represent a
government loan of that amount of money to Ford, allowing him to
spend it now, then pay it back later, interest-free.

Every economist agreed: The energy dollar scheme was too
good to be true. There was no way it could work.

But those criticisms took a few weeks to put together. For the moment, while Ford and Edison were in Alabama, most of the public thought the scheme sounded great. It was another reason to back Ford.

DURING THAT FIRST exciting day of their visit, Ford didn't stop talking to reporters until dinner was served—"a fine lot of quail" delivered to his train car by a local admirer—and after eating he was still wound up. Edison went to bed, but Ford spent the rest of that Saturday night pacing back and forth by the tracks, shaking hands and passing a few words with well-wishers, then taking off to walk the streets of the town, "bareheaded and alone," the local paper reported, stopping at local stores to chat. People in that part of the country seem to have all the time in the world to talk, and they all said wonderful things about Ford. He was having the time of his life.

The next morning was chilly and blustery, weather that worried Edison's wife. She would rather have had her aging husband quiet at home than running around the countryside, clambering over machinery and through cold, empty buildings when he should be reading in his office.

But Edison was determined to see what he'd come down to see. He and Ford started the day off with an hour-and-a-half press conference. A local ten-year-old boy was invited to sit between Ford and Edison, who held forth yet again on the potential of Muscle Shoals and the cleverness of their energy dollar plan. It was Sunday, and a town delegation of ten or so prominent citizens came down to the train to see if the two visitors wanted to go to church. "No," Ford answered, "I'll worship the Lord seeing what he gave us."

Then they took off on a trip farther up the river with a group of local notables, to the proposed site of a second holding dam. Everyone bundled up in overcoats and got aboard a little narrow-gauge railway. "They had this beautiful little coach for guests built out of

walnut stumps," one of their hosts remembered. "It was the pret-
tiest thing you nearly ever saw." As they clacked along, they talked
about farming—everyone shaking their heads about how the bottom had fallen out of prices and how greatly they would be helped
by cheap fertilizer. Edison smoked a pipe and looked at the water.
After returning to Florence for a short rest, everybody headed out for
an old-fashioned barbecue at the country home of Ed O'Neal, scion
of a leading political family and head of the state's Farm Bureau.
It was bitingly cold by the time they got to the O'Neal place, but
there was a big chestnut wood fire blazing in front of his home,
lamb was sizzling, the local ladies and gentlemen were dressed in
their best outfits, drinks were served by Black waiters in suit coats,
and they had quite a party. Ford was, again, as lively as a young boy.
He and Edison split some chestnut logs for the benefit of the press.
Then O'Neal's young son took Ford on a tour of the place, showing
him the hams hanging in the smokehouse and the spring where
they got water. Ford was especially interested in the aging pieces
of Americana scattered around the farm—the big old iron laundry
kettles that still stood in the yard, a cedar bucket and gourd dipper.
He reminisced about his mother toting water and washing clothes in
her yard. "Sell me that kettle," he asked his host when the tour was
over. "Sell me that gourd." The souvenirs were loaded into Ford's car.
He was a very happy man—so happy, O'Neal remembered, that "he
just had a fit about that party."

They all drove back to Florence, where Ford and Edison topped
off the day by sitting down with the press for another hour. "Both of
them are as unaffected as children, as friendly as men could possibly
be," one reporter wrote. They were now talking about building one
hundred dams on the Tennessee—Ford later upped the number to
one thousand—and bringing the benefits of electricity to the whole
region. He wanted people to understand, Ford said again, that he
was not in this to make money for himself—he had all the money

In Alabama, the Ford-Edison plans generated years of front-page news.

he would ever need—but to perform a service for the people of the region and the world, to weaken the stranglehold of gold, and to end war.

Edison, as usual, spoke far less than Ford. When asked about the nitrate plants, he nimbly sidestepped specifics, saying things like "I have been deeply impressed by the possibilities of that great nitrate plant. I went over that place very carefully" and "I can't tell you what the possibilities are, they are so great."

Actually, Edison hadn't the faintest idea of what might be possible when it came to making nitrates. He claimed chemistry as one of his greatest strengths, but he was actually more of an enthusiastic and talented amateur than a real researcher. By 1921, chemistry was a mature science that required years of graduate study to truly master, and Edison had never taken a class. He was gifted with important talents: He was smart, persistent, and patient; he would try substance after substance in his searches related to his inventions. But he had little deep knowledge of how chemistry worked, next to no history of synthesizing chemicals at an industrial level, and exactly zero experience with nitrates or making fertilizers. He could see during his quick walks through the echoing, deserted plants at

Muscle Shoals that the huge facilities had been well maintained, that they were wired for a lot of power, and that all that space and machinery offered possibilities for something, but whether that something was going to be cheap fertilizer was beyond his ability to predict. Still, he made positive noises.

He was there more as a wingman for Henry Ford. So he kept his comments vague, like this answer given when reporters asked him about how nitrates were made: "Nitrates for fertilizer are merely power arrested by electrical and other fixation processes and concentrated into the form of crystals," he said. This was nonsense that sounded scientific. Edison was covering up his ignorance.

Then he would change the subject, telling long stories about his career or commenting on Ford's endless, restless energy. "He's a wonder," Edison said of Ford. "What Ford sets out to do he will do. He permits nothing to stop him." Once he digressed to talk about how his son Theodore had invented a super-weapon during the Great War, a six-foot-high, ten-inch-wide sharpened steel wheel packed with high explosives. They tested it in Key West during the war, Edison told the reporters, spinning the wheel to high speed using a car engine, then releasing it, sending it zooming and bouncing at four hundred miles per hour toward a target, an electric wire unspooling behind it. It could cut through 150 feet of barbed wire. Once it was where you wanted it, you exploded it with an electric signal. It was looking good, but unfortunately the war ended before it could be approved. "Just think what Theodore's invention would have done to the Heinies if it had ever been put to use," his proud father said.

Edison might have been too tired during the trip to Muscle Shoals to do much more than tell stories. His wife, Mina, cautioned Ford not to push her husband too hard. But, she remembered, their host didn't seem to listen. After the barbecue Mina retired to her bedroom and penned a letter to their son Theodore. "I had made the remark that he [Edison] got pretty tired but did not want to admit it," she sighed. But "Mr. Ford assumes the attitude that he knows Papa better than I do."

Their last day was busy again. First Ford and Edison received a delegation of notables from Birmingham. Then they piled into cars again for a last visit to Nitrate Plant #2, where they were met by an enthusiastic crowd of locals. The weather was warming, the southern sun was bright, and Ford was again in high spirits. On their way back to the station they stopped by a local school where their car was swarmed by children asking questions, chattering and laughing, and keeping the two great men occupied so long that they had to delay their departure. When they finally made it back to the station, there was an enthusiastic farewell crowd applauding, crying out support, lifting babies to kiss. As the train readied to pull out, people in the crowd started calling, "Come back, Henry!"

"I'm coming back," he called, waving his hat from the back platform, "if the government lets me."

CHAPTER 8

ROADBLOCK

"THE SOUTH IS with us," Ford told reporters on the train heading home. "The possibilities of the project are greater than we first believed." The Tennessee River valley, he told reporters, was about to enter a "period of wonderful prosperity." For days the newspapers nationwide told stories about what he'd seen and said on the trip, the jobs, the end of war, the energy dollars, the revival on the river. All the news was good news. "I think that Mr. Ford felt a news story on the front page was of much more value than a paid campaign," his personal secretary Ernest Liebold remembered. "He went on the theory of keeping the name Ford before the public, not particularly as an advertising factor so much as it was a means of upholding his popularity. In this way people would have favorable inclinations toward him."

Now, eager to close his deal with Washington, Ford used all his media clout to make a final push for Muscle Shoals. Having Edison at his side had been a brilliant move. The chance to follow two of the best-known men in the world on a momentous trip to a little-known area was catnip for reporters. Every cheering crowd, every child's handshake, had been reported. The Harding economic recovery was beginning to be felt in much of the nation, but around the Shoals it was still hard times. The economy had not recovered from the double whammy of the halt in dam construction and the lingering effects of the agricultural slowdown of 1920.

Ford was seen as a savior, and after his visit with Edison, local news coverage sometimes veered into hero worship. On the front page of one southern newspaper of the day, a large portrait of a benignly smiling Ford was captioned: "Farmer, philosopher, humanitarian, man of big business affairs, and doer of big things, and withal a kindly man of the people." Another paper noted that Ford was being hailed as "the Messiah of Muscle Shoals."

Once they were back, Edison formalized his stamp of approval. "I shall recommend to the people of the United States and to Congress the acceptance of Mr. Ford's offer for the Muscle Shoals project," he said. "If the government is wise, it will accept Ford's offer for this uncompleted dam and the plants that go with it. Ford's offer is liberal. Nobody else will pay as much."

The trip to Muscle Shoals had been a publicity coup for the ages. Now, with Edison's backing in place, it was time to close the deal. After returning to Detroit, Ford sent J. W. Worthington and engineer William Mayo to Washington with a lightly revised offer (no important changes, but a greater stress on how his plans would improve navigation on the river, which meant the federal government should be expected to cover a portion of the costs). The hope was that Secretary of War Weeks would be bowled over by the support shown for Ford's bid, cave in, and approve the revised offer.

But he did not. Weeks, for a variety of reasons, from his personal dislike of Ford to his still-unanswered questions over financing and fine points, was in no mood to talk to the automaker's underlings. Despite his suggestion to take Edison down to the Shoals and see what he thought, Edison's support now did not seem to sway Weeks.

He received the visitors frostily, stood his ground on the money the government would need to finish the dam, and sent Ford's lieutenants back to Michigan empty-handed.

Stung, Ford now presented himself as victim: "The enemies of the project are many. They are powerful, and above all, they are silent, secret, and menacing," he told reporters. "We cannot fight them in the open, because they will not come out. We cannot fight them with our fists because they won't let us. We cannot fight them with argument, for they will not debate. We can fight them with our brains, and that's the only real way to fight, anyway." He was referring to his old enemies, the big-money boys, the Dukes and Morgans and Mellons, the financiers and Wall Street gougers.

And there it was: on one side Ford, selflessly devoted to the good of the nation (especially the South), saving farmers, creating jobs, and ending war. On the other his shadowy "enemies," with an unspoken nod to the international Jew—"silent, secret and menacing."

The battle for Muscle Shoals was not over. It was barely getting started.

WEEKS FUMED AS he saw Ford trying to whip up public support. He knew that Muscle Shoals was a valuable government asset, and he wasn't going to let it go for a song to the first person who showed an interest. By delaying Ford, he kept the door open for other offers, competing bids that might sweeten the pot and move Ford toward more serious negotiations. The Muscle Shoals project already had been sitting idle for a couple of years. Given the money at stake, Weeks was willing to wait a little longer.

Ford was forced to trek to Washington in mid-January to meet once again with Weeks and Secretary of Commerce Herbert Hoover. Again he made minor changes to his original offer—some financing tweaks that didn't amount to much. Weeks counteroffered with a

The Battle of the Shoals: Secretary of War Weeks and Ford, January 13, 1922
Courtesy Library of Congress

compromise on the financing scheme plus an increase to $8.5 million for the nitrate plants instead of the $5 million Ford offered. Neither side would move. Ford walked out of the meeting—the last time he would sit face-to-face with Weeks—knowing that the secretary was still not going to support his bid.

So Ford went back to applying public pressure. Immediately after the fruitless meeting, he walked over to his rooms at the Willard Hotel and started his people working on a press release. In the Ford archives is a draft dated January 14, 1922, that gives a sense of Ford's state of mind. Under the title "Shoals Delay Arouses Ford," it appears to be a carefully crafted argument ghostwritten by Ford's public relations team. "You know, I used to wonder a few weeks ago why the dickens I was bidding for Muscle Shoals," his writers had him saying folksily. "We have never needed Muscle Shoals—always got along fine without it." He had only gotten into it because the government kept "pestering" him to bid. When he took a look in more detail he discovered great waste—"the waste of millions of dollars raised by taxing the people in selling war-built industries for junk; the waste in letting Muscle Shoals lie there uncompleted and idle"—so as a public service he made an offer to help out the government. Then came the delay of his bid, "the waste of millions more of money raised by taxing the people because of the government's dilatory and indifferent ways and methods of doing business generally. . . . More than six months have gone by and we haven't closed negotiations one way or the other. The Government's executives and agents are still puttering around with a lot of preliminary questions which should have been settled months ago."

He added an attack on what he was now calling the "Fertilizer Trust," a group of powerful fertilizer makers he claimed was behind the opposition to his bid. They didn't want the competition from Ford's cheaper product, so they were turning what Ford saw as a relatively straightforward transaction into a political quagmire. As for making fertilizer, Edison was at work on that problem at that very moment, he said, coming up with a better fertilizer at a lower price than Americans had ever seen.

Worthington began a lobbying push, getting Ford's rural supporters and agricultural lobbyists whipped up across the Farm Belt around a rallying cry for cheap fertilizer. Word spread that now was the time for speaking out. An Alabama woman suggested in a letter to her local newspaper that "every man and woman age 21 or over, black or white, rich or poor, educated or illiterate, who favors the government leasing Muscle Shoals to Henry Ford for development, demonstrate that desire by writing a letter to their representatives in Washington." A Methodist official issued an appeal for all Christians to come to the support of the Ford offer.

Pro-Ford letters poured into Weeks's office, the White House, and Congress. One magazine editor estimated in early 1922 that "thousands of resolutions and literally millions of letters have been written by farmers in favor of acceptance." A Georgia farmer wrote Harding that "nine out of ten people have the utmost confidence in Henry Ford." Mass meetings were held in towns and cities across the South. The Tennessee Federation of Women's Clubs declared April 1, 1922, "Ford Day." And the state's governor said that nobody opposing the Ford bid would be welcome in his state.

Politicians continued lining up behind Ford, led by Alabama senator (and future Democratic presidential aspirant) Oscar Underwood, who soon after Ford's visit to the Shoals gave the automaker's bid his "unequivocal endorsement." Harding's secretary of agriculture, Henry Wallace, added his support. One Mississippi congressman summarized his state's view: "We have great respect for Mr. Ford in our country," he said. "We call him 'Uncle Henry' and we believe he will give us cheaper fertilizer just like he has given us automobiles to ride around in."

"There is somewhat of a land slide taking place in Congress in favor of the Ford offer," Worthington wrote Liebold on January 22. "He has everything here, as far as I can see, his own way."

A few days later, Ford's top engineer, William Mayo, rushed the latest version of the Ford bid to Washington on the fastest train out of Detroit. Nothing much had changed, other than some payback scheduling and the suggestion that the president appoint a commission to oversee the profits from the fertilizer part of the deal. Ford helpfully suggested how the commission might be structured: two representatives of the Ford Company and seven chosen by the president from a list of names supplied by leading farm organizations—all of which were supporters of Ford. This was it. There would be no more changes.

Now it was up to Weeks to make his recommendation to Congress. His report would be critical: If Weeks said not to accept Ford's bid, the chances of Congress voting approval were close to zero.

On the other hand, if Weeks strongly endorsed Ford, congressional approval was assured.

In the end, neither thing happened. After having a heart-to-heart about the issue with Harding, Weeks sent Congress a neutral presentation of the facts without a recommendation either way. But he made it clear how he felt by including a laundry list of shortcomings: Ford wanted a hundred-year lease; Weeks said the government should limit it to fifty years in line with national water power policy. Ford said it would take $28 million to finish the big dam; Weeks estimated $40 to $50 million. Ford offered $5 million to buy the nitrate plants; Weeks said the government could get twice as much by selling them as scrap. And he highlighted a new legal snag: The wartime contracts made between the government and the private companies that build the nitrate plants had, buried deep within them, clauses that appeared to put those companies first in line to buy the plants if they weren't used by the government. That would have to be dealt with before they could go to Ford.

The Weeks report stopped short of saying Ford's bid should be turned down, but it came close. Don't worry, Worthington quickly wrote Detroit. He had been counting votes in the committee, and a clear majority of the members were still in favor of the Ford bid. In any case it was no longer up to Weeks. The bid was now in the hands of Congress, where it would be studied by committees in the House and Senate, and once out of committee would go up for a vote. Once it came before the full Congress, Worthington was certain, Ford would get the Shoals.

But the federal government moves slowly. Now that Weeks had made his report, congressional hearings got underway, starting with the House Military Affairs Committee. The first witness called was Weeks, and the imposing secretary of war, his dark suit impeccable, his manner restrained and thoughtful, patiently answered questions for hours. He noted additional concerns about Ford's refusal to commit in writing to producing cheap fertilizers for a set number of years, even if there was no profit to be made. Ford had said he'd limit his fertilizer profits to 8 percent, but what if these profits fell below 8 percent? Could he simply shut down the fertilizer plants because they were unprofitable? The offer did not say. Weeks questioned Ford's rosy predictions, saying, "I think Mr. Ford himself is rather groping in the dark on what the results of his enterprise might be." He added that he was expecting more offers from competing bidders within a week or two.

The next logical witness was Ford, and an invitation to appear had been sent to Detroit. But while Weeks was testifying, a telegram arrived saying that unfortunately other affairs were pressing, and Ford would be unable to accept the committee's invitation. He would send William Mayo in his place. It's difficult to say exactly why, at this critical moment, Ford chose to stay out of it. He never expressed any reason beyond being busy. But it seems likely that several things played a part: Ford's frustration with government officials generally; his distaste, after the Mount Clemens trial, for being questioned by critics; the risk of being caught out on the fine points of his bid. Perhaps he was expecting full-throated support from his camping buddy, the president, and was worried because he hadn't gotten it. He didn't like being put in a position where he wasn't in control. Whatever the reasons, he stayed home and Mayo appeared, to no great effect. The hearings dragged on for weeks.

Things were not going well. But Worthington was still confident that the Ford bid had overwhelming support in the House and Senate. He called Ford's opponents "a crowd of wolves" who were interested in more than Muscle Shoals; they were also out to assail Ford's honor and blacken his name. Still, he wrote Liebold, "I consider the Ford offer and its acceptance by Congress as merely a matter of legislative grind and that there is no doubt about its acceptance—nothing to do but just stick to the job."

The Hand of Politics
Nashville Tennessean, July 29, 1921

When reporters asked Ford if he was thinking about dropping his bid, he said, "You don't know me. I am in this to the finish. If it should take years to reach a decision on my offer for this Muscle Shoals project, I'll be there, fighting to the end. I don't quit."

That was exactly what much of America admired about Ford: his straight, simple answers, his perseverance, his assurance. A lot of voters wished more politicians could be like that. The more the Muscle Shoals fight was in the news, the more Ford appeared like a hero to the forgotten people in the South and Midwest, the farmers and the underemployed. He was a straight shooter who would take on the politicians and the fat cats and fight for the common man. Every time a popularity poll was run, he ended up at the top of the list of the most admired men in America.

Maybe, people began thinking, he should run for president.

CHAPTER 9

PRESIDENT HENRY FORD

IT WASN'T THE first time people had thought about Henry Ford for president. Back in the summer of 1916, a celebrity psychic named Bert Reese—"the man who prophesied the date on which the Spanish-American War would end," his ads read, "whose pow- ers have puzzled the most famous scientific bodies"—predicted that Ford would one day inhabit the White House. "Positively and unequivocally," Reese told reporters. After Woodrow Wilson's second term, Ford was next in line. "He will occupy the White House for a longer period than any other president we have had," Reese said. "He will make the best president we have ever had."

He claimed to have told Thomas Edison about it years earlier, and the great inventor had replied, "Good, Reese! Good!" Edison had been a fan of the psychic ever since sitting down with Reese for a séance, an event that impressed the inventor enough to start him to work on a "spirit telephone" with which he could contact the dead.

Reese was eventually unmasked as a publicity-hungry fake, and Edison gave up his attempts to talk with ghosts. But the prediction

131

about President Henry Ford came closer to coming true than most people realize.

FORD WASN'T MUCH interested in politics. It wasn't even certain what party he was for, although he was a Wilson Democrat in 1912 because they were both for peace. Knowing he was a teetotaler, the Prohibition Party approached Ford in 1916 to be its candidate for president, but Ford rebuffed them. He didn't like politics, didn't much like giving speeches (his voice was high and could sound whiny), and didn't like the endless glad-handing and promise-making that politicians had to do.

By 1916, though, he was so well-known that some fans got his name on the presidential primary ballot as a Republican in a couple of states, and a few "Ford for President" clubs started up. Ford didn't stop them, but neither did he campaign. So it came as a surprise when he won the Republican primary in Michigan and came close in Nebraska. His response was definite: "I do not want anything to do with politics or political offices," he said. "The filing of my name . . . was a joke." He again threw his support to Wilson. But those clubs sprouting spontaneously in the Midwest caught the attention of politicians in both major parties.

Woodrow Wilson knew political potential when he saw it, the Democrats needed all the votes they could get, and in 1918 he asked Ford to run as a Democrat for the US Senate in Michigan. At the time it was an overwhelmingly Republican state. When his friend Edison heard about it, he reportedly told Ford, "What do you want to do that for? You can't speak. You wouldn't say a damn word. You'd be mum." But, perhaps because there wasn't much chance he'd win, and respectful of obeying any presidential request, Ford told Wilson he'd run.

Ford then began one of the oddest senatorial campaigns in American history. His name appeared on both the Republican and

Democratic primary ballots. But once officially in the race, he refused to make speeches or public statements, and spent no money on advertisements. As it turned out, he didn't need to. Everybody in Michigan already knew who he was. Ford won the Democratic primary in a landslide. But he lost the Republican nomination, barely, to Truman H. Newberry, a worldly and wealthy former secretary of the navy.

In the general election, Ford's opponent, marshaling large sums of money for ads, attacked him as a peacenik and an anti-Semite and claimed that his son, Edsel, was a draft dodger. (Edsel had been exempted from service in order to do vital war work at the Ford Motor Company.) The *Chicago Tribune* unsurprisingly backed Newberry, editorializing that "if we had a Senate full of Henry Fords, the best thing the people of the United States could do would be to put to sea in lifeboats." Ford publicly tried to remain above the fray but privately was furious about the attacks.

When the final votes were counted, the margin was razor-thin. Ford, it appeared, had lost by just a few thousand votes out of more than 400,000 cast. Instead of blaming himself for refusing to campaign, he claimed the election had been rigged against him. At fault were the usual suspects: Wall Street financiers, bankers, and an "influential gang of Jews." He charged Newberry with campaign finance improprieties, demanded a recount, paid for private investigators to dig up dirt, and raised such a big fuss that the Senate refused to seat Newberry until it could all be sorted out. Ford took his charges against Newberry all the way to the Supreme Court, which let the new senator-elect off on a technicality. On January 12, 1922, more than three years after the election, the Senate voted to seat Ford's opponent.

But Ford still wouldn't let it go. Laser-focused in his anger, he continued to oppose Newberry, threatening to run against him in the next election. And eventually, in a way, his stubbornness paid off. Rather than face another race, Newberry resigned before the election. His seat was filled by Detroit mayor James Couzens, an early Ford investor and former top Ford lieutenant.

The Newberry fight only seemed to increase Ford's popularity. His stubbornness was seen as a virtue; he looked like a man who would not be cowed by the political elites no matter how high and mighty they were. Here, it seemed, was an outsider who spoke the truth, fought injustice, and would not give up battling for what he thought was right.

But what exactly did he think was right? Because Ford spoke so little about public issues, his positions could be hard to pin down. He was generally pro-business and anti-war. He was in favor of women's suffrage and developing hydropower. He was for Prohibition. He talked about nationalizing railways to make them more efficient, and government ownership of telephone and telegraph services for the same reason. "Beyond this, his beliefs and intentions were mysteries," wrote historian Jeff Guinn, "and for disenchanted American voters, this was part of his allure." The public could fill the void with their own wishes and desires.

It made him in many ways a perfect candidate for president. Thanks to the incredibly positive Muscle Shoals press coverage, Ford was seen in the South as a would-be savior, in the Midwest as the farmer's friend, and across the nation as an appealing choice for anyone who shared his anti-banking, anti–Wall Street, anti-Jewish, anti-alcohol, antiestablishment sentiments.

Muscle Shoals was his springboard for a presidential run. In the spring of 1922, as his bid for the Shoals ground its way through Congress, the occasional civic meetings held in favor of his bid for the Shoals began turning into mass rallies. Five thousand Ford supporters gathered in Mobile, Alabama, in March to support his offer; thousands upon thousands more joined them in towns and cities across the Farm Belt. Pro-Ford petitions and proclamations were forwarded from business clubs, labor groups, civic booster associations, civic officials, and the American Legion. "No single subject since slavery has so roused the South," reported *McClure's Magazine*. "The easiest way to start a fight south of the Mason-Dixon Line is casually to remark: 'Ford's offer is no good.'"

On May 23, 1922, in Ford's hometown of Dearborn, 137 men gathered and put on cardboard hatbands reading, "We Want Henry." It was the inaugural meeting of a Ford for President club. Many more would follow in towns and cities across the nation. A sort of Ford mania swept the South and Midwest. A Ford for President movement started building.

But he stayed silent about the whole thing. Yes, there was something tempting about being able to wield all that power. He could clean up a lot of problems pretty quickly, he thought, and make government more efficient. He could point the US toward proper development for the future. He would be beholden to no one, able to root out some of the big-money corruption in politics. He could push for water power and highways, and fair wages, and new forms of industry. He could better battle his enemies on Wall Street and give power back to the little people. He could reshape America in ways that would allow it to prosper without socialism, without bolshevism, with an emphasis on clean, honest private enterprise, freed from some of the influences of bankers and big-money types. And of course he could solve the Muscle Shoals issue.

On the other hand, he had no time for it. He had a full plate with the Muscle Shoals bid, and getting the huge River Rouge plant smoothed out, and the question of whether to make a new model of car to replace the aging Model T, which had been in continuous production for thirteen years and was beginning to show its age. There were a hundred other issues large and small clamoring for his attention.

During their camping trip the previous summer, Harvey Firestone remembered, President Harding had talked around the campfire of "the vast amount of unnecessary detail imposed upon the office." The number of issues that had to be dealt with every day was smothering, and each issue had many sides that had to be considered.

That kind of detail work was exactly what Ford didn't want. He was a big-picture leader who loved to get out and see things in action, and leave the unpleasant details to men like Liebold. The last thing he wanted to do was sit behind a big desk in the White House all day long, dealing with the fine points of bills and crises and favors and staff and those blowhard politicians. Then there was all the politicking he'd have to do during the campaign, the speeches he'd hate making, the deals he wouldn't want to dirty his hands with. So when reporters started asking about whether he'd run, Ford played coy, pointing out all the other things he was busy with, brushing it off as a joke.

On the other hand, he didn't do anything to stop the spread of the Ford for President clubs. And he made other moves that seemed to be setting the stage for a run. He worked with a writer on a laudatory autobiography, *My Life and Work*, which became an instant bestseller in 1922. He opened himself to interviews with other friendly writers interested in writing other pro-Ford books.

And he stopped the International Jew articles in the *Dearborn Independent*. He said it was because he wanted to throw all his efforts into currency reform and fighting the gold standard. But he never did much in that arena and left it to Edison to find ways to argue for their "energy dollars" scheme.

The likely reason for stopping the anti-Semitic screeds was more political. Complaints about the series had been growing louder, especially in the Jewish community, and, observers noted, the Jewish

Once a political movement, now an auction item

vote was important in winning New York and Ohio, two states vital for any presidential candidate.

Ford, it seemed, was seriously considering a run.

WARREN G. HARDING himself offered another reason for Ford to think about running. The affable, handsome president was making a career out of doing very little. His administration had been marked by a devotion to big business, a blind eye for corporate misdeeds, and an emphasis on bringing back good times. There were rumors of cabinet members using their positions to line their own pockets. There were rumors that Harding had a mistress, that he was in the pocket of big-money contributors, that he had participated in sexual shenanigans in the White House.

One of the many things President Harding was doing little about was Muscle Shoals. He had good reason to ignore it. It was a mess, for one thing. It was a southern issue, and he was a northern president. Ford's bid was being pushed by Democrats, and Harding was a Republican.

He was already thinking about the next election, about how his party might square up against the Democrats, and, increasingly, about the wild card that was Henry Ford. Ford had run for Senate as a Democrat, and his push for Muscle Shoals and his growing popularity among rural and southern voters made him look like a Democrat again. There were murmurs about Ford running for president. If Ford decided to get into the 1924 race and run against him, Harding was in for a fight. He couldn't afford to alienate the automaker.

At the same time, he couldn't give him Muscle Shoals. If Ford got it, his popularity, already soaring, would skyrocket. Breaking ground on Muscle Shoals would confirm his status as Savior of the South and Friend of the Farmer; those two huge blocks of national votes would be his for the asking. It might serve as a launching pad for a campaign against Harding.

So the president hung back. His cabinet members, too, limited their activity to neutrality (as in Weeks's refusal to either recommend or not), muted support (Hoover at Commerce and Wallace at Agriculture), or dodging the question entirely. There was no need for fast action anyway: The economy was shaking off the recession of 1920–21; unemployment was down, the stock market was up, the nation's gross national product was growing along with consumer spending. Given the way the economy was booming in most of the nation (although not in Alabama), Harding figured that doing nothing about the Ford bid might be the best thing to do.

His attitude was noted in the press, and by mischievous observers like the anonymous poet who sent his local newspaper this bit of doggerel:

Said Henry Ford to Warren G.
"Complete that dam down there for me,

Across the river Tennessee,
I'll give your reign prosperitee."

Said Warren G. "You know I would
Gladly do so if I could,
And I know that I should
Build it for the nation's good.

"The fellows who opposed the dam
Helped put me where I am;
They're the ones who gave me the dough
And that is why I'm going slow."
(Slow curtain with soft music)

Anonymous poem, Ford Archive

The president's reticence gave Ford another potential reason to run. If Harding and his Republicans were going to do nothing to advance his bid for the Shoals—were, in fact, doing what they could to slow him down—then running as a Democrat might bring a measure of revenge. Not that revenge was the first thing on Ford's mind. This wasn't the Newberry race. He just didn't like how Harding was ignoring him. Everything was taking too long. The seemingly neverending congressional grind seemed designed to keep anything from ever being decided. This was a simple business matter; it should be decided quickly, as business matters usually were. Harding could make that happen. But he didn't.

PART II

BOOMTOWN

CHAPTER 10

SWAMPLAND AND WHISKEY

WHILE WASHINGTON, DC, seemed to be in a coma, the Shoals region was coming to life.

"Florence and Muscle Shoals have lately been placed on the map, and in great big letters," announced the *Florence Times* in 1922. The bad times of the past few years had been reversed. People from all over the nation were again flocking to the Shoals, drawn by little more than Ford's words and the enticing ads of real estate developers.

Few doubted that Ford was coming, which meant that property values would go through the roof. Real estate companies from New York, Detroit, and Chicago sent their buyers down to snap up large tracts of land anywhere near the nitrate plants. They started purchasing vacant lots, old farms, cotton fields, anything that could be subdivided into building lots.

The boom times were back. As Norris ran his hearings, real estate offices were popping up in the Tri-Cities, and chartered trains filled with prospective buyers were running between New York and the Shoals. "You can imagine the excitement we are having here over the Ford offer," a Sheffield woman wrote her friend. "The Muscle Shoals district is one seething mass of excited humanity. It is full of prospectors and speculators, and property is changing hands and rising in value every hour."

Developers began platting new housing developments, putting in paved streets, sidewalks, and streetlamps. Whole towns were being planned, with names like Nitrate City.

The old Tri-Cities were growing, too. Under the title of "The Tri-Bulation Cities," a political cartoon of the day showed a typical Main Street now plastered with signs—"Fried Fish and Real Estate," "Soft Drinks and Real Estate," "Washing Taken In and Real Estate"—as elephants paraded through town advertising lots for sale. There was national display advertising from the real estate companies, too: "Muscle Shoals Most Desirable Site Found in America," "Greatest Real Estate Opportunity," and maps of the "Splendid Location of Our Properties" near Muscle Shoals.

"I know of two Sheffield men who bought up some swampland and a couple cases of whiskey and got on the train for New York," remembered one local. "They were going to unload the swamp on unsuspecting Yankees. But the longer they sat and drank and planned their sales program, the better the land sounded to them. By the time they got to New York they had decided it was too good to sell and caught the next train for home."

A company called the Muscle Shoals Intelligence Bureau appeared in New York City, advertising the "chance of a liftime [sic] to become financially independent" and "You have not the opportunity to affiliate yourself with Mr. Ford's successes of the past, but you may profit and prosper by his operations of the future." Those interested were invited to send in a reply card for the latest information. When they sent in their cards, they were put on a mailing list to receive promotions from the New York real estate firm Howell & Graves.

The metropolis that never was, as promoted by a big real estate company.

No speculators exemplified the real estate rush of the early 1920s more than Howell & Graves. The firm set up elegant offices in midtown Manhattan, plastered their display windows with promises of riches, and ran endless Muscle Shoals ads. Passersby who wandered into the showroom found themselves face-to-face with large photos of the revered Ford and Edison, with signs below them saying, "I Will Build a City 75 Miles Long at Muscle Shoals—Henry Ford" and "2428 Industrial Buildings Ready for Workers Today" and "It Will Insure Fortunes for Early Investors." Then one of the company's scores of well-groomed sales representatives would strike up a conversation.

The Better Business Bureau said Howell & Graves bought $24,000 worth of low-cost Alabama land and quickly turned it around for $600,000. "Mr. Howell and Mr. Graves," said one observer, "two of the larger land speculators, developers, shysters, thieves, manipulators, or whatever you might want to call them—I think all of those terms would fit." One buyer testified at a trial later that he had been drunk when a Howell & Graves salesman talked him into buying land in Alabama, telling him that his lot was so close to the nitrate plant he'd be able to stand on his front porch and throw a rock into land that had cost the government $110 million to develop. The buyer signed away a large part of his savings. The next day, when he sobered up and asked to get his money back, Mr. Howell himself told him it was impossible.

Ford and Edison were both unhappy about the misuse of their images. They didn't want unscrupulous real estate types profiting off their names and reputations. Ford asked Liebold to look into it, and before long Ford men were posing as potential buyers at Howell & Graves, then reporting back about the sales techniques. Edison and Ford wrote cease-and-desist letters to the real estate company. Then the firm was hauled into court on a charge of false advertising.

The company took down Ford's and Edison's pictures, then replaced them with a large three-dimensional scale model of Muscle Shoals that filled one side of their showroom. It was a masterpiece of landscape modeling, with pointers to the locations of the dam, the nitrate plants, and the company's planned developments. Behind it, "covering the wall space from ceiling nearly to floor," a Ford Motor Company manager wrote Liebold, was a painting of an imaginary city, a "magnificent representation of bunk realism," he wrote, with "big business enterprises, beautiful homes, rolling away into a dim haze. . . . Muscle Shoals, as displayed and depicted here, looks good to the shoal of suckers for whom Howell & Graves have spread their nets."

They were not the only ones hoping to catch a few suckers. A Chicago real estate firm bought a big chunk of land near Nitrate #2 for about $250 an acre, broke it up into lots, and sold them for many times the price. Among the buyers who were told that they'd reap fantastic profits by holding on to their land for a year or two were two middle-aged sisters from Detroit who put everything they had on the investment. One of them, Ellen Johnson, went to see their land in the fall of 1922, riding down on one of the real estate firm's "excursion" trains to the Shoals.

The trip south was a hard-sell hotbox. Prospective investors were seated, then sweet-talked all the way from Chicago to the Shoals by a polished squadron of salespeople. Don't worry, they were told, their firm was so closely tied to Ford that their president and the automaker were on a first-name basis; it was "Hank" this and "Hank" that. Investors without a lot of funds did not need to buy all at once. There were alternative schemes that required less money up front, with options where buyers didn't have to do much but pay some fees and a monthly installment, leaving the worrisome details in the control of the real estate firm, which would sell the land later at higher prices, making tremendous profits for all. Get in now while the best lots, closest to the plants, were still available. Look, those people across the aisle are already signing a contract. According to Johnson, $25,000 worth of land was sold on that train before they got to Alabama; word was that within a year a million dollars' worth had been sold by this one Chicago-area firm alone.

The Johnson sisters bought their lots outright, but when Ellen tried to secure their deeds so they could resell some of it themselves or at least get a loan, she ran into problems. The initial surveys and mapping, she was told, seemed off. There was some sort of lawsuit going on with the government. The deeds kept getting held up.

Ellen, who had worked for years in the business world, was no pushover. She went back to the Shoals by herself, hired a lawyer in Sheffield, got her land resurveyed, then went home and marched with her sister into the offices of the Chicago firm that sold it to her. After a four-hour meeting with the president to lay out their complaints, he said, "Ladies, I am amazed, yet grateful, to learn all this." Then he blamed all the problems on other people. After they left, he did nothing to help them, and they did not get their money back.

The sisters were now short on money to pay their lawyer and unable to sell the land they thought they had purchased. With no other recourse, Ellen wrote Henry Ford himself to ask for help. Liebold saw her letter first. Normally he would not have bothered the boss with such a small matter, but something about the sisters' plight touched him. He knew how much Ford disliked hearing his name linked to the questionable business tactics of land speculators (there is little evidence that Ford himself was involved in buying or selling land in Alabama beyond the purchase of some distant tracts of natural resources), so he passed Ellen's letter to the boss.

Once Ford read it, he told Liebold to check it out and help if he could, and Liebold put Worthington on it. It turned out that the Chicago firm did not itself have clear title to the land it was selling; the issue was mired in foreclosure litigation with the government. Worthington wrote Liebold that the real estate firm was "a gang of thieves."

"These women have been criminally mistreated and if you will provide the necessary funds to redeem the property I will get the best lawyer at Muscle Shoals to straighten out the case," he wrote. Ford and Liebold decided to help the sisters out.

But even backed by all the power of the Ford Motor Company, it took a few more months and a lot of pressure before the Johnson sisters were able to claim their land. In the end, they finally did. And eventually, it appears, they even made a bit of profit.

CHAPTER 11

A PARTY OF ONE

MUSCLE SHOALS REMAINED Henry Ford's top priority. Now that his bid had pushed through the roadblock that was Secretary John Weeks, now that public support was peaking, the only thing standing in his way was Congress. J. W. Worthington kept assuring Ernest Liebold and Ford that they had the votes there they needed. All they had to do was get the bid through the initial committee reviews—one in the House of Representatives, one in the Senate—and then it was on to the floor for a vote and inevitable victory.

But Weeks had done his damage. His "neutral" report to Congress on the bid contained so many criticisms that it slowed all further consideration. The House Military Affairs Committee hearing stretched out for months as testimony was taken from a long list of dam engineers, power experts, Alabama boosters, fertilizer makers, and farm activists. They went over everything from water flow to money schemes, new advances in nitrate production to power distribution. One open issue was exactly what Ford planned to do with all the extra electricity he'd control, beyond using a fraction of it to make fertilizers. His top engineer, William Mayo, caused a stir when he testified that all surplus power would go to automobile parts production. That meant Ford would be hoarding all the power for himself, not sharing it with the rest of the region. It would be February 1922 before the hearings finally closed.

On the Senate side, no one was sure which committee should review the Ford offer. Some argued for Appropriations, others for Commerce or Judiciary. But in the end, in something of a surprise, the bid went to Agriculture. It made sense because of the fertilizer component, and the Committee on Agriculture and Forestry was powerful, given the importance of farming to the nation and the fact that half the voters were rural, but otherwise it seemed an odd choice.

In fact, the assignment to Agriculture appears to have been made under pressure from Oscar Underwood, a big, handsome, smooth-talking Alabama senator who was all for the Ford bid. Underwood was a powerful and popular political figure in the South, and also had the blessing of the Farm Bloc, the nation's most powerful agricultural lobby. The Farm Bloc, too, was all for Ford. Its leaders might have figured that they could quickly persuade the Agriculture Committee to do what they wanted.

But taking it to Agriculture would prove a historic mistake. The reason was simple: The committee was chaired by a senator that no one could push around. His name was George Norris. And he was about to become the fiercest and most effective enemy Henry Ford would ever have.

GEORGE NORRIS, LIKE Ford and Edison, grew up a Midwest farm kid. His parents spent twenty years carving a place out of the woods and rocks of Ohio, trying to make it yield enough crops to support a large family. His mother gave birth to twelve children; seven of them survived to adulthood. George, born in 1861, was number eleven. They lived the backbreaking life of pioneers: cutting trees;

gouging out stumps; prying up boulders; building homes, barns, and fences; turning soil; planting; harvesting; repairing. And repeat. It was a life that demanded hard work, stubbornness, and hope.

Norris grew up exemplifying all three. When he was a toddler his father died of pneumonia, making George the last male in the family. (An older brother had been killed in the Civil War just months before his father died.) He grew up doing his best to take care of his mother and sisters. He was good at school, not particularly intelligent but capable of endless, patient work, and he drove himself to success through sheer study. Every spare hour before and after school and in summers he worked the farm. That persistence eventually got him into law school, where he made plans to become a small-town attorney.

The law was going to be his way of helping the common people like his parents. Like many farmers, he was appalled at the excesses of the robber barons, the Gilded Age speculators and corporate brigands who reaped enormous profits off the backs of farmers; the railroads that charged too much to haul their products; the banks that foreclosed on farm loans; the politicians who made laws that were stacked against the poor and powerless. "As a boy I saw with my own eyes the struggles of a democracy," he wrote. His idea of democracy was that the government should work for the people, not the elites. He was drawn to populism, a loose political movement that swept the prairie states in the 1880s and 1890s by championing social and economic justice for the many over profit for a few.

After earning his law degree and making sure his mother had enough to survive, Norris moved west, practicing law, serving a stint as a district judge, and settling in McCook, Nebraska, where he earned respect for his independent thinking and straight-from-the-shoulder talk. He got involved in politics and was elected to the House of Representatives. Ten years later, the people of Nebraska sent him to the Senate.

That was in 1912. By then prairie populism and agrarian activism had been absorbed into the broader movement of Progressivism, championed by Teddy Roosevelt. Progressivism started with the ideas of the prairie Populists, then added trust-busting, consumer protection, and an emphasis on caring for natural resources. For a while Progressive Republicans made a lot of good things happen, establishing national parks, criticizing corruption, reining in big business, and cleaning up Washington. Norris was an eager part of all that. But once Teddy Roosevelt's second term was over, the Grand Old Party changed, shifting toward a more pro-business fiscal conservatism. The old Progressives were marginalized.

By 1921 Norris seemed like a relic of an earlier age. He lived in a modest boardinghouse within walking distance of the Capitol, wore old-fashioned black suits with bow ties and a heavy gold watch chain, smoked big black cigars, and sported a drooping "weeping willow" mustache. He was no great orator, no backroom dealer. He

Senator George Norris
Courtesy Library of Congress

often seemed tired and sad, and could work himself to exhaustion. He suffered from bouts of depression. But he made his way through the Senate just as he'd made his way through school, by grinding away, working harder than anybody else, studying the issues more deeply than anybody else, then using his growing reputation as an incorruptible moral force to persuade others. The people of Nebraska kept sending him back.

If Henry Ford was born to make machines, George Norris was born to make laws. He was a "master of parliamentary maneuvering," as one historian put it, coupling the political instincts of a Solon—a natural dealmaker—with the patience and stubbornness of a farmer. He slowly and patiently worked the system, found allies across party lines, formed effective committees, knew how to compromise when needed, knew when to back off and when to move things forward. While he "voted his conscience whatever might be the consequences," as his friend Supreme Court justice Hugo Black said, Norris also "clung to principle while yielding on minor points to help make the principle turn into reality." He was a practical idealist, a man with his head in the heavens and his feet planted on the ground.

Sometimes Norris was able to turn seemingly lost causes into victories. In the House, for instance, he helped lead a successful revolt against one of the most powerful politicians of his day, stripping the czar-like power of Speaker Joseph Cannon and returning it to the body at large. He found allies among a splinter group of Progressive Republicans who followed Wisconsin's "Fighting Bob" La Follette—they were called "the Sons of the Wild Jackass"—who managed to expose some corruption and get some laws passed.

But it was getting tougher. His party, under Harding, had become completely pro-business. "The early twenties brought the American people to their knees in worship at the shrine of private business and industry," Norris remembered. "It was good, and accepted by millions of Americans, that private enterprise could do no wrong." Norris found himself so far out of the Republican mainstream, he could just as easily have been a Democrat. Not that he cared much. Norris was a maverick. He thought for himself, reached his own conclusions, and voted the way he believed was right, regardless of what the party wanted. He would do everything he could for the rights of the common people against the privileges of the wealthy. He was a party of one.

WHILE NORRIS'S AGRICULTURE Committee began reviewing the Ford bid in the Senate, the military committee in the House, under the chairmanship of California representative Julius Kahn, was getting bogged down in details. The more he looked into Muscle Shoals, the more Kahn found himself up to his eyeballs in a mire of competing claims, accounting and contractual fine points, arguments over engineering, ceaseless lobbying, and relentless media attention. His committee members were bitterly split about what to do with Ford's offer. It looked like it would require years to hash it all out.

On top of everything else, there was now a new sticking point in the form of the big coal-fired steam power plant that had been built during the war to provide interim power to the nitrate plants while the dam was going up. It was called the Gorgas plant, and Ford's bid demanded it as part of the deal. But Alabama Power, which had built the plant during the war, insisted that its construction contract gave it a prior right to purchase. The company's claim looked legitimate. Kahn tried to convince Ford to strike it from his bid.

But Ford refused. His bid was his bid, he said, and nothing major was going to change. Alabama Power dug in its heels. There were no easy answers. Kahn kept his hearings running until late

May, hoping for some kind of resolution, but then he threw up his hands. Given the Gorgas impasse along with everything else, his committee decided they could not accept Ford's bid as written. Instead, Kahn's committee put together its own recommendation for a bill that looked very much like Ford's, but without the Gorgas plant and with more detailed assurances of fertilizer production. When Kahn summoned Ford's men Mayo and Worthington, along with the president of Alabama Power, to explain his decision, nobody left happy—except, perhaps, Representative Kahn, who had successfully passed the buck to the full House.

At the same time Ford's backers launched a competing bill in the House that presented Ford's bid as written. When the Speaker of the House and the House majority leader met with the president to see what he wanted to do about the two competing measures, Harding refused to back Ford; according to some reports he spoke against accepting the Ford bid. The Republican House managers resigned themselves to a long summer of debate.

MAYBE THE REPUBLICANS figured that making Norris chair of the Senate's Committee on Agriculture and Forestry would make it difficult for him to stir up much trouble.

They were wrong.

He had seen what floods and drought could do to Nebraska farmers. He believed the answer was public control of waterways, putting government money into projects that would protect the land and the people. These public improvements, he thought, should not be left to private corporations, because the natural tendency of a private corporation was to make as much money as possible. That's why they existed. It wasn't necessarily a bad thing—stockholders deserved a return on their investment—but neither was it necessarily in the public's best interest. The public deserved to benefit from their nation's rich public lands and waterways, getting the most goods at the lowest price.

Norris was not antidevelopment. He just thought that the development of the people's resources should benefit the people, not corporations. He'd fought against corporate interests and in favor of public control of the Hetch Hetchy Reservoir in Yosemite to bring fresh water to the people of San Francisco (in doing so drowning one of the most beautiful valleys in Yosemite); for publicly owned electrical systems in Nebraska; and for government completion and oversight of the great dam at Muscle Shoals. He believed that America's rivers were "the common heritage of the people."

He also thought Ford's bid should have gone to Military Affairs instead of becoming a headache for his Agriculture Committee. When it ended up on his desk, he wrote, "I found myself confronted with a responsibility which I did not want." But there it was, so he devoted himself to it with his usual close, patient, meticulous attention. Norris read everything he could find about dams, river navigation, fertilizer, and electric power generation. He reviewed the Weeks critique. And the more he read, the less he liked the Ford offer.

When his committee opened hearings on the issue on February 16, 1922, Norris started things with a bang by announcing that the members would consider two bids, not only Ford's, but another he had crafted himself proposing government ownership of Muscle Shoals. The Agriculture Committee would weigh them side by side. It was a clever move, making sure that each of Ford's ideas was constantly measured against a public alternative.

Then he made sure that his hearings lasted a very long time. Weeks kept hinting that other bids were coming in; Norris intended to delay Ford's bid until they did. He dragged his hearings out over four long months, hour after hour, session after session, probing and pulling apart the Ford bid. He and his panel quizzed what seemed like an endless procession of engineers, military officers, politicians, fertilizer experts, power company representatives, investment bankers, and farm organization figures. They pored over charts, graphs, photographs, estimates of fertilizer production, crop yields, electricity production costs, and the fine points of contract language.

The chairman requested testimony from Senator Underwood, who, in his deep, reassuring Alabama tones, told the committee that the development at the Shoals was something the people there had wanted for a hundred years. "It is the dream of their lives," he said. The way to make that dream come true was to accept the Ford offer. He himself was very happy to support Ford's "great patriotic act" of paying the government so that he could give farmers cheap fertilizer.

Norris brought in Worthington and raked him over the coals. The panel questioned the hundred-year lease, asking if Worthington thought Ford would be alive in one hundred years to make good on his promises, and if he wasn't, as seemed more than likely, who would then be in charge of the operation? The deal was being made with Ford; how could someone else be held to account? Then there was the question of existing federal law on the management of public waterways. How could the government be expected to abrogate its own fifty-year limit on water power if the outcome was so uncertain? Norris didn't trust Ford's promises on fertilizer, and he argued with Worthington over whether the bid required the automaker to put even a penny into fixing up the aging nitrate plants. They tangled over whether Ford, after using cheap government money to finish the dam, could then simply sell the electricity to whoever he wanted to, at whatever price, for whatever purpose, without any government oversight at all. They argued over whether Ford or the government would be best able to oversee the project, and under what contract restrictions.

After two days of testifying, neither side had given up any ground. Worthington summed up his feelings with a frank admission: "I have been talking about power development in the United States since 1910. As far as talk goes, I am ready to quit. I think it is time to do something."

But getting something done quickly was looking more and more unlikely.

The more Norris's committee quizzed experts, the more tangled the issues seemed to get. Ford's people repeated simple, often vague arguments about Ford's proven management skills, the farmers' need for fertilizer, and the evils of the government getting into private business. On the other side, disquieting testimony came from technical men who disputed Ford's chances of making cheap fertilizer at the outdated nitrate plants, questioned Ford's financing scheme, and dismissed Ford's engineers as being experts in cars but untrained in dams and chemical plants.

Among the critics was Charles Parsons, the man the government had sent on a whirlwind wartime tour of Europe to review nitrate factories. Parsons, who knew the industry inside and out, had nothing but disdain for Ford's proposal. The fertilizer question was nothing more than camouflage, he said, "a mere shibboleth. . . . Those interested in the power, and especially land speculators, have painted a beautiful mirage for the farmer, which will fade utterly on approach." It looked like Ford was using fertilizer not because it made any economic sense, but for political advantage, building support among farmers for his bid. Don't be fooled, he warned: Ford's real aim was to get his hands on all that electricity.

Then Parsons made his own offer to take the failed experimental Nitrate #1 plant off the government's hands for $600,000 so he could gut it and put in a system that would work. His offer was politely ignored.

Other private bids were now starting to come in. Some, like Parsons's, from individual entrepreneurs or small companies, were easily dismissed. The project was too big for them. But one, from Alabama Power, was a full-fledged, serious contender. AP was a big corporation with deep pockets and powerful allies, and its bid was attractive, promising to abide by the fifty-year lease rule and offering what appeared to be a stronger dollar return to the government. It looked like a better deal. And AP was accustomed to playing hardball. Its move on the Gorgas plant had shown that it was willing to use anything it had to take down the Ford bid.

Ford had to pivot now to battle this competitor as well as Norris's government ownership idea. He painted AP as part of the old Duke cabal of trusts and moneylenders, the East Coast elites he was trying to defeat. It wasn't a hard case to make: AP was certainly tied to other private power companies, and it was easy to draw lines from this "power trust" to the "fertilizer trust" and then to Wall Street and the treasury secretary's aluminum investment portfolio. It looked to Ford like they were all ganging up on him. "If it's the last thing I do in this world, I'll exert every resource and influence at my command to keep the hands of Wall Street off Muscle Shoals," he said.

That sounded good to his supporters. At the same time, however, Ford's name was being linked with the shady land speculation around the Shoals. Once the media started reporting on the land boom and the chicanery around it, Ford's cause in Congress suffered. Senator Norris, in particular, saw this sort of naked profiteering as symptomatic of what happened when great natural resources were put in the hands of private developers. It was another reason to argue for government oversight.

Then Norris, now firmly anti-Ford, threw another curveball: He quietly tucked into a huge army appropriation bill a small $7.5 million earmark for continued construction of the dam at Muscle Shoals. The bill passed, and suddenly there was government money flowing

back into the dam. It wasn't much—just enough to fund construction through the summer of 1922—but it was a demonstration to
folks at the Shoals that the government could get things done, too.
Henry Ford wasn't their only option.

ON MAY 20, 1922, the star witness of the Norris hearings walked
slowly into the Senate hearing room. He was accompanied not by a
lawyer, but by an assistant whose job was to shout every question into
the witness's one good ear. Thomas Edison, now seventy-five years
old, had presumably come to testify on behalf of his friend Ford's bid.
But what he said didn't sound much like an endorsement.

He was seated, welcomed, and asked a question about what he
thought of power development at Muscle Shoals. Edison replied,
"That is out of my line. I don't know anything about that. I have not
been in the power business for many years." It was not an answer
anyone expected. Edison then begged off answering any other broad
questions about the Ford bid, saying that his friend had brought
him down to Alabama to take a look at things only in "a narrow,
technical way."

By which he meant fertilizers. Ford had been hinting about
"secret" methods of cheap fertilizer production, and said various
times that Edison was at work on the problem. When a senator asked
Edison if he knew of any new and better ways of making nitrogen
fertilizer, Edison flatly replied, "No sir. I have not worked on any."
He described how Ford had asked him to figure out if he could
create a "full fertilizer" from resources available around Muscle
Shoals—not just nitrogen from the nitrate plants, but also potash and
phosphorus—and how he had worked with local geologists to assess
mineral deposits for one hundred miles around. He'd found deposits
that could be worked to get the substances they wanted, he said, but
the methods needed to refine them hadn't been commercialized

yet and were still a bit expensive. He was working on better ones. When asked what specific methods he planned to use, he dodged. "Well, I don't think I had better. I might fail. I have never yet eaten any boiled crow—all my stuff has worked—and I don't want to start now. Wait until I get through experimenting." One of the few things he seemed to know for certain was that cheap fertilizer was going to be important. When he was down in Alabama, he'd taken a look at a cotton field. "What I saw down there in those poor little starved places near the falls is awful," he said. "The land is all right. It wants fertilizer, and it has got to be awfully cheap." And that was the end of his testimony on the matter.

The senators tried exploring the "energy dollars" idea Edison and Ford had endorsed. Edison had indeed been working on that, he said. "Mr. Ford says to me, 'Why can't we put this money in Muscle Shoals and issue currency against it? It is good security,'" Edison testified. "It looked all right, as a great many things do, on its face. So I tried to work out whether it would be all right, and I have been at that in addition to these other things."

After coming back from Muscle Shoals he had run the idea past a number of economists, bankers, and financial experts, sending out questionnaires and tallying answers. But he was no economist, his ignorance showed in the questions he asked, and the responses he got back had not been encouraging. (In fact, after looking at Edison's questionnaire, one professor at the University of Wisconsin refused to fill it out, writing back instead, "At your age and what seems to be your present state of mind, it would be worthless to attempt to teach you.")

Then he destroyed the idea of energy dollars. "I have been trying to make that thing work," he testified. "It don't go. Although there is plenty of security behind that money, it won't work. I am very disappointed." The committee members were floored. Edison had publicly repudiated Ford's financing plan.

The whole thing was puzzling. Instead of supporting his friend Ford, Edison seemed to be undermining him.

One of Ford's biggest boosters on the panel, Senator J. Thomas "Cotton Tom" Heflin of Alabama, tried to get things back on track. He asked Edison, "You don't know the details of Mr. Ford's offer, and, of course, you don't know the others?"

EDISON: "No. I don't attend to his business."
HEFLIN: "You know that Mr. Ford wants to get Muscle
    Shoals?"
EDISON: "Yes. He seems to want it. I don't know why. He
    has got enough work now. I think he would be very
    foolish. His wife thinks so, too."

The elderly inventor's testimony then wandered off into musings about factory automation, electric automobiles, and tips on how Congress might better make legislation.

After forty-five minutes, the panel let him go.

What had happened? It is possible that the inventor was tired of his old friend using the Edison name to gain favor for his bid. People kept asking him about fertilizers, and he knew next to nothing about them. His wife, Mina, didn't like the way Ford was pushing him into things, Clara Ford was unhappy about her husband wasting his time on the huge Alabama dream, and the whole energy dollars scheme had fallen embarrassingly apart. He was unhappy about the way his name and face were being used by real estate speculators to lend credibility to their schemes. Muscle Shoals had done little but waste Edison's time and damage his reputation. He was getting too old for this kind of foolishness. In his simple, straightforward way, he was bowing out.

It was the end of Edison as a force in favor of Ford's bid. After exiting Norris's committee room, Edison rarely spoke again about fertilizers, or alternative money schemes, or Ford's dream city. He began spending more of his time in the more benign climate of Florida, where he had a house next door to Ford's winter home, and where he could tend a semitropical garden filled with plant species he hoped to use to create artificial rubber.

J. W. WORTHINGTON WAS beginning to worry. As Ford's man in Washington, Worthington had been promising his boss swift passage of his bid through Congress. Now, a full year after Ford first sent his offer to Weeks, it was beginning to look like they were no closer to their goal.

With the House stymied and the Senate Agriculture Committee looking like it was about to vote thumbs-down, Worthington threw a Hail Mary. He and a powerful farm lobbyist, the American Farm Bureau's Gray Silver, decided to talk Senator Edwin Ladd of North Dakota—a strong farm advocate and member of Norris's committee—into introducing a competing bill backing Ford's bid as written. Worthington remembered having to sweet-talk the reluctant Ladd, who insisted at first that most members of the Agriculture Committee were fixed on at least amending the Ford offer before sending it on, and it would be useless to try and preempt their work. Worthington and Silver argued that Ford wouldn't go for any changes and it would have to be his bid as written or nothing. Then they gently reminded Ladd of the "personal advantages and prestige" that he would gain from leading the pro-Ford fight. It was easy for Ladd to interpret what those words, coming from representatives of the nation's richest industrialist and one of its most important political blocs, might mean. Within a few days, Ladd announced he was introducing a bill in the Senate to accept Ford's offer without any changes.

The moment that happened, Norris ended his months of hearings and, in mid-July, released his committee's findings. The vote was 9 to 7 against Ford's bid. In his lengthy majority report, Norris released a broadside, calling Ford's grab for the Shoals "piratical" and saying that its acceptance would constitute "the most wonderful real estate speculation since Adam and Eve lost title to the Garden of Eden." He listed each of the high points of Ford's offer and demolished each one in turn: No, Ford was not actually guaranteeing cheap fertilizer; yes, Ford's hundred-year lease would destroy the Water Power Act; no, his offer would not ensure endless electricity for the people of the area; yes, he would use the low-cost, government-subsidized electricity from the great dam the taxpayers were building to power his own industries. In exchange for Ford's offer of a small amount of income spread over a century, a private corporation would be allowed to rob the public of both its enormous wartime investment in Muscle Shoals and all potential benefits from its future development. "The mind is dazed at the unreasonableness of the proposition, at the enormity of the gift," Norris said. "The acceptance of Mr. Ford's offer turns back the clock of progress and opens the door wide for the use of natural resources by corporations and monopolies without restriction, without regulation, and without restraint."

On the other hand, Norris's committee did not endorse the chairman's own plan for government operation (indeed, the minority report savaged Norris's idea as nothing more than socialism thinly disguised), but he was willing to wait on that. The important thing was to stop Ford.

Soon after Norris unleashed his barrage, Senator Ladd was called away to Geneva to be the US representative to the Inter-Parliamentary Union meetings. This long European trip would effectively prevent him from pushing forward his own pro-Ford bill. Without Ladd to lead the charge, his Ford bill languished.

Ford's great campaign to take the Shoals had started the previous December with his triumphant visit with Edison to the Shoals.

It had continued with a blitz to build public support through the spring. He wanted to get congressional approval before the summer recess of 1922 so he could start construction while the weather was good.

But somehow an aging relic from a nothing state, a marginalized old prairie Populist named George Norris, had found a way to checkmate him.

CHAPTER 12

THE 75-MILE CITY

WHAT FORD DECIDED to do next was to go directly to the people. Publicity had always been Ford's friend; now he would use it to force Congress to act on his bid. The trick was going to be making his Muscle Shoals bid sound too good to turn down. He wasn't going to pay the government more money. What he was going to do was enhance and embellish the benefits he would bring—package them and sell them so attractively that Congress would be pressured into accepting them.

All stops were pulled out to get a new string of pro-Ford Muscle Shoals articles into major newspapers and magazines designed to juice up public support for his bid, with the side benefit of keeping Ford on the front pages looking like a force for national good and, perhaps not coincidentally, presidential. Taken together, they also offer the most complete look available at exactly what Ford was planning for his utopia on the Tennessee.

Ford was fascinated by the idea of using hydroelectricity to power industry. He'd played with the idea on a small scale for years, even putting in a low dam to power his home on the River Rouge. He liked how clean it was—there was no smoke-belching, coal-powered steam plant to worry about—and how self-sufficient it made him, freeing him of the tyranny of the coal companies.

He was a small-dam man at first, thinking about little dams on smaller rivers and streams to power small operations and small areas. But the big dam at Muscle Shoals expanded his vision. With that much power, he could do much bigger things over a much wider area.

Dams, electricity, and transmission lines formed one part of the picture. The other part came from his cars. Access to cars meant that workers didn't have to live within walking distance of their jobs. They no longer had to pack into housing crowded around a factory. They could spread out and drive to work.

Everything could be stretched out. Instead of living in major cities—Ford hated big cities—people could live in small towns or villages, each with its own small electrically powered factories linked by smooth, modern highways and telephone and power lines. What emerged was the idea of weaving these villages together into a ribbon city along the river, with workers scattered over a green landscape, commuting to their jobs. While there had been talk for years among planners about creating garden cities and using village models for living, there had never been a concept on the scale of Ford's, because there had never been the inventions—the electrical power, the big dams, the cheap cars—needed to make it happen. It was a new way of living made possible by new technology.

In an interview with the Associated Press in January 1922, he expanded his ideas. The resulting story ran on front pages around the country. "Muscle Shoals Site Selected as Ford Utopia," read one headline, followed by the text, "The Muscle Shoals plan of Mr. Ford contemplates one of the greatest undertakings in the history of industrial America." He was proposing to create a city seventy-five miles long (twice as long as the New York City of those days), stretching from the Tri-Cities all the way up the river to the city of Huntsville. This, the story explained, would be "in line with the manufacturer's view that men and their families should live in small communities where benefits of rural or near-rural life would not be entirely lost."

Ford added that he had been spending most of his time working hard on Muscle Shoals plans for weeks, holding meetings with his engineers and putting together detailed plans. One worker at the company remembers many meetings being held about it, the tables covered with maps and blueprints. (If extensive plans ever existed—and I believe, given Ford's working methods, that they probably did—they are not publicly available. My search at the Henry Ford Archive for maps, blueprints, or detailed descriptions of his Muscle Shoals plans turned up very little. Either they were lost after Ford's death, or they are locked away in the company's private executive files.)

One young southern journalist and Ford enthusiast, Littell McClung, got so caught up in the stirring vision of Ford's Muscle Shoals plan that he devoted himself to writing about it. In April 1922 he published a long feature article, "What Can Henry Ford Do with Muscle Shoals," in *Illustrated World* magazine. It was written with all the enthusiasm of a born promoter. "An enterprise of the most gigantic, revolutionary, and far-reaching import ever conceived by human mind," it read, "a conquest such as Alexander, Caesar, or Napoléon never visioned . . . an ambition unique in conception, humanitarian in purpose, staggering in proportions. . . .

"Henry Ford is a new and great force in the destinies of men," McClung wrote. "There has not been and is not another like him. . . . What won't Ford do? What can't he do?"

McClung followed up in September 1922, just in time for the reconvening Congress, with a second feature story, published this time in the more sober *Scientific American*. Titled simply "The Seventy-Five Mile City," the story's editors cooled off McClung's overheated prose—no more Napoléon, no more miracles—and instead presented a wealth of detail. The key was not Ford's mighty factories, but his revolutionary new way of structuring society. Put simply, "Mr. Ford would have the factory and the farm working hand-in-glove," the story explained.

It illustrated the idea by telling the tale of an imaginary "Bill Jones," a typical factory worker with a young family, tired of trudging to the factory from his big-city apartment, who moved to Ford's Muscle Shoals and invested in a mortgage on forty acres of farmland a couple of miles up the river from the dam at fifty dollars an acre. Bill gets a job at a new Ford factory. But he and his wife also have time to care for their new farm. When it's time to plant wheat, Bill is given two weeks' unpaid leave from his factory job, "more if needed; and another man, trained in his work, takes over his machines for this time. Bill goes a-planting." He doesn't know much about farms, but no problem: "An experienced farm demonstrator is on hand to aid him. Tractor, plows, pulverizer, harrow, grain drill are rented from the factory management." By renting the machines he needs just for the time he needs them, Bill doesn't have to go into debt buying equipment that would sit idle most of the year. "Two weeks of Bill's time—or at most three, depending on the state of the weather—here, and a few odd days later on, are all of Bill's time that is invested in the crop," the story explains. With his seed in the ground, he returns his rented machinery and goes back to his factory job.

On evenings and weekends—thanks to Ford's five-days-a-week, eight-hours-a-day schedule—there's plenty of time to grow his crop and care for his place. When the wheat's ready, he again rents the equipment he needs, brings in the harvest (in the fastest, most efficient way possible, "with the farming instructor at his elbow"), and transports it by barge or tractor to the local grain storage elevator, where he gets a fair price for his product, minus the rental charged for the farm implements.

"The result of these systematic and intelligently directed operations is that Bill Jones has made a crop surprisingly cheaply, and has made an excellent profit on it. He did not have to buy horses or mules and feed them through the year. He has had no money tied up in machinery. . . . And the farm demonstrator, without cost to him, has prevented him from making foolish or costly mistakes," McClung wrote.

And that's just the start. Gradually Bill and his family improve the place, putting in fruit trees and vines, enriching the soil with Ford's cheap fertilizer, and making more money all the time. Soon Bill has a boat and a new car to carry his goods. And there are benefits for his wife, too. "A woman home demonstrator will show Mrs. Bill Jones how to can and preserve the fruits for winter use," McClung promised. And of course there would be endless cheap electricity for every farm, which meant labor-saving home appliances, an electric stove, and electric heat. The Jones family would live a clean, green country life, never experience the sins of the city, and never have to buy coal again.

When it came time to retire, Bill Jones would have his Ford pension. But more important, he would have his own land and his own house. The kids would know the benefits of living on the land. The Jones family would be "about four times as prosperous and six times as contented as it would have been in the ordinary run under the old industrial dispensation."

The whole region would flower.

There were other promises as well—a Ford-funded agricultural and industrial school to teach local boys hands-on skills with machines, woodworking, and farming, and give girls instruction in cooking, sewing, and food preserving; cheap aluminum and cotton and fertilizer; and the staggering long-term economic benefits that would accrue by increasing crop production a few units per acre. (Added up over the whole region, this improved productivity would create "additional wealth beyond the comprehension of the average man," McClung wrote. "The automobile industry would be a pigmy beside it.")

This remarkable article went far beyond puffery. It summarized and detailed a powerful set of ideas that Ford had been thinking about for years. It envisioned a new future that would maintain the values of the past by transforming them with the technologies of the present. "Factory and farm close together, yet cooperation between them," McClung wrote, "satisfying and lasting opportunity to tens of thousands of capable, ambitious workers—this is Mr. Ford's purpose and plan."

It was a grand plan. The scale was breathtaking. The purposes were noble. Ford, like many others in the 1920s, was concerned about the fracturing of American society, the rise of organized labor, the threat of bolshevism, the vice and dirt of the ever-growing cities, the loss of old farm values. This was his way of piecing America back together. Muscle Shoals would be his grand test case. When it worked he was going to export the system to the rest of the nation, starting with the Mississippi Valley. He was going to engineer the future the way he had engineered the making of the Model T: efficiently, practically, and with an eye toward the well-being of everyone.

Muscle Shoals would be his model for a new kind of nation, a Ford America.

UNDERLYING HIS PLANS was Ford's personal vision of a perfect American town. It was much like what he thought an idyllic New England village would have been like in the early 1800s, built around a green with a whitewashed Protestant church at one end, a small main street with a few brick businesses at the other, a schoolhouse, an inn, a lot of trees, and a mill on the pond powered by a waterwheel. This was the America of Emerson, Thoreau, and Whitman. This is what he wanted for his workers.

At Muscle Shoals the old villages would meet the future. They would be linked into a city, the tidy houses expanded to small farms; the water wheels would become giant dams, the grist mills electrically powered factories. All this would be made possible by machines, too, but not the old heavy, metal, steam-powered machines of the dark early industrial era. The new machines would be personal gasoline-powered cars and electrical devices.

Electricity was the key. In 1922, despite all of Edison's and Westinghouse's efforts, the majority of Americans still had no electricity in their homes. Only one in five were wired for anything more than lighting—they didn't have the heavier circuits needed for heating or major appliances. The numbers were worse the farther you got from cities. The Muscle Shoals plan to bring cheap electricity into every worker's home meant more than convenience. It meant new ways of getting work done, in home workshops, in kitchens, and in barns. It meant new ways of refrigerating and preserving food. It meant less labor spent on cutting stove wood or hauling coal. It meant telephones and phonographs and radios in each worker's home, opening the door to more communication and richer cultural lives.

The Ford scheme also, in his mind, had the advantage of turning renters into homeowners. Most big-city factory workers rented, and renters were not invested in their communities the way owners were. Owners were motivated to maintain and improve their homes. They had a stake in local politics and education and health. Here again, new technologies made more things possible. In the old days, farmhouses had to be big, rambling affairs, with big kitchens and space for hired help. The Ford model of electrified, mechanized small farming could be run from a much smaller house—a bungalow, much cheaper to build and more affordable for more workers with smaller incomes. That would open ownership to more workers, including Black laborers. In Detroit, the Ford Motor Company employed hundreds of Black workers, mostly in lower-end jobs, but many in skilled positions. In Muscle Shoals, his jobs would help raise the living standards of everyone, Black and white alike.

Ford (and Edison) were certainly not the first utopian thinkers in America. The nation's history was rich with experiments in creating perfect societies—some political, many religious, from socialists to Shakers. Edward Bellamy's influential 1888 utopian novel *Looking Backward* had been a blockbuster bestseller, influencing many readers to think about how life might be made perfect. And Ford was not the first to think about moving people out of big cities and into small villages—a "garden city" movement to do just that had been rattling around for decades. But Ford was among the first to translate the fuzzy concepts into concrete, large-scale industrial/technological terms, with power sources and lifestyle changes matched to factory designs and living conditions.

Ford's appreciation for what cars made possible and Edison's deep knowledge of electricity's potential role in society made them the ideal pair to dream up this new kind of techno-utopia. The post–World War I atmosphere, with its worries about money, about Communists, about vice and moral decay, was a perfect time to look for the kinds of solutions they were offering.

The idea of the seventy-five-mile city had long-lasting effects. A young polymath named Lewis Mumford was inspired by utopian writers like Bellamy in general and Ford's vision specifically; he put the effects of new technology at the center of much of his influential writing about the design of cities. To Mumford it was about more than healing the urban-rural divide; it was also about maintaining a sense of place, of breathing new life into regional cultures and preserving the environment. Mumford was part of a loosely linked group of thinkers who, during the 1920s, were seeking fruitful ways to integrate fast-changing technology into the ways real people lived.

Mumford and Ford both helped to inspire Frank Lloyd Wright, a young architect who championed the idea of a decentralized America with village industries, rural prosperity, and people living in harmony with their natural settings. Of Ford himself, Wright said, "He is a man of common sense. He is a man that has really contributed a great deal to our country. He has successful ideas. His proposal for Muscle Shoals was one of the best things that I have heard of."

And Wright, in his designs, often echoed Ford's themes. "Modern transportation may scatter the city, open breathing spaces in it, green it and beautify it," Wright wrote, "making it fit for a superior order of human being." Wright at one point designed a model for the future of urban and rural life that he called Broadacre City. It consisted of a constellation of one-acre farms connected by high-speed roads and small commercial centers. It looks a lot like the real estate promotional illustrations for Ford's Muscle Shoals.

FORD NOT ONLY understood how to make great automobiles. He also understood what the automobile meant to America. He started out wanting to make life easier for farmers. But by the time he was bidding for Muscle Shoals, he saw that auto ownership could change how all Americans lived. Personal cars and better highways made longer-distance commuting more likely, and longer-distance commuting meant that populations could be dispersed. Scattered populations meant more green spaces and access to land. Cars would alter the shape of society.

The new utopia would not be religious or political. It would be scientific and technological. Machines would, from this point forward, drive change.

With Muscle Shoals, Ford was taking one giant step into that future. But his other foot was still planted firmly in the past. He yearned for a society that would adapt to and benefit from new technologies while at the same time using them to strengthen old values. He wanted the village green of the 1820s, but he wanted it powered by the machinery of the 1920s. If he could pull off that trick, he could reshape America for the coming century.

It is easy to see in Ford's ribbon city some of the elements—the small houses on green lots, the emphasis on cars and highways, the commuting, the electric homes—that would, after World War II, sprawl across the landscape in the form of the great American suburbs. Later historians trace the roots of the 'burbs back to the late 1940s or 1950s, or perhaps earlier to the installation of electric trolleys that allowed wealthier city residents to move to outlying neighborhoods. But a small number are beginning to appreciate a less known father of the suburbs: Henry Ford.

CHAPTER 13

GUTTERS OF POLITICAL FILTH

WHEN CONGRESS GATHERED in the fall of 1922, Muscle Shoals was still at the top of the to-do list. In fact, Ford's bid and the various bills and bids around it seemed to constitute about half of everything on the list. It was a problem that would not go away.

During the summer Ford seemed to have strengthened his position. Ford for President clubs continued to spring up in towns and cities across the South and Midwest; Ford for President buzz was growing; and Ford kept reassuring his backers that he was "in the Muscle Shoals project to stay. We haven't started to fight." He announced that he was thinking about expanding his efforts along the Tennessee to include more industries, tractor manufacturing, new metal alloys, or a giant plant bigger than Highland Park to make a revolutionary new model of car. Those speaking against him, like the big-money players in the power and aluminum industries, he told reporters, were "just plain liars."

The topic was too hot to do much with until after the midterm elections in November. But when those results were in, Ford's chances seemed better than ever. Ford's strongest ally, the Farm Bloc, had more backers elected to Congress. They would take office in January. And it was then, Ford expected, that one of the bills supporting his offer would finally be passed. Then he could start work.

But Ford's opponents were also strengthening their case. Early environmentalists formed a group to defend the nation's Water Power Act, and affirming its fifty-year limit on leases for hydroelectric dams would be a major blow to Ford's hundred-year lease requirement. Alabama Power continued lobbying for its competing bid, and articles critical of Ford were starting to appear more often. "The combination of interests against Mr. Ford's getting Muscle Shoals is the most powerful that ever got together in this country," J. W. Worthington wrote Ernest Liebold in September. But he remained confident of victory. With the farmers behind him, Ford would win the battle. "I still believe we are going to whip the greatest combination of interests ever arrayed against one man," he wrote. "Long ago the fight ceased to be about Muscle Shoals; it is just a fight against Henry Ford the man."

That wasn't exactly true. Ford's major opponent in Congress was Senator George Norris, and Norris didn't have anything much against Ford the man. He was opposed to Ford the bidder on Muscle Shoals. Norris had kept studying the issue through the summer, and in the fall of 1922 was more firmly convinced than ever that the only good answer was public ownership.

Ford was interested in building dams to power his industries. But Norris's studies had shown him that dams were much more than that. They were ways to deepen navigation channels, improving trade up and down the river. They were ways to provide irrigation water to farms in the dry season.

And, perhaps most important, they offered ways to control floods by trapping water when rainfall was high. The Tennessee River could still be a wild one, with destructive floods every decade or so that washed away houses and people, stripped topsoil, ruined farms, and damaged cities. There had been truly epic floods in 1847, 1867, and 1902—the kinds that people tell their grandchildren about.

And on the Tennessee they could happen fast. After four days of rain around Chattanooga, the water in 1867 rose a foot an hour, until the city was under fast-moving water as deep as a man was tall. The flood washed away the town's major bridge, destroyed its telegraph system, and sparked days of looting. Dead bodies floated through the streets. Norris wanted to dam the river in ways that would stop that from ever happening again. To do these jobs adequately—commerce, flood control, irrigation—Norris knew he would need to build a series of dams that could work together to maximize the benefits.

Norris had a broader vision than Ford. And as Ford and Alabama Power slugged it out in print, he found more and more supporters. When the new Congress convened, he was planning to introduce another bill to move Ford aside and let the government take over.

The *Wall Street Journal* was now calling the fight over Muscle Shoals "the battle of a generation." And there was about to be a final showdown.

WORTHINGTON TALKED A very positive line, but he could sense Ford's momentum slipping away. Too many criticisms were being leveled by too many people at the faults Norris had pointed out, and Ford was adamantly unwilling to respond by improving his bid. When the new Congress convened after the midterms, despite the increased Farm Bloc power, the Ford effort failed to gain traction. Instead, senators and congressmen began peeling away in ones and twos, convinced by Norris's dogged criticism, Alabama Power's continued lobbying, and persuasive arguments from fertilizer makers who tore apart Ford's claims about what might be possible at the nitrate plants.

Ford kept going anyway. The prize was too great to give up. He was now thinking of the project as a grand, integrated, region-wide industrial empire, a factory the size of a small state, full of metal ores and eager workers, powered by endless, cheap electricity, connected by rail and ship with Ford's factories in the north and the Gulf of Mexico to the south. It could be a like an assembly line stretching from Michigan to Alabama, sucking in iron, aluminum, timber, cotton, and chemicals, turning them into parts and fabrics, then putting them together to create a flood of next-generation cars and tractors. Each of the factories strung along the seventy-five-mile city would be like a stop on the line. Composing this symphony of industry, designing the parts and arranging the sites, smoothing the connections and getting the whole thing to function efficiently, would put the Ford Motor Company so far ahead of its competitors that they could never catch up.

At the same time, Ford was also investing in other pieces of the puzzle: railroads, coal mines, timberland, iron mines, steamship lines, steel factories, glassmaking plants, and on and on. Muscle Shoals would be at the center of it all.

Viewed this way, all his talk about making fertilizer and putting workers on small farms seems like a smoke screen. The real prize was owning the Niagara of the South and using it to create the Detroit of the South. Worthington kept telling him there was a good chance still that Congress would back him. And it wouldn't cost much to stick it out a little longer: a few dollars for Worthington and his public relations people, some reprinted pamphlets of his bid to pass out, and an occasional pep talk to the press. He was a very rich man, and this was a low-cost gamble.

He got support from other quarters as well. Ford didn't want his name associated with the scandalous land speculation going on around the Shoals, but he didn't complain when plans for a new city were announced in the spring of 1923 by a company called the Muscle Shoals Railroad and City Development Company, which had purchased more than three square miles of farmland along the river. Its plan was to turn the land into a complete small city with five major boulevards, a forty-acre central square, a big hotel with golf and tennis, a boat club, and building sites for eighteen thousand houses. They were calling it Ford City.

He also had continued strong support in the Farm Belt and across the South. And his communications operation chipped in: No fewer than seven laudatory Ford biographies were published in just two years, 1922 and 1923. The "Ford Clubs" that had started sprouting up across the South and Midwest to support his Muscle Shoals bid continued turning into Ford for President clubs, and speculation about his political plans kept his name in the papers.

If he did run, it would likely be Ford versus incumbent Warren G. Harding. And the timing seemed auspicious. Even though the economy was booming, Harding's administration lost political support in the midterms, in part because of rumors of corruption and graft at the highest levels. (The rumors would soon turn into the Teapot Dome scandal.) Harding had proven no friend to Ford in the Muscle Shoals affair, instead aligning himself with Wall Street and bankers, the Republican old guard that Ford felt was fighting him every inch of the way.

"Ford looms today a powerful figure on the political horizon," the *New York Times* wrote in the spring of 1923. He appealed to rural voters, to southern voters, to laborers in Michigan, and to anti-Harding voters everywhere. He was the richest and best-known man in America. And he was among the most admired. He managed to accrue wealth faster than Rockefeller but was never tarred as a robber baron. He ran an open shop at his factories but paid so well, the labor unions left him alone. He was all for the common man. And many Americans seemed to think he was a magician, capable of solving any problem, conjuring every answer.

His quiet right-hand man, Liebold, noted the increasing number of letters urging the boss to run—at one point it grew to two hundred per day—and passed a few on to Ford. One that ended up in the Henry Ford Archive gives a sense of the sentiment of the day. A Pendleton, Oregon, woman wrote: "Dear Sir, Please run for President. The farmers are all going broke and me along with the rest. We need you, for you are the poor peoples friend. I am farming 1,500 acres alone, been a widow for nine years. Could you please help me with some money. I shure need help. I would bless you."

Despite the growing support, Ford played coy. When Liebold talked with the boss about running for president, the response he got was "You do all you can to keep me out of this thing. I don't want to have anything to do with it."

Note that Ford did not say he was not a candidate. He just didn't want to go out and act like one. He allowed the speculation about his political future to percolate.

Perhaps it was because he knew that the threat of a presidential run could be used as a bargaining chip to get Muscle Shoals. He was in an enviable position. As the *New York Herald* reported in the spring of 1923, "The astonishing growth of popular sentiment for Ford for President is causing deep concern to Democrats and anxiety to Republicans." On the Democratic side, potential challengers to Harding were already beginning to test the water, an equation difficult to calculate without knowing what Ford might do or who he might support. On the Republican side, Harding's people worried that Ford might get enough votes to rob them of another four years. The result was that Ford had political leverage in both parties that could be used to push through his bid.

In June, Liebold let it be known that Ford would consider the offer of a presidential nomination and did not object to activities supporting him. That spurred some news coverage. But just as in his Senate race years earlier, Ford shunned active campaigning, refusing to get out and make speeches or shake hands or even state directly that he wanted to be elected. He kept everybody guessing, rumors flying, and papers selling.

It reached a pitch in the summer of 1923. Political pundits of the day opined that even if Ford lost the industrial Northeast and the West Coast, he could still sweep Middle America and the South, winning the Electoral College even if he lost the popular vote. But he had a good shot at winning the popular vote as well. As historian Reynold Wik wrote, "Convincing evidence exists to prove that had a popular referendum been held in July 1923 to elect a president of the United States, the winner would have been Mr. Ford." He based his conclusion in part on a large straw poll published in *Collier's* magazine in July that showed Ford defeating Harding by a huge margin.

Not everybody was for Ford, of course. Edison weighed in with a brief statement that he thought Ford would be better off sticking to his business. His former business associate James Couzens, now sitting in the Senate seat Ford lost in 1918, wrote of a Ford run, "How can a man over 60 years old, who has done nothing but make motors, who has no training, no experience, aspire to such an office? It is most ridiculous. . . . I want to save Ford the greatest humiliation of his career and save the United States Government the humiliation of him as President." Couzens and Ford had ended their business relationship unhappily, which might account for part of the outspoken snark. But the greater part was straightforward: He knew Ford well enough to judge him unqualified for the presidency.

Perhaps the most important force against a Ford run was his wife, Clara, who thought her husband had plenty to do without running for a political office. "I do not want him to go through the awfulness of a political campaign," she said. She called Liebold and reportedly told him, "Since you got him into it, you can just get him out of it. I hate this idea of the name of Ford being dragged into the gutters of political filth!"

Collier's followed up its straw poll by asking Ford for an interview and help with an article to be titled, "If I Were President." Surprisingly, Ford said yes. He handed the project off to his communications office, which cut and pasted bits from his columns in the *Dearborn Independent* and supplemented them with carefully selected quotes from an interview with a *Collier's* writer. At the same time, the Ford Motor Company's motion picture department put the finishing touches on a laudatory special feature, a summary of his life and successes called *The Ford Age*.

Ford didn't quite say he was officially launching a run, but, buoyed on a swell of popular support, it looked like he was getting closer.

Then, just days before the *Collier's* feature was set to appear, everything changed.

CHAPTER 14

THE LAST MEETING

WARREN G. HARDING was not a well man. The president was overweight, smoked too much, drank too much, and suffered bouts of chest pain. And he had political worries as well: Stories of graft and corruption were swirling around his administration, centered in part on rumors about his cronies making money off of sweet-heart deals for oil in a federal reserve called Teapot Dome, and in part about his sexual peccadilloes, including salacious rumors about extramarital affairs (true), an illegitimate daughter (true), and sex in a White House closet (maybe). His wife was not a happy woman.

And neither were voters, who, despite the good economic news, had seemed to turn against his policies and defeated his conservative candidates in the midterm elections.

In the hot, sticky summer of 1923, Harding fled Washington, DC, and embarked on a long goodwill tour of the West. His plan was to visit cities from Juneau down to San Diego, then take a Navy ship back through the Panama Canal and return in August. It would be a chance to get away from the scandals and enjoy a public relations bonanza of warm civic welcomes and applauding crowds.

It started out well enough. He became the first sitting president to visit Canada, then the first to Alaska. But his staff had arranged a brutal schedule, tightly packed with speeches and receptions, with little time off. While in the Pacific Northwest, Harding suffered what was thought to be a bout of food poisoning from bad crab. Visibly fatigued, he hurried through a speech in Seattle, then walked off the stage without waiting for applause. His physicians couldn't agree on what was wrong with him. The next day Harding managed to board a train to San Francisco, but once he got there he could barely walk the few blocks from the station to his hotel. He made it to his room and collapsed.

His doctors diagnosed heart problems worsened by mild pneumonia. He needed to clear his schedule and stay in bed for a least a few days more. But he never left the hotel room. On the night of August 2, 1923, Harding was hit with a massive stroke—what was at the time called apoplexy—and was dead within minutes.

Everyone started scrambling. Vice President Calvin Coolidge, who was visiting his parents in Vermont, was quickly sworn in by his father, a notary public, and rushed back to Washington. The nation was only a year away from the next presidential election. Coolidge was now both the president and the Republican Party's new next candidate. In many ways, the conservative and squeaky-clean Coolidge was a stronger candidate than Harding.

Democrats were eager to take advantage of the sudden political shift, but how? Three or four established politicians were interested in running. But they were all asking the same question: What was Henry Ford going to do?

The answer, it turned out, was: go camping. As Harding was touring the West, Ford, Edison, and Firestone were scheduling another of their annual Vagabond trips. When they learned of the president's death, they altered their plans just enough to make it possible to attend Harding's funeral in Ohio.

The usual gaggle of reporters followed them everywhere, photographing Ford and Edison standing behind Coolidge at the funeral, then following them on their woodsy trip to Michigan's Upper Peninsula. When they asked Ford about running for president, he laughed it off, leading them to infer that, as one wire service reported, "he was not going after the presidency, but . . . would be willing to accept the honor if it were conferred upon him."

But he was going to have to make a move. When the Prohibition Party asked him to run as its candidate, he said no. Then Democrats started jockeying for the nomination, starting with Alabama senator Oscar Underwood. Others would quickly follow. In the fall, the leaders of Ford for President clubs from two dozen states announced they were going to hold a national conference in Dearborn on December 12 to push their man toward the White House. It was time to make a decision.

And still he would not commit. One moment Ford would say something like "I don't have a political mind and I don't see any sense in my attempting political leadership." The next, he was cracking jokes about which of his executives might make good cabinet members, or saying things like "I'd like to be down there [in Washington] for about six weeks to throw some monkey wrenches into the machinery."

There were several reasons for his ambivalence. As always, he hated the idea of politicking. He was still a poor public speaker. It is also likely that Ford, based on his own comments and those made by people who knew him best, realized that at some level he simply wasn't suited for the job. He was a business tycoon accustomed to one-man rule and fast decisions. "If our government were an absolute monarchy, a one-man affair," wrote the former head of one of Ford's departments, "Henry Ford would be the logical man for the throne." But the government wasn't a monarchy, and his autocratic tendencies would not serve him well in Washington.

Some observers began whispering that Liebold was more interested in the presidency than Ford was. Fred L. Black, business manager at the *Dearborn Independent*, recalled, "From various things he said to me, I think if Mr. Ford had been elected, Liebold expected to run the country. He was terrifically ambitious. And, if Mr. Ford had been elected, Liebold practically *would* have been assistant president."

But for the moment, playing the sphinx suited Ford's interests. By staying on the sidelines, he allowed speculation to run wild, which meant more newspaper coverage for Ford. And that was always a good thing.

DURING HIS FIRST month as president, Coolidge set up a meeting with Ford. The Fords, father and son, along with chief engineer William Mayo, arrived in Washington in early September 1923, hoping that the new president would at last make a deal.

There were good reasons for it to happen. Coolidge wanted two things: to clear Muscle Shoals off his plate and to neutralize Ford as a political opponent. Supporting Ford's bid for the Shoals might allow him to do both at the same time. Once Ford was focused on building his great city, he might be too busy to run for president. If he took the Shoals and stayed in the race as well, a case could be made that there were fatal conflicts of interest between Ford's business dealings and his political ambitions. That could help neutralize a potential rival.

On the other hand, Coolidge had inherited John Wingate Weeks as his secretary of war. And Weeks was as adamantly critical of Ford's bid as ever. Ford didn't help his own case by digging in his heels. He still refused to make the smallest change in his offer. His bid was his bid, take it or leave it.

So when they all sat down together, Coolidge tried to play peacemaker. Their discussion eventually focused on one major sticking point: the Gorgas steam power plant. Ford insisted on taking the plant as part of the deal, but Alabama Power planned within the next few weeks to exercise its legal option to buy it back. Coolidge asked Ford if he could give up his insistence on Gorgas, dangling the bait of his possible backing if he could. Ford asked for some extra time to think about it. Congress had spent almost two years delaying his bid. The White House could certainly give him a few more months before selling the Gorgas plant.

No deal was settled, and nobody was happy after the meeting. Ford got a little extra time, but not as much as he wanted. Less than a month later, Weeks announced that he was going to sell the Gorgas plant to Alabama Power for $3.5 million (an amount that made Ford's $5 million bid for the much more costly nitrate plants look weak). Coolidge had approved the sale. "Ford Dream Collapses," ran a typical headline. But it wasn't quite true. In early October, Coolidge assured an unhappy farm lobbyist that Ford wasn't out of it yet, that he thought a solution could still be found that would be satisfactory to Mr. Ford, although he didn't know yet what it was.

Ford lashed out at Weeks, hinting that shadowy "other parties" were pulling the war secretary's strings, saying he couldn't get a fair hearing because "John W. Weeks and scores of corporation lawyers have exerted their cunning game to prevent me." By blocking his bid, Weeks was making it possible for the water power and fertilizer financiers to retain the endless millions they made through exorbitantly high pricing. Ford would have nothing more to do with him. Then he announced flatly that he was staying in the fight, that his bid was still alive.

The secretary of war responded that Ford's statement was "filled with reckless assertions," that the sale of the steam plant was a good deal for the nation, and that the proper place to take up the issue was not in the pages of newspapers, but in the US Congress. He did make one concession, likely at Coolidge's insistence, delaying the final signing of the Gorgas sale until December. But that was all he could do.

The walls were closing in on Henry Ford. His bid was still under relentless attack by Norris and his growing number of allies in the Senate; his congressional support was weakening; the Gorgas plant was being sold; and, most important, the big dam—thanks to Norris's ability to keep construction money flowing—was finally nearing completion. They were planning to name it Wilson Dam, after the president who had started the project. Once it was up and running, however, the entire financial structure for Ford's bid, with its repayment schedule based on projected construction costs, would be rendered obsolete.

So Ford made a final play. Just before the final papers for the Gorgas plant were due to be signed, he came to Washington for one last meeting.

In early December, President Coolidge, Secretary Weeks, Ford, Ford's engineer Mayo, and the ever-present Ernest Liebold sat down together. Official records of the meeting are not available. But from what participants later said and what the newspapers put together, it appears that Ford started by telling Coolidge and Weeks that he was not going to give ground on the Gorgas plant. His offer, as delivered to Congress in the last session, still stood. The president tried to interest him in an alternative in which Gorgas was sold, as it was required to be, but a second big power plant was built in its place, which Ford could have with proper adjustments of the bid. Ford rebuffed the idea. No other details of the meeting are known.

But when it was over, Ford seemed unusually chipper. Instead of trying to avoid the reporters standing outside the White House, he waded right into the scrum and teased them, saying, "You fellows are a damned nuisance." "So are your flivvers, Mr. Ford," a photographer shot back (referring to a common nickname for the Model T).

Ford wouldn't answer any questions about what had been decided in the meeting, When a reporter asked about his presidential ambitions, Ford said, "Hmph. That would be funny, wouldn't it?" Then he and his entourage walked off.

The meeting lasted twenty minutes, and Ford emerged in an uncharacteristically good mood for someone who had made no headway on a problem that had bedeviled him for years. It seems likely that more was discussed in that meeting between the president and the automaker than anyone wanted to make public.

Both Ford and Coolidge were eager to make something happen. Coolidge, unlike Harding, was doing more than ignoring the question. He was trying his best to come up with a solution. He didn't want to run against Ford for the presidency, and when it came down to it, Ford didn't much want to run against the well-respected and apparently popular Coolidge. If Ford was going to get in it, he intended to win, and Coolidge looked like he would be a tougher opponent than the scandal-ridden Harding. Given the situation, it is possible, even likely, that Coolidge made it clear in their meeting that while he was certainly in favor of private control of the Muscle Shoals project, he couldn't risk political capital by publicly supporting Ford, a move that would anger radical Republicans like Norris. He needed to keep his party together until after the election. Then, possibly, he could find a way to support the Ford offer and help push it through Congress.

If, that is, Coolidge was elected. If Ford ran against him or publicly opposed him, if he made Coolidge's election more difficult, it would be a different story. Coolidge would then be justified in doing what he could to deny Ford the prize he sought. However the discussion went, Ford emerged from the meeting realizing that he was being given a choice: He could either make a run for the White House, or he could get control of the Shoals. He could not have both. It was up to him.

If it happened that way, it made for an easy choice. He didn't much want the presidency anyway. He went for the Shoals.

In the absence of contemporaneous notes or other records of the meeting, it's impossible to say exactly how these issues were discussed. What is clear, however, is what happened next.

THREE DAYS AFTER the meeting, Coolidge put out the word that he was in favor of selling Muscle Shoals to a private party, a statement that members of the Senate interpreted as an endorsement of the Ford offer. Soon after, just a few days before the Ford for President clubs were scheduled to hold their big meeting in Dearborn, Ford asked them to call it off.

Then, on December 19, 1923, Ford issued a formal statement. He announced officially that he had no intention of entering the presidential race. Instead, he threw his support to the Republicans. "I would never for a moment think of running against Calvin Coolidge for President on any ticket whatever," he told reporters. "In this present situation, I am for Coolidge."

It was a shock to both Democrats and Republicans. The president immediately wrote Ford a flattering telegram noting his many good works and thanking him effusively for his support.

Just like that, the Ford for President boom was over. There was grief and lamentation among the Ford faithful. One disappointed backer from Minnesota wrote that Ford had "chickened out, leaving us who thought we had a leader for the great Armageddon, the fight between right and wrong, between man and money, between freedom and slavery, between Christ and Satan. We now wonder if we haven't been worshiping a Tin God."

But others were pleased to hear the news. Coolidge, of course, was elated, and most Republicans along with him. Clara Ford couldn't have been happier. Many higher-ups in the Ford organization were glad to see the boss clear a major distraction off his desk. And other candidates for the Democratic ticket now had a clear path to the nomination without worrying about Ford.

Across the board, just about everybody took it for granted that Ford had traded his candidacy for Muscle Shoals. Some of his backers said so. At least one Democratic candidate for president agreed. Newspaper editors treated it as obvious. "Ford's decision to support President Coolidge . . . has caused quite a stir in political circles," one editorial observed. "We're now ready to bet a plugged nickel that Henry gets the Muscle Shoals plant."

And it looked like he had cleared the path to do just that. Republicans in the House of Representatives voted by a hefty majority in March 1924 to approve Ford's bid—without Gorgas, but with a new plant to be built in its place—and sent the bill to the Senate. This win for Ford set off rejoicing around the Shoals, where factories blew their whistles, drivers honked their horns, bonfires were lit, and crowds gathered on courthouse lawns. Some people said it was the biggest celebration they'd seen since Armistice Day. There was only one more step to go, Senate approval, before Ford's bid would be sitting on the president's desk for a final okay.

Everything was finally lining up.

But people seemed to forget that before it went to the Senate floor, the House's Muscle Shoals bill would have to be reviewed by the Senate Agriculture Committee and its chairman, George Norris.

CHAPTER 15

SCANDAL

SENATOR GEORGE NORRIS had come out of the 1922 midterms stronger than ever. A few more of his allies had been elected to the Senate—enough to make Norris's and Bob La Follette's little group of radical Republicans an essential swing vote. They numbered seven senators now, just enough to make the difference between passing and stopping legislation. If they aligned with the minority Democrats, they could outvote the Republican majority; if they voted with the Republicans, there was no way the Democrats could get anything passed. The old-guard mainstream conservative Republicans had to keep the radicals happy, and Democrats were always after them to make deals. Norris was suddenly a key player.

And he took advantage. In March 1924 he cosponsored a bill that would create a new approach to the oversight of public lands, placing the people's rich natural resources, ores and oil, under the control of a federal commission appointed by the president. It would help avoid scandals like Teapot Dome. It was also in line with Norris's ideas for government control of the Tennessee River.

His more immediate problem was the rumored Ford-Coolidge deal for Muscle Shoals. If it was true that Ford had pulled out of the presidential race in exchange for the Shoals, there was very little time to waste. Once President Coolidge formally announced his support for Ford, the game would be over.

But Norris had one last move. It was not his style. It was scandalous and a little underhanded. But it was all he had to knock Coolidge and Ford off balance.

IN THE SPRING of 1924, somebody brought Norris a tip. The Nebraska senator thought about it, then acted on it. He sent a subpoena to the telegraph company, demanding certain records. He checked the White House visitors' logs. And once he saw the replies, he called a new round of hearings and started calling witnesses. He invited Ford and Ernest Liebold to appear. And then he added someone new to the list, an aging hack reporter named James Martin Miller.

Miller was an old-school newsman who never went to journalism school but learned his job by getting out there and doing it—traveling the world and writing about what he found, selling reports to newspapers, magazines, book publishers, whoever would pay him a few dollars. He worked his way up the journalistic ladder, working for some decent papers, interviewing admirals and cabinet secretaries. Miller could drop into a new part of the world, mix with any crowd, and talk on any subject. Whatever kind of reporter the assignment called for—war correspondent, travel writer, current events—he was ready. He became something of a specialist in churning out quickie books on current events and notable people, including biographies of figures like William McKinley, Teddy Roosevelt, and Pope Leo XIII. He churned out copy fast and became a regular at press clubs around the world, the places where journalists gathered to socialize and drink. He was something of a fixture at the

National Press Club in Washington. Now past sixty years of age, he could be found there propping up the bar, sporting an impressive walrus mustache, looking like a harrumphing British lord from the movies, telling entertaining stories to anyone who would listen. He claimed to have been named to diplomatic posts in France and Germany, and said he had served as US consul general to New Zealand. He talked about meeting Japanese warlords and French socialites. Like any good reporter he had gotten into a bit of trouble as well, and had been accused at various points of everything from bouncing checks to skipping out on warrants.

Recently he'd been working for Liebold and the editors at Ford's *Dearborn Independent*. He'd been taken on there after writing a fast Ford biography published in 1922, *The Amazing Story of Henry Ford: The Ideal American and The World's Most Famous Private Citizen; A Complete and Authentic Account of His Life and Surpassing Achievements.* The text was as fawning as the title. He'd gotten Ford's personal cooperation on that project, and when it was done he'd been hired to write an article or two for the *Independent.* He also became part of what some people called the "Ford secret service," a loose, shadowy collection of reporters, detectives, and informants used by Liebold and Ford to keep Dearborn informed of what was going on in Washington, DC, and do whatever needed doing. Like a lot of Liebold's contacts, Miller was not officially an employee of Ford but was somehow paid; he communicated with headquarters but often in ways that did not leave a record.

The incident that brought him before the Norris committee had taken place in October 1923, back when Weeks announced he was selling the Gorgas plant, and in response Ford attacked Weeks publicly. The morning the Ford attack on Weeks was printed, Weeks met with the president to agree on a response. And as soon as Weeks left, in something of a surprise, Miller was called into the president's office for a lengthy one-on-one interview.

Norris became very interested in that interview. He heard that as Miller was getting ready to leave, Coolidge had stopped him and said, unprompted, "I am friendly to Mr. Ford but wish someone would convey to him that it is my hope that Mr. Ford will not do or say anything that will make it difficult for me to deliver Muscle Shoals to him, which is what I am trying to do."

Miller knew what that meant. Coolidge was making it clear that he was going to help Ford get his bid accepted, but that Ford should stop attacking his cabinet members and stirring the pot. He was asking the reporter to pass along the thought. Miller hustled out of the White House, went to a telegraph office, and sent the president's words to both Liebold and the editor of the *Dearborn Independent*—this was the communication Norris had subpoenaed from the telegraph office. Within days Miller was called to Detroit to meet personally with Liebold and Ford, setting the stage for the deal that Coolidge and Ford supposedly struck a few weeks later.

Oddly, Miller never wrote any sort of article based on his long interview with Coolidge. Nothing about his visit appeared in public for months, until Norris somehow found out about it and called him to testify.

How was it that months later Norris found out about the interview? Miller himself might have tipped the committee. The aging newsman had recently fallen out with Liebold over money he thought he was owed, and had quit the Ford organization in January. Maybe letting Norris know about his telegram was Miller's way of getting even.

However it happened, it was the only hard evidence Norris had of Coolidge's intent to work on Ford's behalf. It smelled of a quid pro quo between the president and Ford, a deal trading political favors for economic benefits. It might not be much, but it would make it look like the president was ready to do what needed to be done to get Ford the Shoals as long as Ford quit making waves about the

Coolidge administration. It made Coolidge look less like a president and more like a man dedicated to doing Ford's bidding.

In April, Miller entered Norris's committee room, was sworn in, and began testifying. What was his job with the Ford organization? He had been hired by Liebold to be part of the *Dearborn Independent* team to act "as an observer of things political relating to the manufacturer's presidential boom." He was no lobbyist, he testified; he was a reporter and had had nothing to do with Muscle Shoals. Yes, he met with the president at the date and time mentioned; yes, his telegram to Liebold had presented the president's words accurately; and, yes, he had sent the telegram immediately after the meeting.

It was bombshell testimony. As soon as the reporter's testimony was splashed across the front pages of the nation's newspapers, Coolidge released a lengthy statement denying the whole thing. Well, he couldn't deny meeting with Miller—that had been entered in the White House log—but the supposed quote, the promise "to deliver" the Shoals to Ford, that had never happened. "I have never said I was trying to deliver Muscle Shoals to Mr. Ford, or to anyone else," Coolidge stated. He wanted each bid for the project to be considered fairly, on its merits.

Then Norris called Liebold into the committee room. Ford's personal secretary tried to undercut Miller, saying that the newsman had never officially been on any Ford payroll, had done no more than write a few articles for the *Independent*, and "never was authorized to act as Mr. Ford's agent in any matter." No mention was made of the admiring Ford biography Miller had written. Liebold said he really didn't remember much about the journalist; he thought Miller might have sent telegrams to Dearborn on various matters, but he couldn't really remember much about them. Norris had requested that Liebold bring with him all telegrams or other correspondence between the president and Ford; Liebold testified that he had been unable to find anything.

The only thing he was definite about was that he certainly did not remember receiving the telegram in question about Coolidge's views on Muscle Shoals. And he certainly did not have a copy of it. "If any such telegram was received, it was regarded as of no practical importance and no attention paid to it," Liebold said. "It is quite probable that we did receive that telegram, as we frequently received wires from many sources, but I have no recollection of it." He was pretty sure that if it had been received, he had never shown it to Ford.

Norris himself took the lead in questioning Liebold. He asked several times about other direct communications between the president and Ford (an indication that Norris thought other evidence existed). He asked about Miller's trip to Dearborn days after the telegram. Liebold said that Miller made the trip on his own volition. "Did he have an interview with Mr. Ford?" Norris asked. "Mr. Ford may have talked with him," Liebold answered. The man who prided himself on knowing everything that went on in Ford's office had gone suddenly vague.

Norris had hoped to ask Ford the same questions, but again Ford refused to appear before the committee. The process had gone on long enough, he wrote in response to his invitation. The committee knew everything they needed to know about his bid. He had made his associates available. "We are further inclined to this course by the recent effort of Chairman Norris of the Senate Committee on Agriculture to reflect upon the integrity of the president of the United States in connection with our effort for Muscle Shoals," he wrote.

Over the next few days, anti-Miller pieces started appearing in the press, bringing up his checkered reputation, noting his "vivid imagination," his lack of ethics, and his money troubles with the Ford organization.

But it didn't matter. Norris had succeeded in his major goal: getting Miller's testimony into the public record. He made Miller's telegram look like a smoking gun, seeming confirmation of collusion between Ford and the White House. He made the relationship between Ford and Coolidge look scandalous.

Norris used his hearings to keep hammering at the issue. Didn't Ford issue a "cutting statement against the Administration on last October 12?" he asked one witness, referring to Ford's public attack on Weeks. Clearly Ford was angry with Coolidge in October. But did he not then pay a friendly visit to the president a few weeks later on December 3? Was it not "almost inconceivable" that Ford would suddenly change his whole attitude toward Coolidge unless he had some very good reason for changing?

After both Ford and Coolidge loudly denied Miller's testimony and attacks on him began to appear, Norris called the reporter back to the stand to defend himself. Miller declared flatly, under oath, that he had "correctly and truthfully" related what had happened. "The president himself brought up the Muscle Shoals question at our conference, and he cannot deny it," the newsman said. After essentially calling the president a liar, Miller went on to say that the government had no secret service greater than Ford's.

Norris jumped in to add, "I have no ill feelings toward anyone in connection with Muscle Shoals. . . . Mr. Ford's statement, published in the papers, that I have been trying to reflect upon the integrity of the president is simply an attempt to shift the attention of the public from the real question at issue. . . . I am simply endeavoring to save for the people of the United States the valuable inheritance of our national resources and I will continue to do this regardless of results and regardless of who may be involved," he told the committee. "I do not want a controversy with the president, or with anyone else. But I will not deviate from what I believe to be my duty in bringing out the proper evidence before the committee, regardless of what the effect may be, either upon me or upon anyone else. . . . The committee and the Senate, as well as the public, can draw their own conclusions."

In what was for him a long piece of oratory, Norris summed up his findings for his colleagues in the Senate. He compared the politicians around him to chemists, who could take seemingly common ingredients and mix them in ways that made explosives or poison gases. In the same way, enemies like Ford and Coolidge might suddenly undergo a reaction and become friends; northern Republicans, if mixed the right way with southern Democrats, might find themselves backing the Ford bid. The catalyst for this strange political chemistry was Ford, "the magic of whose very name causes millions to go insane with enthusiasm for any crazy notion he may ever possess."

"So with the political chemist," Norris said. "He can put together men of different political faiths, of different interests, and make a product that will make poisonous gas that will smell to high heaven."

His main message had been delivered. He used the remainder of his committee's hearings to bring forward witnesses attacking Ford and supporting his plan for government ownership.

Ford's supporters, seeing Norris once again gaining the upper hand, brought in one last surprise witness, an Alabama socialite, E. A. Edmundson, who testified that during one of Norris's visits to the Shoals two years earlier, the senator had promised to support Ford's bid if he got a kiss from one of the pretty girls at a barbecue. A smiling teenager had stepped up and delivered.

Norris rose from his chair, his face "as red as an American Beauty rose," the *New York Times* reported. He thundered "Did Senator Heflin [a Ford supporter from Alabama] know in advance that you were going to come here and tell this story? Was this fixed up in advance to browbeat me?"

"Why senator," she said, "I intended it only as a little pleasantry. . . . I did not think the revelation of the little story would hurt you so."

"The story you have told is a falsehood," Norris said. "I know a blackmail plot when I see it. If you were not a woman," he said to the witness, "this would not be the end of this, I tell you. I did not kiss that girl. She kissed me."

The other senators and the audience erupted in laughter. A prank was being played on the generally humorless Norris. "Cotton Tom" Heflin was needling him in front of his own committee. Heflin laughed it off as "simply a pleasant incident," and confirmed that as far as he knew the local beauty had indeed kissed the senator, not the other way around. "It is also true," he added, "that every other member of the Joint Committee who was present was genuinely and sincerely envious of the Chairman."

NORRIS GOT WHAT he wanted out of his hearings. Miller's testimony, with its hints that Coolidge was a man willing to deal away public resources for political gain, got wide play and made Ford's bid for the Shoals look just enough like the Teapot Dome scandal to stop Coolidge from jumping in to back Ford's bid. Without Coolidge's public support, the Ford bid was likely to stay stuck in Congress. Norris had once again outfoxed the automaker.

In late May his Agriculture Committee voted against sending Ford's bid—the one that had passed the House—to the full Senate, forwarding in its place Norris's own bill for government ownership. There was not much chance that Norris's bill would go much farther—even if by some slim chance it got enough votes to pass the Senate, Coolidge would certainly veto it—but whatever time the senators spent on the Shoals would be spent on the merits of public ownership, not Ford.

As Worthington wrote Liebold, the Norris bill would be argued to death for the next few months. Any last-ditch attempt to introduce a Ford bill without the Agriculture Committee's backing would go nowhere. When Congress reconvened after its summer break, everyone would be up against the 1924 election, and nobody would want to be on record one way or another until after November 4. They couldn't look for any forward movement until after the election. Once Coolidge won, he would no longer have any need to deal with Ford.

The Ford faithful were still ready to stand and fight. "I just finished a long talk with Senator Underwood, who is my personal friend for many years, and he is strong for the Ford offer, and intends to use every effort to win," one of them wrote Liebold. "But he frankly says that he will need some help from the Republican side, and that President Coolidge is the only one who can induce the regular-line Republicans to vote right. Therefore, I suggest to you that if there is anything you know to do, it must be done quickly."

But there was nothing much to do. Norris's strategy of delay had worked. Coolidge was too close to the election to risk a Ford-related scandal now. Norris had succeeded in keeping enough funding flowing for the dam construction that it was now a matter of months until the mighty Wilson Dam would start producing electricity—for the people, not for Henry Ford.

Ford waited through the summer, hoping, perhaps, for some faint signal of support from Coolidge. He never got one. So he made his final decision. In the fall of 1924, three years after he had first looked at the half-finished dam on the Tennessee and saw what he could do with it, and a few weeks before the presidential election, Ford (along with one of his biographers, Samuel Crowther, and his communications team) put the finishing touches on a magazine story titled "Henry Ford Tackles a New Job." It was set to run in the October 18 issue of *Collier's* news weekly.

It was written as if Ford had decided to open a new chapter in his career. But in reality, it was a surrender. He was saying farewell to Muscle Shoals.

It was a wandering and vague piece, without any of the stirring, focused vision of his seventy-five-mile-city rallying cries. In Ford's telling, Muscle Shoals was no longer needed. He had passed beyond it. Thanks to the government delay, he was now setting up to install his own dams and coal-powered electrical plants wherever he wanted, to power his own industries "in our own way entirely outside of all political influence or political meddling," he was quoted as saying. "That is why we have lost our interest in Muscle Shoals."

Ford wrote a simple one-page letter to President Coolidge, timed to arrive at the White House the day the *Collier's* article appeared. In it, after pointing out how long his bid had been considered, he wrote, "Inasmuch as so much time has already elapsed we are unable to wait and delay what plans we have any longer for action by Congress, and I am, consequently, asking that you consider this as a withdrawal of said offer."

It was over.

Coolidge wrote back a one-paragraph note saying that he understood, adding, "I trust, however, that should the Congress conclude that it is best to restore this property to private ownership you will at that time renew your interest in the project."

Liebold, who had been unable to get the project rolling for his boss, wrote a brief, cryptic note to Worthington. "There seems to be considerable disappointment over Mr. Ford's withdrawal of his offer on Muscle Shoals," he noted. "But upon second thought I am sure that the people will come to the conclusion that it is for the best of all concerned."

It certainly seemed the best for Ford. In the years since he had first faced the adoring crowds at Florence, much had changed. Part of it was the near completion of Wilson Dam. Part was the loss of his presidential bid. But more general scientific and technological progress had also undone Ford's efforts. Advances in the making of fertilizers, the adoption of the Haber system, and the evolution of the cyanamide process rendered the old World War I–era plants at the Shoals obsolete, robbing him of a potent argument for keeping them running. The art of dam building had advanced, too, with the giant dam on the Tennessee serving as a model for proposals to build more across the country, on the Colorado and Columbia Rivers and in a dozen other places. The flood of cheap electricity that was going to power the Detroit of the South would become commonplace. Instead of powering utopia, the electricity would be used to light up Vegas.

And perhaps Ford, like Edison, was just getting too old for grand dreams. Now in his early sixties, a time when many people are thinking of retiring, Ford had plenty to do without Muscle Shoals. He was fending off a growing number of competitors to his motor company; thinking about gearing up for the production of a new model; moving into more international markets; thinking of building manufacturing plants in England and Germany, among other places; perfecting production at River Rouge; and keeping his company at the forefront of the auto industry. He had three grandchildren now, and a legacy to ensure for them. There was enough for any man.

Muscle Shoals no longer captured his mercurial interest. Let the government have it, or Wall Street, or whoever wanted it. He no longer saw much future in it. "There is small promise now that it will ever be a national asset," he wrote in his goodbye piece in *Collier's*. "More than likely it will be a national expense."

Which raised another question: Without Ford, what would become of Muscle Shoals?

PART III

TVA

CHAPTER 16

THE ALABAMA GHOST

GEORGE NORRIS'S POLITICAL roots were in old-style prairie populism, the farmers' revolution against big railroads and rapacious banks. Then he grew into Progressivism, with its crusades for clean government and control of monopolies. Now he was a radical Republican. The one thread that tied it all together was his dedication to taking power away from the rich and influential and giving it back to the common people.

That was what Muscle Shoals was all about. It was a tremendous source of power made by a big river, and in Norris's view all that power and that whole river belonged to the people. He wouldn't let it be taken over by rich financiers and corporate titans. Henry Ford wasn't his enemy. He had nothing against him personally. He was just a plutocrat, and plutocrats were who Norris battled. There were many others. He had killed Ford's bid, but that didn't end the fight. It simply cleared a spot for the next contender.

Next in line was Alabama Power, which had gotten into the game late and then ran competition for Ford. AP had been circling around Muscle Shoals since the early days, when it bought

Worthington's and Washburn's little hydroelectric company (along with many other little power companies in the state). It was now a big, rich, powerful force in the state, cozy with the region's politicians, connected with all sorts of other power companies, banks, and corporate interests, from American Cyanamid and the Morgan banking empire to Mellon's aluminum companies. Many people around the Shoals despised AP because it raised rates seemingly without reason and was slow in bringing electricity out to farmers and small towns in the state's rural areas. But it was the big dog in the state when it came to electricity, and once a private utility built and owned the state's electrical system, it was hard to beat.

Senator Oscar Underwood of Alabama had shifted his allegiance from Ford to AP and back to Ford, and now rose again as AP's champion in Congress. After Ford bowed out, Underwood pushed forward AP's bid for Muscle Shoals. It was slightly more palatable than Ford's. (It leased Wilson Dam, for instance, for only fifty years instead of Ford's one hundred, putting it in compliance with federal law.) Former Ford backers around the Shoals, eager to finalize the long-promised development, swallowed their distaste and began backing the AP bid.

In the months after Ford dropped out, it looked like AP would run the project. Underwood, with his enormous pull in the region, backed the firm. Accepting the bid would provide a simple way out

Wilson Dam, 1924
Courtesy Library of Congress

of the Muscle Shoals problem. The Senate was sick of debating it. Coolidge would have no objection.

But Norris refused to fall in line. AP's bid might have been marginally better than Ford's, but it added up to the same thing: Once private interests controlled the big dams and built the transmission lines, nobody could compete with them; they could pretty much charge consumers whatever they wanted. These big regional power trusts like AP were snapping up all their smaller competitors, a move that would leave America's power system in the hands of an interlocking group of wealthy private interests, a "power trust" that could squeeze consumers for whatever it wanted.

Norris saw it coming. So he took on Underwood and the AP the same way he had taken on Ford—by outworking them, outstudying them, and outmaneuvering them in the Senate. During the next year he used every parliamentary trick he knew to stall the AP bid. Norris pushed the idea of the "power trust" as the enemy of the common people, then refined and reworked his ideas about public ownership as the strongest possible alternative. He undercut Underwood wherever he could, benefiting from the Alabama senator's shift of attention to a run for the 1924 Democratic nomination for president. He didn't get it; in Ford's absence the Democratic nomination went instead to a former ambassador named John W. Davis, and Coolidge won in a walk.

Underwood and AP were still using the cheap fertilizer line, promising to use power from the dam to restart the nitrate plants, which put Ford's old allies in the farm lobbies on their side. It was the old Ford team back together again, minus the automaker.

Despite Norris's efforts, the AP bill did get passed by the Senate and sent to the House, where Norris's allies bottled it up until it died. Norris meanwhile built his own network of support for government ownership, finding allies like newspaper magnate William Randolph Hearst, who pushed the idea that Underwood was in the pocket of the power companies and the railroads, and called AP's bid a "steal" and "a greater scandal than Teapot Dome." Coolidge refused to get back into it, limiting his comments to things like "The problem of Muscle Shoals seems to me to have assumed a place all out of proportion to its real importance. It probably does not represent in market value much more than a first-class battleship."

This left Norris with a clear field to push his own plan. When a southern senator called his government plan "socialistic and Bolshevistic," Norris replied that it was nothing of the sort, merely good government. Norris had never advocated for direct government control of the project—the sort of bureaucratic, centralized state planning that was being tried in the Soviet Union—but instead wanted the project overseen by a government corporation. This model (which had already been used in a limited way during the Panama Canal construction) allowed public funds to flow to projects overseen by a more or less independent board of directors who were allowed leeway to run things as they saw fit. It would avoid management by politicians, with its risk of graft and party cronyism, and allow top experts, free from pressure, to make decisions based solely on what worked best.

The choice of directors was critical. They would be presented with goals and guidelines, but other than that were supposed to be nonpolitical, shielded from direct pressure from Washington as long as they did their jobs. The president might pick the directors, but once in place they were semi-independent—able to hire, fire, and make policy. The structure offered both a degree of freedom from strict government agency regulations and more financial flexibility to sell stock or borrow on credit, but would still be a government undertaking, with access to public funding and responsibility for carrying out a public mission.

By building his proposal around this structure, Norris was able to deflect not only charges of Russian-style control, but also criticism about the government unfairly meddling in and competing with private enterprise. One example was fertilizer. Fixed nitrogen was "first in war, first in peace, and first in the hearts of demagogues, politicians, lobbyists, professional farmers, and other honest and near-honest persons," as one writer put it. Norris, seeing that new technology was rendering the issue moot in any case, focused attention away from the production of nitrates, where it might get into tangles with private companies, and toward government research on fertilizers in general, with the aim of developing cheaper, better versions for farmers. His newest bill proposed using the old nitrate plants as sites for fertilizer experiments that would benefit agriculture and get cheaper food to more Americans. That was hard to argue with, and it helped Norris weaken farm opposition to his plan.

But that was secondary. As Norris recognized, the issue was not fertilizer, but power. With unaccustomed oratorical grace, he said, "If we should properly develop this project, we would tap this lightning that man has called electricity and convert its destructive and ruthless forces into a friendly power that would turn the countless wheels of toil all throughout the South and bring happiness and comfort to thousands of humble homes." He proposed establishing a Federal Power Corporation that would both oversee the production of electricity and the use of some of the power for fertilizer research. Like Ford, his plan foresaw not just completing one dam, but building a whole string of them up the river, creating a "super power district" that would rationalize and organize power production, flood control, and navigation for the entire region.

It was a great dream—as great in its own way as Ford's seventy-five-mile city, but it was unlikely to happen as long as Coolidge was in the White House. Norris was strong enough to delay the AP bid the same way he delayed Ford, but he was not strong enough to override a likely presidential veto.

So the debates ground on. Tired of congressional delays, Coolidge set up a commission to study the issue; after arguing and splitting over approaches, the members narrowly decided to back Underwood's AP proposal. Even with that weak endorsement, the AP bid couldn't manage to win a majority vote in the House. "Muscle Shoals as a Hot Air Plant," read the snarky headline in a 1925 issue of *Current Opinion* magazine. "The Muscle Shoals debate is a splendid instance of the impotence of a democratic government in handling a highly technical problem."

Again, as it had for the past seven years, the Muscle Shoals debate was going nowhere. Perhaps as a joke, some friends of Coolidge that year gave him an "electric horse," a mechanical exercise device like a little merry-go-round, with a mahogany horse that he could ride up and down, around and around, endlessly.

BY 1926, THEY were calling the never-ending issue "the Alabama Ghost." It simply would not die. Once more Coolidge attempted to attract and review fresh bids—there were rumors that Ford himself might jump in again—but Ford was smart enough to stay out, and the attempt ended without a clear winner. The top two contenders now were AP and American Cyanamid, which spent time attacking each other's bids, giving Norris the chance to promote his own plan.

By 1927, it was clear that no more private bids would be forthcoming. Norris packaged his third major proposal for government operation and multipurpose development (including navigation, flood control, and experimental fertilizer development along with power) and, in a long-awaited victory, managed to get it passed by both houses of Congress. It went to the White House—where Coolidge refused to sign it, resulting in a "pocket veto" that doomed the bill.

Norris kept at it. He was now in his mid-sixties, and Muscle Shoals had become the center of his legislative life. He simply ground down his opponents with sheer stubbornness and the power of his ideas. Ford had given up. And now Oscar Underwood, sick and tired of the fight, announced that he would not run again for the Senate, and retired to private life. Only Norris, still doggedly walking to the Capitol day after day, still battling bouts of depression, still fighting the good fight, kept at it, month after month, year after year.

The 1928 election brought him no joy. It delivered yet another conservative Republican to the White House, this time Herbert Hoover, secretary of commerce under both Harding and Coolidge. And Hoover was just as dead set against government ownership of the Shoals as his predecessors had been. He was bound to veto any Norris bill for public ownership.

But larger forces were again going Norris's way. He was working a new angle. The demand for electricity was skyrocketing across the nation, and there was growing interest in building more giant hydroelectric dams on more of America's big rivers—dams large enough to power entire states, with reservoirs big enough to irrigate vast swaths of arid land, like Boulder Dam on the Colorado and a string of giant barriers across the Columbia. Norris called for a government survey of all major dam sites across the nation to find the best spots, and got Congress to fund it.

The great Wilson Dam was at last completed and churning out electricity, which the government was, for the moment, selling to Alabama Power for distribution. It served as a model for the new generation of giant dams—projects so big that no private company could build them, and so necessary for irrigation and power that the government had a stake in making sure they got done.

That didn't mean that the private power companies were on the wane. All through the 1920s, private power companies had been growing, too, building smaller dams and coal-powered generating plants, electrifying one city after another, and sinking millions into wires and poles to get their product to consumers. Private power companies insisted that they were not gouging the public, that they were selling electricity as cheaply as they could. Whenever questioned by government officials, they marshaled stacks of facts and figures to prove their point. Opponents charged that the opposite was true—that the privates were inflating their costs, keeping their rates too high, and raking in unconscionable profits. Many in government became convinced that private companies were getting too big and too entrenched to properly regulate. A vigorous public power movement sprang up, demanding better control of rates and availability.

Were private power companies overcharging consumers? It was hard to tell, because the only figures people could study were provided by those same companies. What was needed was a way to prove just how cheaply electricity could be made and sold. There was talk of the government building a system that would offer a "yardstick" to measure the claims of the private companies.

Norris's plan for Muscle Shoals could help accomplish that. Build and operate dams efficiently without thought of profit, do a fair job of accounting, and the government would know exactly how much it cost to produce electricity. That would be the yardstick, the number that would show the private company's rates to be accurate or extortionate, giving the government the arguments it needed to regulate the industry as a whole.

And that wasn't all. With a fair system, you could charge a rate that would allow for building transmission lines to small rural communities and isolated farms. The private companies had been arguing that the costs of rural electrification were too high and the expected income too low. But with public oversight of the dams and power lines, it might be possible to bring electricity to the farmers and demonstrate just what cheap electricity could do for rural people.

Norris's arguments were continuing to make headway. But it took a disaster to get them widely accepted.

IN THE FALL of 1929, the Roaring Twenties crashed to a halt. The cause was a stock market plunge that kicked off a global economic contraction. It was the start of the Great Depression. And it changed the scene decisively for Norris.

In 1930 the Corps of Engineers finished a comprehensive survey of the Tennessee River valley, an effort that had taken eight years and resulted in the finest engineering overview of a large region completed to that time. The final report detailed potential sites for seven big additional dams, outlined how high they should be, and estimated what they could do for navigation and flood control. It was a master plan for taming the river, and it would take the government to do it.

Norris used the Corps' plan later that year when he pushed through yet another bill for public ownership. This time it went to Hoover for a signature, and Norris thought he had a real chance.

But Hoover's rejection was definitive. "I am firmly opposed to the Government entering into any business the major purpose of which is competition with our citizens," the president wrote, echoing the sentiments of the previous two presidents. He called the bill "the negation of the ideals upon which our civilization has been based," and added, "the real development of the resources and the industries of the Tennessee Valley can only be accomplished by the people of the Valley themselves."

"This was flattering to Southern pride," historian Willson Whitman wrote, "but there is a Southern saying that you can't do nothin' when you ain't got nothin' to do nothin' with."

The veto was painful to Norris. But it might have been a good thing for his bill. If Hoover had signed it, the great series of dams would have become a Republican project. The scale and scope of Norris's ideas would have been chipped away in negotiations with Republican managers.

But the public was finally getting ready to turn away from the old Republican mantra of "the business of America is business." As the Depression deepened, they became ready to try new things.

After a decade of maneuvering, stalling, proposing, and vetoing legislation over Muscle Shoals, things were about to start happening very quickly.

CHAPTER 17

A NEW DEAL

MOST OF THE folks in the Tennessee Valley were farmers, but they didn't own their land. They were either tenants who paid large landowners some kind of rent for the right to farm, or sharecroppers who farmed a piece of somebody's land and paid for it, as the name says, with a share of the crop. More than half of all Alabama farmers in 1930 were sharecroppers.

Cotton was what most of them grew, and cotton was still the blessing and the curse of the South: a blessing because it was a cash crop, a curse because prices on the world market jumped up and down; a blessing because the southern climate was perfect for it, a curse because it was a hungry crop that demanded costly applications of fertilizer. "What most strikes the explorer in the cotton country is that it makes so many poor and so few rich," wrote a northern journalist in 1930. "For cotton is something more than a crop or an industry; it is a dynastic system." The large landowners, the inheritors of the old pre–Civil War plantations, could make big money when the cotton market was good. But the tenants and sharecroppers working their land never did. Farmers who couldn't afford the fertilizer saw their crops shrink, year after year, until they couldn't make enough money to live on. They didn't own their land, so they often had to pull up stakes and move on.

It wasn't that they were bad farmers. They were just poor—too poor to afford a tractor or a new plow or adequate fertilizer. Overall farm income in the region averaged about $2 a day ($30 a day, or less than $4 per hour, in today's dollars), and sharecroppers made significantly less than that. One report estimated that most were living on as little as ten cents a day ($1.50 in today's dollars). There was no way to crawl out of poverty.

So they wore rags and lived in leaky, weather-beaten shacks provided by the landowners, most without electricity or running water. The kids started on chores when they were five; the teenagers got up at three in the morning so they could get their chores done before walking to school. Many dropped out of school as soon as they could so they could help out their families. But few of them complained. These were quiet, tough, proud, independent people. They viewed hard work as a badge of honor, and charity as an insult.

Despite all the excitement about Ford and Muscle Shoals, at the end of the 1920s Alabama was still one of the poorest states in the nation, and the Tennessee Valley was one of the poorest regions in the state.

"Before the crash we didn't have much, but we did have hope of making a living," remembered one local resident. "Not long after the market crash, we lost that hope." The cotton market went into a tailspin, and everybody suffered. By 1931, many families in the region were eating nothing but cornbread and beans seven days a week. It got so bad that some people started eating red Alabama clay, which at least contained some mineral nutrients.

Stores began to shut down on the Main Streets of all the little towns. The real estate market around the Shoals plummeted, with all that Ford land speculation money disappearing. There was no money for anything.

By 1932, a quarter of the people in Lauderdale County, Alabama (on the Florence side of the Shoals) were unemployed, and many others could find only part-time work. Some lived in tents or shipping crates along the railroad tracks, where they could at least gather a little bit of coal that fell off the trains. Others pawed through the hay in barns, looking for stray peas that might have dried with the harvest.

And Florence was doing well compared to the rest of the region. Another study of the Tennessee Valley during the early part of the Depression estimated that more than 50 percent of the people depended on some kind of government relief. Only three farms in one hundred had electricity. Literacy was alarmingly low. Malaria and hookworm were becoming endemic.

"The worst part of it was that President Hoover would not do anything to help people," remembered one local. "I mean he would do nothing."

The homeless started calling their growing shantytowns "Hoovervilles." The penniless men would turn out their empty pockets and call them "Hoover flags." And the president seemed unable to do anything to end the misery. He received death threats, and when he went campaigning for the 1932 election his train was pelted with eggs.

By comparison, his opponent in that election, Franklin Delano Roosevelt, looked the way a fresh, cold river looks to people dying of thirst. He was a Democrat, he was an optimist, he promised to end the Depression and give everybody a New Deal, and when the election came he whipped Hoover so bad, there wouldn't be another Republican president for eighteen years. After the votes were counted and it was seen that Hoover had won just six states, there were rumors that he had been arrested trying to escape Washington aboard Andrew Mellon's yacht, which was carrying gold raided from Fort Knox.

FDR was only the third Democrat elected to the White House since 1860, and he was by far the most daring. He was going to put the government to work for the people. And Muscle Shoals was one of his top priorities. FDR liked Norris's government corporation approach but wanted it bigger and faster, with a quick infusion of government dollars, accelerated construction, and lots of job creation. While campaigning, he talked about building more dams, creating a larger channel for navigation, and employing 200,000 men. Muscle Shoals, he said, would "herald the birth of a new America, from which unemployment would be completely lifted." Norris thought FDR's plans dwarfed his own.

But FDR could also sound like Ford when he talked about making cities more country-like, moving more people back onto the land, and healing the divide between cities and farms by offering a third option. "I believe we can look forward to three rather than two types in the future," he said, "for there is a definite place for an intermediate type between the urban and the rural."

His test case would be Muscle Shoals.

After winning the election, one of the first things FDR did was take a victory lap through Alabama. His arrival in January 1933 was the first time in a century that a president had visited the area. Ecstatic crowds gathered wherever the train stopped to greet the popular new president-elect and the other politicians in the train with him—including the graying, serious-looking George Norris, whom FDR introduced as "the father of Muscle Shoals." In Sheffield, fifty thousand people gathered to greet them. When FDR announced to the crowd that he was going to be "putting Muscle Shoals back on the map," pandemonium broke out, the crowd whooping and hollering, shouting praises to the Almighty, dancing and hugging each other.

It had been twelve years since Ford and Edison had gotten a similar welcome. Crowds lined the presidential motorcade's path across Wilson Dam and through Florence. FDR rode in an open car, waving and smiling as Boy Scouts directed traffic. People hung out of windows and climbed on rooftops to get a glimpse, fathers hoisted children on their shoulders, women waved handkerchiefs, local drum and bugle corps marched, flags and banners flew, and jars of moonshine were passed around.

That ride across the dam was a signal moment for George Norris. He could finally, after a dozen years of battling, draw a breath of relief. "From the first gun to the last, there was no armistice, no breathing space, and no truce," he remembered about his Muscle Shoals fight. Congress had considered no fewer than 138 Muscle Shoals–related bills during those dozen years, and Norris had been involved one way or another in every one of them. Not long ago he had been everyone's enemy in Alabama; they'd hanged him in effigy when he opposed Ford's bid. But now here he was, sitting next to the president, riding through the joyous crowds, hailed as a hero.

"From that very day I could see things getting better," said one resident who saw the motorcade. "Everyone felt better. Everyone knew that Mr. Roosevelt would get us out of this Depression. And he did."

Taking a slightly different view, a local banker said, "We looked on it like Christmas. Santa Claus was coming. There wasn't anything to do but hang up our stocking."

Norris was finally going to get his bill passed. Once FDR took office in March, the latest version of the government ownership bill quickly passed both the Senate and House. After the president signed it into law on May 18, 1933, he gave the pen to George Norris. That night, the people of Florence, Alabama, danced until dawn.

Norris (standing, far right) triumphant: Roosevelt signs the Tennessee
Valley Act.
Courtesy Library of Congress

EVERY PRESIDENT GETS a honeymoon period—a few
months after first taking office when it's easier to get big projects
going—and FDR made Muscle Shoals a honeymoon priority, a
showcase project, a demonstration of the benefits that would flow
from his New Deal.

He was a little vague on the details—he would leave those up
to Norris and the project directors—but he was big on how it would
play politically. When Norris asked the president, "What are you
going to say when they ask you the political philosophy" behind the
bill—was it for federal control of public lands, cheap power, jobs, government relief, or what?—FDR answered: "I'll tell them it's neither

fish nor fowl, but whatever it is, it will taste awfully good to the people of the Tennessee Valley."

To manage the project, Norris's bill set up the new Tennessee Valley Authority (TVA), a public corporation under the direction of a three-member board of directors. These three would set priorities, manage strategies, and map progress; they would hire the workers, set the timelines, and distribute the money. Next to the president, they would be the three most powerful men in the region.

Picking the right directors was critical. And FDR already had his first choice in mind, a pioneering university president named Arthur E. Morgan. On paper Morgan looked great: He had both extensive practical experience with dam building (he started his career designing large-scale flood control and irrigation systems) and an idealistic sense of how to build a better America. After moving from dam building into education and becoming the president of Antioch College (now University) in Ohio, he pioneered a new approach to higher education, one in which students were required to do real-world, hands-on work on local farms and in factories along with their studies.

FDR was breaking new ground with his federal control of Tennessee Valley power, and Morgan looked like just the sort of revolutionary thinker—part engineer, part visionary—that he wanted to head it. Norris approved.

In their enthusiasm and eagerness to break ground, they ignored some warning signs. When he first arrived at Antioch, Morgan had fired most of the old faculty, clear-cutting his way to creating a new kind of education. He became known as something of an autocrat on campus, willing to root out anything that stood in the way of his ideal structures. Tall, thin, bespectacled, and balding, he might look like an old professor. But he could be fierce and unyielding in his actions. If people didn't move fast enough, he was likely to drag them into his idea of the future.

He lived by a strict moral code; demanded honesty, sobriety, and hard work from those around him; had zero tolerance for greed or graft; and was fueled by an almost evangelical belief in the use of technology to smash old social systems and create a better world. With Morgan in charge, everything the TVA touched would be clean, straightforward, and fair. Political favors and paybacks were out. No congressmen's nephews or local commissioner's cousins would be taken on simply because they had connections. Hires would be made strictly on the basis of merit. Morgan and the first round of managers he hired—fervent followers who thought the TVA would serve as a global model of honest management—would devote their lives to making TVA into a sort of secular crusade for good government.

He led by example. One of the first things he did after he was hired was present Roosevelt with a careful inventory of his personal possessions and investments; it was his way of demonstrating that he was coming in clean. His first long talk with FDR made him think they were of the same mind. The president, like Morgan, seemed to believe that the TVA was much more than a series of dams. It was a way to reshape local communities, to educate the local people, to improve farming with the latest scientific techniques, to bring a backward region into the twentieth century. The two of them "talked chiefly about a designed and planned social and economic order," Morgan remembered. "That was what was first in his mind." Morgan also left the meeting thinking that he was the top dog, that he would be not just a member of the three-person board, but its undisputed leader.

He started by helping pick the two other directors: Harcourt Morgan (no relation to Arthur Morgan), an agricultural expert who had risen to president of the University of Tennessee; and a dynamic young lawyer, just thirty-three years old, David Lilienthal, who had made a name for himself taking on power companies. It looked like a well-balanced team: a dam builder, an agricultural authority, and a power system lawyer.

But things did not start well. Arthur Morgan was ready to go the moment the act was signed. While the other two directors wrapped up other business—Harcourt Morgan finished a vacation and Lilienthal closed out pending legal matters—he began hiring top aides, structuring the main office, and taking the first steps in building his first dams. For almost two months he ran the show solo, the former president of a small college now in charge of tens of millions of dollars for everything from dam construction to farmers' cooperatives, fertilizer research to job creation, land reclamation, forestry, industrial development, power production, educational programs, and just about anything else he thought the TVA should be doing. The mission of the TVA, as laid out in Norris's act, was fairly vague, including virtually anything related to "national defense and for agricultural and industrial developments and to improve navigation in the Tennessee River and to control the destructive flood waters in the Tennessee and Mississippi River Basins." Within that charter, the TVA had the power to buy and sell land, produce and ship fertilizers, construct powerhouses and erect transmission lines, arrange educational systems for teaching vocational skills, make deals with industrialists, and earn its own money and decide how to spend it. All that, and a flood of taxpayer dollars, too. It was immense in scale and reach.

It was mid-June before all three members of the board gathered for their first meeting. They were close to total strangers. Harcourt Morgan and Lilienthal had never met. And they were both unpleasantly surprised when Arthur Morgan jumped into the lead, inundating them with details about priorities he had already set, projects he already had underway, and forty employees he had already hired. He was unhappy to find that his co-directors were not up to speed on every aspect. He was puzzled whenever they questioned or debated his decisions. It was as if they did not recognize his authority.

In fact, they were three very strong, very different men—"two elderly college presidents named Morgan and a very lively young lawyer named Lilienthal," as the writer James Agee described them—none of whom were inclined to take a back seat. And their duties as outlined in Norris's TVA act were fuzzy enough to allow them to define things the way they wanted, not only as Arthur Morgan had decided they should be.

Their first meeting was an endurance test that lasted eight hours. When it was over, Arthur Morgan complained to his wife, "Ours is one of the few agencies in the government that is being run by a debating society instead of by one man." He had a very clear idea about who that one man should be.

Harcourt Morgan and Lilienthal met separately soon after, and shared their concerns with each other. They decided that, rather than structuring the board as a hierarchy with Arthur Morgan at the top, they should divide management of the TVA into three broad areas, with one director responsible for each of them. Arthur Morgan would be in charge of building dams, Harcourt Morgan would handle everything to do with agriculture, and Lilienthal would oversee legal and electrical power issues.

It seemed reasonable. But Arthur Morgan saw it as a betrayal. He was a loner by nature—many group photos show him off to one side by himself; he preferred long solo walks to making small talk or playing golf—and he thought the president had put him in charge. He was especially mistrustful of the energetic, aggressive, outgoing young Lilienthal, who was as sociable as Arthur Morgan was solitary, and proved very good at making political allies.

There were cracks in the board from that first meeting on. But no one expected them to get as wide and deep as they did.

CHAPTER 18

"I'M GOIN' TO DIE FOR THE GOVERNMENT"

THE DAMS CAME first. Rather than build a string of dozens of low dams, as Ford had talked about doing, Arthur E. Morgan was in favor of raising seven high dams, modern wonders designed for maximum electrical production and efficient flood control. It made engineering sense. But those high dams would also make deep lakes that would drown thousands of acres and displace tens of thousands of people. Whole towns would be submerged. To Morgan, that was the price of the future. To the longtime residents, it was something else entirely.

TVA engineers started going around with buckets of white paint, marking high-water points on trees and rocks. Behind one dam they painted the height above sea level the water would reach: 1,020 feet. That number was soon displayed on so many buildings and along so many roads that, a local story went, a tourist went into a store and asked for a bottle of that 1020 medicine he was seeing advertised everywhere.

The government planned to buy the land it would submerge at a fair price. Deals were made with landowners, but when deals couldn't be made easily, condemnation proceedings were held, and the land was paid for and taken anyway. Everybody got more or less what the land was worth. But there were some who didn't want to move no matter how much money the government threw at them, and there were plenty who didn't own their land and were simply told they had to relocate. Before it was done, the TVA moved about twenty thousand families from land along the river bottom. Most were farmers. Sometimes the government helped set them up someplace new. Other times, they were left on their own.

Many of those forced to move were tenants or sharecroppers who had few possessions, minimal education, and no savings. Most had been farming the area for years, even if it was for next to no money, and their lives were built around the old system. It didn't matter how often the TVA folks came out and explained why they needed to go. It didn't matter that the government tried in many cases to find new living places higher in the hills. Trying to farm in those hills was a different thing—the soil was different, the water was different, and there would be fewer big farms to work on. What were they supposed to do?

Some simply refused to go unless they could take everything with them. One local farmer took apart his smokehouse board by board, pried up the stepping-stones from his yard, pulled up his fence posts, and hauled every bit of it with him up into the hills. Then he told the TVA that he wanted to take his fireplace, too. He told them that the fire in it had come to the valley with his family more than one hundred years earlier and had never gone out. The government ended up helping him move the whole thing, fireplace and fire alike.

Up one of the flooded valleys, one story went, lived a woman called Aunt Rachel. When the TVA buyers came to tell her they were going to give her a fair price for her land, she told them, "I ain't goin' to sell, but I ain't goin' to give you no trouble. I am just goin' to set here in my rocking chair and let the waters come up around me and drown me." When they urged her to cooperate, she said, "Cooperate! I'm goin' to die for the government. What more do you want?"

The living presented one set of problems, the dead another. The people in the valley were deeply religious, their land held thousands of graves, and almost nobody wanted to leave their ancestors behind. To avoid trouble, the TVA dug up and moved as many remains as they could to higher ground; in the end some 20,000 graves were moved and twice that many were flooded. Entire cemeteries were relocated. But that still wasn't enough for everybody. At least one local hanged himself in his barn rather than move.

In the end, though, what could anyone do? As one historian wrote of the relocated residents along the river, "They simply lacked the resources to resist." Most of the relocated families didn't go far, staying within a county or two of their lost homes, and there were benefits for many of them. There was often access to better schools for their kids, and there were more jobs in the area, which meant more money coming in every month. Many of the homes were built through government programs, and were new, electrified bungalows instead of old kerosene-lit cabins. But the farming wasn't as good up in the hills, and they had to get used to new neighbors, and their old way of life was gone.

An unfortunate but unavoidable necessity, Arthur Morgan thought. The dams had to be built, which meant the lakes had to rise, which meant people had to move. In its place he would offer those people a new, better way of living.

He envisioned a network of cooperative villages built around local industries and handicrafts, a dream not unlike Henry Ford's, but with basket weaving and hand-carved furniture in place of car factories. He and Ford shared something of the same nostalgia for a small-town, small-farm America. They both had a special fondness for the old ways—regional crafts, things that drew on the cultural heritage of the region. But Morgan's approach was more intellectual and artistic than industrial.

Morgan also believed in education. Displaced farmers could be retrained for modern jobs. He worked with a local teachers college to create an adult education program that eventually enrolled hundreds of people in occupational training courses, learning new-century skills like blueprint drawing.

He was intent on creating, in the Tennessee Valley, a way of living somewhere in between unfettered big business and European-style socialism. "The Tennessee Valley is the first place in America where we can sit down and design a civilization," he wrote. "We are looking to a Valley inhabited by happy people, with small hand-work industries, no rich centers, no rich people, but everybody sharing in the wealth." He saw a sweet spot between the freedom-loving but poverty-stricken tenant farmers and the mass movements of fascism and bolshevism. The Morgan way "won't be capitalism. It won't be socialism; it won't be communism; it won't be individualism," he wrote. "It will be none of these things, yet some of all of them. It will be a new Americanism."

His new America would also be healthy, both physically and morally. He was devoted to preventing the erosion of farmlands and the destruction of timberlands, at one point advocating the forcible purchase of property that was being misused, which the TVA would then resell to more responsible owners. He wrote an ethical guidebook for the staff of the TVA forbidding the acceptance of gifts or favors and emphasizing honesty and openness in all dealings. Intemperance, habit-forming drug use, and loose sex were to be discouraged. Anyone demonstrating "calculating, selfish ambition, or habitual cheapness of conduct" would be dismissed. He and his team were going to "make the Valley over," one journalist noted, "brand-new and right."

Arthur Morgan might have been an amateur civilization builder, but he was a master with dams. The first project he put up was on a tributary of the Tennessee, the Clinch River, about three hundred miles upstream from Wilson Dam, across the state line in Tennessee. It was an important piece of the larger puzzle of regulating the flow of the system. By damming the Clinch, the TVA could ease floods by holding extra water in the winter, then release it in the summer to keep electricity production high.

Norris Dam
Courtesy Library of Congress

They named it Norris Dam, a tribute to the man who, more than any other, made the TVA possible. And Morgan was intent on making both the dam and the workers' town next to it living demonstrations of the TVA at its best.

The dam was impressive: twenty-six stories high, with stupendous sheer surfaces and clean angles and lines, as spare and striking as an abstract painting. The adjoining town, also named after Norris, was Morgan's dream village. The most current design and technology was used to create its three-hundred-plus houses and dormitories. The homes were small, simple, and all-electric modern bungalows built using local stone and cedar on curving streets, with none of the gingerbread of earlier eras. The central area, built to be pedestrian-friendly, was surrounded by a greenbelt with poultry, dairy, and farming operations; it boasted the first all-electric creamery in the world and the first direct-dial telephone system in Tennessee. Each home had access to land for communal gardening (a nod here to Ford's ideas) and rents were set at an affordable 25 percent of income. Workers could buy a meal for a quarter at the big cafeteria and had their maladies treated in a small hospital. There was a cooperative school that offered night classes for adult education and centers for training in trades and domestic sciences. It looked like no other town in America: TVA designers paid attention to everything from open spaces for kids' play to the look of streetlamps, the curve of roadways to the positioning of homes (many facing away from the street and toward each other).

Morgan wanted this to be a self-sustaining town, not just a temporary workers' camp, so he tried to start industries in addition to dam building. He made plans for reforesting the hills to create a long-term timber industry, and insisted on public ownership of the land along the newly formed lake to encourage leisure activities. He built a ceramics workshop where local clay was made into teapots and vases with a regional look.

The town of Norris was isolated in the hills north of Knox-ville, and a new highway had to be built to reach the site. But Mor-gan didn't want just any highway. He and his designers wanted to avoid the sprawling development that marred America's roads, with the unregulated mess of gas stations, cheap eats, and billboards that sprang up wherever cars were common. The TVA owned the land. So the TVA built a new kind of highway—wide, banked for fast travel, with few intersections and maximum natural beauty. The twenty-mile stretch of road—James Agee called it "TVA's Freeway"—would become a model for the big national highways built during the 1950s and 1960s.

For a few years Norris drew visitors from around the world who wanted to see this ideal modern town in the American wilderness. And as long as the dam was going up, it flourished. But when Norris Dam was finished in 1937, there weren't enough jobs to keep workers busy, and they began to drift away. The ceramics plant closed down. The planners were unable to attract enough industries to keep the town going, and in 1948 the entire town was sold at auction to a private developer. Today it's a bedroom community for Knoxville.

THE TWO OTHER directors were far less ambitious and somewhat more practical. The other Morgan on the TVA board, Harcourt, was a people person, a born teacher, both a respected agricultural expert and somebody the farmers in the valley could talk to man-to-man. He was more comfortable in overalls than he was in a suit, and would rather crack jokes in a field than argue in boardrooms. He believed not in model towns but in fighting pests, rotating crops, preventing erosion, and the liberal application of fertilizer. He saw what decades of cash crops like cotton and corn had done to the dirt of the Tennes-see valley, and he figured that the TVA gave him a chance to make it right. A TVA survey estimated that 80 percent of the farmland in the

The newly created TVA board: (left to right) realist Harcourt Morgan, idealist
Arthur E. Morgan, and ambitious David Lilienthal

valley was eroded to one degree or another, scarred by deep gullies
and washed out by winter rains. Harcourt Morgan and his teams
of workers oversaw a program to stop it by building fifty thousand
little "gully dams" and laying down countless wire mats of brush to
catch the dirt before it was washed away. They showed farmers how
to terrace and plow to minimize soil loss.

Harcourt Morgan worked to get farmers to diversify their crops.
There was a big push to put fields into clover, which added nitrogen
to the soil naturally, and grow livestock rather than the usual corn
and cotton. Small co-ops were set up to demonstrate techniques
for canning and processing fruits and vegetables. As electricity
became more common on more farms, he introduced the wonders
of electric refrigerators for keeping meat and dairy fresh, freezers for

preserving food, electric washers, electric stoves, electric everything. It opened up new possibilities. Farmers could now raise strawberries and fast-freeze them for market, start a small dairy farm and keep milk and eggs fresh longer, or use electric heaters to dry meats and electric grinders to make flour. They could diversify.

He also changed the kind of fertilizer they used. Cotton and corn needed a lot of nitrogen, so the emphasis in the Ford days had been on making cheap nitrates. But the new farms, with less cotton and more grass fields for growing livestock, needed a fertilizer rich in another element, phosphorus. The TVA slowly moved the emphasis away from the old nitrate plants, now nearly two decades old, and toward research projects designed to make cheaper, better phosphate fertilizers. The great nitrate factories, once the cause of so much noise and worry, would never again be fired up. Their machinery would be scrapped and sold, and they would be turned to other uses. Instead, Harcourt Morgan preached "the phosphate gospel" and put money into phosphate research.

Talking about all that soil science and new electric gizmos didn't matter much to old-time farmers. They couldn't be told something worked. They had to be shown. "Dirt farmers will not accept a new order imposed rudely from above, no matter how beneficial it might be," Harcourt Morgan said. Instead of bringing in some egghead to explain the world to them, he focused on setting up "demonstration farms," thousands of them up and down the valley. It was a chance to see what would happen if a farmer took the government's advice and help. There would be crops growing where a washed-out gully used to be, or two plots, side by side, one using a new fertilizer or planting technique, one without, and farmers could see the difference with their own eyes.

"In the early days of our program, you could drive through these rural communities in which these farms were located and you could pick them out just as far as you could see them," one TVA man remembered. "They were sort of like oases in the desert as compared to other farms." The TVA would make social occasions of the open houses, which offered a chance not only to see a neighbor's place in action, but maybe to see a demonstration of a new electric appliance or piece of new farm equipment. And of course there would be experts around to offer advice. They became popular ways to spend part of a day.

WITH NORRIS, THE dam and the town both, under construction, and plans laid and ground being cleared for the next dam, and the next, and the next, the region began coming to life. Only this time it was not just around the Shoals, but all the way up the river to the middle of Tennessee, where the TVA built its headquarters in Knoxville.

There were jobs now, thousands of them—blue-collar, white-collar, and pink-collar, for men and women, Black and white. Applicants flocked to Muscle Shoals by train or bus if they could afford it, riding the rails, hitchhiking, or walking if they couldn't. Many of them were highly educated and trained, and the TVA soon boasted "one of the most over-qualified work forces ever put together," as historian North Callahan put it. Competition was stiff and getting hired wasn't easy. There were openings for librarians and agronomists, research chemists and welders, cooks and secretaries, plumbers, mechanics, teachers, and loggers. There were paths forward for untrained workers, too, with training available for learning blacksmithing, auto repair, woodworking, and bookkeeping. Many people changed their lives by taking those classes. The TVA seemed to be doing a little bit of everything: spraying for mosquitoes and draining swamps to prevent malaria; growing hundreds of thousands of trees and planting them to reforest the hills and stop erosion; moving bodies; building towns; laying down roads; you name it. Mistakes were made, too: The TVA brought in an Asian plant called kudzu to control erosion and planted it by the millions. "There is no danger that kudzu will become a pest," the government said at the time. Today there is kudzu everywhere; some wits have dubbed it "the plant that ate the South."

At the end of 1933 the TVA employed about three thousand people. By the next summer, it was nine thousand. A year later, in the summer of 1935, it was sixteen thousand workers. It was an enormous enterprise, an unprecedented experiment in physical, economic, and social transformation. The TVA got a reputation for attracting honest workers with high ideals, people who followed Arthur Morgan's example, creating in many cases a highly motivated, exceptionally efficient work team. Labor relations were excellent. There was a spirit of public service, a sense of doing good for the nation.

And the whole thing was being run on the fly. "We got into TVA with no tradition. We didn't have a pattern," Harcourt Morgan said. "Nobody had ever set up the idea of integration of natural resources—water, land, air, and everything else, including human ability." Nobody could really give them advice from the outside, so the three directors grabbed the reins and figured it out themselves. They were smart, honorable, science-oriented men. They were eager to transform the region, to modernize the valley, to help make FDR's New Deal a success, and to make the TVA a model for other projects.

They succeeded, in great part.

CHAPTER 19

ELECTRIC NATION

ARTHUR MORGAN PLAYED with town building and Harcourt Morgan helped stop erosion, but in the end, it was all about power. The TVA's purpose, more than any other, was to make cheap electricity for the same reasons Ford had wanted cheap electricity: to create industries and jobs. Flood control and navigation were important, too. But the TVA had one additional goal, Senator George Norris's and FDR's goal, which was to demonstrate just how much private power companies had been gouging the public on rates.

"Roosevelt believed that the public was being systematically milked by private utilities, which set their rates artificially high" is how one historian summarized it. The utilities argued that high rates were necessary in order to cover the costs of building steam plants and dams, transformer stations and transmission lines, to carry the juice to customers. Their businesses were complex, and their stated costs were easy to disguise or inflate. FDR wanted a comparison he could rely on, a government yardstick that showed the true costs of electricity. If the government rates were far lower than private companies claimed were possible, he could use his yardstick to beat the privates into lowering their rates. Lower rates meant higher use and more benefits from electricity. Everyone would benefit.

David Lilienthal was put in charge of the yardstick, which gave him an important role among the three TVA directors. He was the man who dealt with electrical rates and legal matters, which put him at the forefront of dealings with private utilities. And he was a young wolf, full of energy and eager to mix it up.

Lilienthal was a lawyer both by training and by temperament. He worked endlessly, charged hard, and debated fiercely, "a terribly intense young man, ambitious and impatient to enter the contest between labor and capital," TVA historian Thomas McGraw wrote. He was also a skilled writer and speech maker. He was persuasive and smooth. And he had a taste for battle, which made him a needed counterpoint to the lofty morality of Arthur Morgan.

It came as a surprise when he was asked to join the TVA board of directors—he was half the age of the other directors, had no ties to the South, and had no engineering background—but he had been recognized as something of a whiz kid in the legalities of electrical power, an up-and-comer who greatly impressed one of his mentors, Felix Frankfurter. It was Frankfurter who recommended Lilienthal to FDR as the guy who could best fight the private power interests. Once asked, Lilienthal threw himself into the work.

After that first eight-hour board meeting, when he saw how Arthur Morgan planned to run the show, he made sure that he had control of his own area of the TVA.

Then he and Arthur Morgan started jostling for position. Their conflict was constant for the next three years. The two men differed on their attitudes toward private utilities. Morgan was in favor of getting along with the privates, selling them TVA electricity at wholesale prices and letting them distribute it. Lilienthal wanted the TVA to control the whole system, from dam to home. Only that way, he argued, would it be possible to clearly establish the yardstick the president wanted. Morgan tended toward telling people in the TVA region what to do; Lilienthal (like Harcourt Morgan) emphasized cooperation and flexibility. Arthur Morgan wanted to avoid conflict with the private utilities; Lilienthal welcomed it.

The key was endless, cheap electricity to drive economic growth. Provide the power, and industries would be built, farms would thrive, people would work, and prosperity would follow. More availability would mean more use, which would spur investment in making more electricity, which would help keep prices down. "What had proved to be a good business principle for Henry Ford in the pricing of his first automobiles, what was good business in the mass production field generally, would be good business in electrical supply," Lilienthal wrote. The TVA was on track to produce unprecedented amounts of electricity. But in order for the system to work, somebody had to buy it. America had to use more electricity.

He encouraged FDR to make a push for an "Electrification of America" program to encourage, among other things, the purchase of more home electrical appliances. The problem was that most home appliances were seen as a luxury and sold for high prices. Selling more appliances would draw new manufacturers into the field, resulting in more jobs for workers and more choices for consumers. More consumer choices would mean more sales, which would increase competition that would push down prices. And the cycle would continue, with cheaper prices, more appliances in every home, and greater consumption of electricity.

But the whole scheme had to be jump-started. Americans in the Depression didn't see the need for new gadgets. Electricity was still a novelty in much of the nation outside of the cities, and folks on farms seemed to be happy with the ability to run a few electric lights. They'd gotten along fine without anything more. If they had extra money, they'd rather spend it on a car or something they could use to boost next year's harvest.

Lilienthal worked to turn that around. TVA outreach teams began teaching homeowners about the benefits of electric freezers and refrigerators, and low-interest loan programs were made available for buying them. The TVA encouraged manufacturers to lower their prices. The government push included traveling displays and demonstrations of appliances, movies, radio spots, and assistance for dealers. In 1934 one appliance manufacturer said, "The TVA is the grandest piece of promotion that has ever broken for the electrical industry."

Getting electricity out to farms was the next piece of the puzzle. In 1935 FDR created another New Deal program, the Rural Electrification Administration (REA), to speed the installation of electric lines throughout rural areas. When the TVA started, 90 percent of the nation's farms still had no electricity, a shortcoming that slowed economic recovery and threatened America's agricultural competitiveness. The private power companies were slow to build lines out into rural America because the costs were so high and the returns too low. But with the REA in place, workmen fanned out to raise thousands of poles and string miles of wire connecting farmhouses and barns to the growing grid. By the 1950s, the numbers had reversed, and 90 percent of rural America was electrified. As one writer put it, "Nobody but Uncle Sam would run a mile of wire so a farmer could screw in a twenty-five-watt bulb."

AS SOON AS Lilienthal got his office up and running at the TVA, he started throwing elbows with the men who headed private power companies in the US. Chief among them was the dynamic young head of the Commonwealth & Southern Corporation (C&S), a tall, charismatic businessman named Wendell Willkie. C&S, headquartered in New York, was a huge holding company whose subsidiaries controlled electrical production in much of the South. One of those subsidiaries was Alabama Power.

Willkie was not your typical Wall Street Republican. He had been raised a Wilsonian Democrat in Indiana, believed in the League of Nations, and had voted for FDR in 1932. His parents were both lawyers (his mother was the first woman to pass the Indiana Bar exam), and he followed in their footsteps, starting out representing electrical utilities and then moving to New York City as counsel for C&S. He loved New York, saw Broadway shows whenever he could, read ten newspapers a day, and impressed the chairman of C&S so much with his legal skills and personal charm that he was quickly kicked upstairs to the head office. Willkie was smart, articulate, and smooth—"a big, well-read, quick-thinking, supremely self-confident man," one observer described him. He was named president of the company in 1933, just after his fortieth birthday.

He and Lilienthal were well-matched opponents: both skilled lawyers, both fast climbers who had been elevated to high position while still relatively young, both hungry to win, both deeply committed to their missions. But their missions were antithetical. Willkie's job was to keep C&S in the forefront of electrical power, including the Tennessee Valley, and to make money for his private investors. Lilienthal's was to move C&S aside in the valley and replace it with TVA power so he could show just how much cheaper true public electricity could be. Lilienthal hated the way big private monopolies and trusts worked to control markets, raise rates, and push around consumers just to make a few more bucks. When it came to providing electricity, he was fervently committed to public oversight of "those reckless men [who] played with this essential community enterprise as if it were the stakes in a game of roulette."

That included men like Willkie. They met for the first time at the Cosmos Club in Washington, DC, in October 1933, "two exceedingly cagey fellows," Lilienthal remembered, sitting across from one another, sizing each other up. Their discussions were about complex matters, made more complicated by the fact that they had to do business together. The TVA was in charge of selling electricity from Wilson Dam, and its number one customer was Alabama Power—which meant Willkie had to be kept happy. If he stopped buying, the TVA would be in trouble. They were cordial and careful, verbally sparring and jabbing, gauging each other's moves like a pair of prizefighters. Willkie treated Lilienthal to a display of cocksure confidence at first, coming on strong as they talked about rates and charges. Then Willkie tried to throw a haymaker. He told Lilienthal that the public was eventually bound to react against public power schemes like the TVA, it would lose its taste for these New Deal programs that competed with private companies, and when that happened, Congress might be convinced to pull funding for finishing the just-started Norris Dam. It might stop funding for all the TVA's planned dams. Then Lilienthal would have nothing to sell. It went without saying that if C&S wasn't happy with the TVA, it was likely to lead a public relations campaign to make sure federal funding dried up.

Before the whole house of cards came tumbling down, Willkie said, it would be better for Lilienthal to make a fast deal. C&S could guarantee healthy wholesale payments for all the electricity the TVA could produce as long as Lilienthal gave up the idea of selling directly to consumers. They could put the whole thing to bed right then.

Lilienthal held his tongue. He now knew his opponent's initial offer. And he knew how he was going to deal with Willkie. He ended the meeting pleasantly but without any commitments or promises, went back to his office, and started planning.

The two men had more meetings over the next few months, with Lilienthal arguing for pure TVA power, start to finish, so the president could get his yardstick of the real cost of electricity, and

Willkie countering that any such comparison would be false because the TVA enjoyed so many benefits as a semipublic agency, from financing to taxation, that comparing its costs with a private corporation would be ridiculous.

Neither man gave much ground. They fought each other to a draw. And in the end, they compromised. The five-year agreement they signed in January 1934 allowed the TVA to buy some electrical systems in the TVA region from C&S with options for others; constrained the TVA from making further incursions into C&S markets; and included a mutual pledge to promote the use of electrical appliances. Within a prescribed area, the TVA would be able to make, transmit, and sell electricity directly to consumers. It seemed like a happy ending.

But a few months later, shareholders of C&S mounted legal proceedings against the TVA, arguing that the government had no business selling electricity in competition with private companies. There was suspicion that Willkie himself helped engineer the suit,

Aerial View, Wilson Dam, near Florence, Ala.

The mile-long Wilson Dam after completion

although he loudly denied it. The case wound its way through the legal system until early 1936, when the Supreme Court ruled in the TVA's favor. The government, they said, wasn't building dams to get into competition with private electrical utilities. It had the right to build the dams for navigation and flood control. If it could offset costs by harvesting electricity along the way, it had the right to sell it, just like it had the right to sell any government property. Private utilities, the justices declared, had no legal right to claim freedom from competition.

Both men emerged from their long battle with their reputations burnished. Lilienthal had what he needed for his yardstick and was in a stronger position than ever at the TVA. Willkie became a Republican nominee for president, running unsuccessfully against FDR in 1940.

All through the legal fight, Lilienthal kept the pressure on by offering towns in the region the chance to buy low-cost Wilson Dam electricity directly from the TVA. It was up to each community to decide whether to switch to government power or keep its privately run system. The private companies did everything they could to keep local residents from voting to change, placing newspaper ads, sending letters, and quickly running electric lines out to rural areas. Voters in Birmingham turned the TVA down in late 1933 because of worries about inefficient management, political interference, and higher taxes, while Knoxville voted in favor of the TVA later that year.

The first community to actually link directly into the TVA power system was Tupelo, Mississippi, and when the new service started in early 1934, electric rates plummeted by two-thirds. Within six months, the average use of electricity in the town rose more than 80 percent; two years later it had tripled. There were criticisms that the TVA's rate had been set artificially low in order to encourage sales (and there was evidence that government support for the TVA did indeed help push costs down; as Willkie put it, "Whenever a householder in Tupelo, Mississippi, switches on a light, everybody in the United States helps to pay for it").

It soon became clear that any sort of clear, simple "yardstick" comparison was impossible. There were too many variables to consider. The TVA could brag—and did—about how cheaply it could sell electricity to a town. Its opponents could assert—and did—that it was only possible because taxes somewhere were going up to pay for it.

But there's another way of looking at it. Communities who bought power from the TVA in the 1930s saw significant decreases in costs to consumers. Once people in nearby areas realized that, they put private utilities under pressure to do the same. Within a few years of the TVA's start, private companies in the area somehow found a way to dramatically lower their consumer prices (31 percent drop by C&S subsidiary Alabama Power, 35 percent drop by Georgia Power, 46 percent drop by Tennessee Power). The yardstick might not be perfect, but it had its desired effect in getting prices down.

And Lilienthal's idea of lower prices spurring more use—the same approach Ford had used for his cars—was also proven correct. The lower consumer costs got, the more electricity they bought, and the more electric appliances they used. Consumption shot up around the TVA region within a few years (increasing 44 percent in Alabama and almost doubling in Tennessee).

The effects rippled out nationwide. An analysis by historian Thomas K. McGraw found that, in general, the farther away you got from the Tennessee Valley, the higher the electricity rates were. "A more convincing evidence of the yardstick's success," he wrote, "would be difficult to conceive."

CHAPTER 20

A SIGN IN THE SKY

DAVID LILIENTHAL'S SUCCESS in defending the TVA's turf helped give FDR the data he needed to get the public lower electricity rates, and boosted the young director's visibility and prestige. It also increased the tension between him and Arthur Morgan. The sun was shining on Lilienthal now, and the older man did not appreciate the shade.

The two directors found themselves at odds on any number of issues. Morgan had been in favor of cooperating with private utilities; Lilienthal was combative. Morgan pushed his agenda from the top down; Lilienthal favored letting solutions percolate from the bottom up. Morgan believed jobs would come from small cooperative communities engaging in local handicrafts; Lilienthal thought jobs would come from big dams, cheap electricity, and larger industries. "I am against 'basket weaving' and all that it implies," Lilienthal said. "It must be plain to see that I do not have much faith in 'uplift.'"

As Lilienthal's star rose, the rift between the two deepened. Morgan was an introvert, a deep thinker, and unskilled at debate. "I had no time for political conflict, even if I had desired to spend my time that way," he said. Lilienthal, a people person, was articulate, ambitious, and persuasive. He was constantly in meetings, traveling here and there, scoring points, and making friends. By 1935 everywhere Morgan looked he saw Lilienthal's name, quoted in the newspapers, talking to congressmen, giving speeches to civic groups. "Since Mr. Lilienthal had relatively few duties except those relating to the transmission and distribution of TVA power, the technical aspects of which were admirably administered by [a man] whom I had found for him," Morgan complained, "he had much time for contacts in Washington." Morgan didn't trust the younger man. He worried that Lilienthal was accruing power so he could push his own plans over Morgan's. He was hearing whispers about Lilienthal criticizing him in private meetings. And gradually his mistrust turned to paranoia. He thought Lilienthal was giving jobs to the relatives and supporters of various politicians, undoing the TVA's reputation for clean hiring. He thought Lilienthal was sabotaging his communication with the president. "The President and Senator Norris were regularly and deeply impregnated with untrue stories about my disloyalty, which eroded and eventually eliminated their warm friendship and trust for me," Morgan later wrote.

As the TVA offices began to fracture into pro-Morgan and pro-Lilienthal factions, the third director, Harcourt Morgan, tried to stand aside and, wherever possible, play peacemaker. The job of the TVA was too important to let personal enmity get in the way.

When they were first hired, each director was given a different term of service so their terms wouldn't all be up at the same time. Lilienthal's was the shortest, at three years, which meant he would be up for reappointment in May 1936. And Arthur Morgan wanted to take advantage of the moment to force him out. He started complaining about Lilienthal to anyone who would listen, pointing out weaknesses, trying to get others to back him in a move to get the younger man off the board and appoint someone else. Lilienthal heard about the effort and mounted a counterattack. "Intrigue thick," Lilienthal's wife wrote in her diary.

In the end, the president sided with Lilienthal. The Supreme Court had just ruled in favor of the TVA, ending the long challenge by the private power advocates, and Lilienthal was seen as the man who had won the case. Still burdened by an economic depression that refused to lift, FDR found Lilienthal's pro-industry, pro-job arguments more appealing than Morgan's idyllic, cooperative village workshops. Lilienthal got reappointed to a full nine-year term. At that point Arthur Morgan went a little crazy. He refused to attend board meetings for a month. Then he put forward a plan to reorganize the TVA around himself, firming up his power. After FDR rejected the idea, Morgan's health began to decline and he took a long vacation; when he came back, he seemed more suspicious than ever. He wasn't sleeping well and he was losing weight. "It is very disturbing to feel that one's every act is watched by a keen, shrewd lawyer who is aiming to build up a case and to achieve personal dominance," he wrote.

He could have resigned with dignity. But Arthur Morgan was beyond reason now. He thought Lilienthal was in the pocket of Alcoa, the big aluminum manufacturer. He thought Lilienthal was conspiring with Harcourt Morgan. "To Mr. Lilienthal's mind I was an obstacle to his establishing personal control of the TVA," Morgan later wrote. "It was essential that I be eliminated." Charges began flying, with Lilienthal accusing Morgan of trying to override majority decisions, and Morgan charging Lilienthal with making deals with politicians and betraying the core values of the TVA. Their fight boiled over into public speeches, magazine stories, and interviews.

By early 1938, it was clear that something had to be done, so FDR called the three TVA directors in to meet with him and talk out their issues. The president liked nothing better than to use his personal charm to solve problems. But Morgan was never in the

Arthur Morgan laying out his many complaints in public testimony
Courtesy Library of Congress

mood to be sweet-talked, and he was no longer thinking clearly. He wrote back to the president saying that such a meeting could serve no purpose. Then, astonishingly, he told FDR he would not come. When the president, incensed, issued a second invitation, Morgan again refused, calling instead for a congressional hearing. After a third, even more pointed invitation, Morgan, like a sulking schoolboy, finally showed up—and then refused to participate.

The meeting of the three directors with the president and secretary of the interior Harold Ickes did not go well. When the president asked Morgan a question, he got back nothing beyond a prepared answer. At one point Morgan asked FDR not to interrupt him until he was finished speaking. "Really insolent" was Ickes's summation of Morgan's attitude. The president did his best, outlining the problems as he understood them, then asking Morgan to state his specific charges against the other two. The only answer he got was "I am of the opinion that this meeting is not, and in the nature of the case cannot be, an effective or useful fact-finding occasion." And then Morgan again called for a congressional hearing.

The president heard from the other two. Discussions went on over and around the uncooperative Arthur Morgan for six long hours. It ended when FDR told Morgan that he could have a week to change his mind about giving a more useful response, and the group was dismissed. When they met a week later, Morgan again would do nothing more than read a prepared statement, rebuffing the president's attempts to get him to answer questions. The president gave him three more days to come around. Three days later, Morgan again refused to speak.

So FDR fired him. Arthur Morgan was told he was off the board effective March 23, 1938.

Even after being removed, Morgan still behaved bizarrely. He wrote the president, "I do not recognize your order for my removal as within the power of the president. I am, therefore, notifying you that I am still a member and chairman of the Board of Directors of TVA." His note made no sense—and made no difference. He was out. He had to clear his office. Months later, when he finally got his much-desired congressional hearings, they ended with the conclusion that Morgan's charges against Lilienthal were without foundation.

When it was over, Morgan simply shifted his attention to another attempt to make a perfect society, working first to start a small utopian experiment in the mountains of North Carolina, then embarking on a long career as a community organizer. He lived to be ninety-seven years old. And during all those years he never appeared to have second thoughts about any of his actions. "The personal tragedy of it all," wrote future attorney general Francis Biddle, "was that Dr. Morgan might have gone down to posterity as a great man."

Instead, he was for the most part forgotten. And in 1941, David Lilienthal was named chairman of the TVA.

ARTHUR MORGAN'S DEPARTURE represented, in many ways, the end of twenty years of grand visions for the Tennessee Valley.

But it was just the start of what later was called the myth of the TVA.

Under Lilienthal, federal money continued to pour into the valley for the construction of dams and distribution of electricity. By the early 1940s, the TVA had tamed the Tennessee River by completing sixteen new dams and improving five others, installing locks for navigation, and coordinating the whole system to control floods in the winter and provide plenty of water in the summer. It was an amazing achievement, its size and scale dwarfing even the Panama Canal—"the largest job of engineering and construction ever carried out by any single organization in all our history," Lilienthal boasted.

He, like Henry Ford, knew the value of publicity. Under his leadership, the TVA's public information arm released a steady stream of photos, news releases, pamphlets, and short films that made the TVA's work look heroic and transformational. Speakers were sent to hundreds of civic meetings. Dams were turned into tourist destinations, with visitors' centers, informational plaques, and written guides. Visitors by the millions arrived to marvel at the huge, beautiful structures with their stories of rivers conquered and economies revived.

Lilienthal himself was the TVA's main booster. He marshaled phalanxes of data to convince government agencies that their TVA money was not being wasted. He wrote a popular book, *TVA: Democracy on the March*, that lauded the TVA's effects on commerce, community, and the economy. It, too, was fact-filled: The TVA had cleared more than 175,000 acres of land and excavated enough dirt and rock to build the seven pyramids twelve times over. It had constructed more than 1,200 miles of highways and 140 miles of railroad track, poured almost three times the amount of concrete used in the Panama Canal, and employed 200,000 workers at one time or another. The destructive floods were gone, the river turned into a string of dams, power plants, and beautiful lakes, the "Great Lakes of the South," creating 9,000 miles of new shoreline—more than the entire coastline of the US. The Tennessee River—"an idle giant and a destructive one," in Lilienthal's words—had been put to work. Quiet cotton towns were now busy river ports. Change was written in "the records of new private industries established in the valley, or failing enterprises revived, more money in people's hands, less tax delinquencies, increased bank deposits . . . new public library services or state parks established . . . more hospitals, county health units almost doubled, less tuberculosis and malaria," increased average wages, increased retail sales, and on and on.

He waxed poetic when writing of the TVA demonstrating "the oneness of men and natural resources, the unity that binds together land, streams, forests, minerals, farming, industry, mankind . . ." It was the first government agency of its kind, he wrote, devoted to the total benefit of a large region. "What the TVA . . . has sought to do," he wrote, "can be simply stated: to accept an obligation to harmonize the private interest in earning a return from resources, with the dominant public interest in their unified and efficient development . . . to make affirmative action in the public interest both feasible and appealing to private individuals."

It was stirring stuff, and it had its effect. The nation and the world saw the TVA as an unalloyed success story, a demonstration that a democratic, capitalistic society could mount great projects for the common good. The TVA was a shining example for the world. The eminent historian Henry Steele Commager called it "probably

the greatest peacetime achievement of twentieth century America."
A 1943 study of its effects concluded, "To friend and to foe, the TVA
has seemed a sign in the sky, an indication of the shape of things
to come." One newsman said it represented "the new heaven in the
old earth."

BY THE END of World War II the valley had changed dramatically. It had been two generations since J. W. Worthington and Frank
Washburn first dreamed of a great dam across the river, twenty-five
years since Henry Ford and Thomas Edison had rolled into the
Shoals, and fifteen years since FDR and George Norris had paraded
in triumph through the streets of Florence and across the Wilson
Dam. The region had prospered during the Second World War, using
its abundant electricity to make munitions, fertilizers, aluminum for
planes, and a hundred other needed items. Some of it was used to
purify the elements used to make the atomic bomb, and some went
toward rocket research. After the war was over, Wernher von Braun
and other German rocket scientists were flown to the Huntsville
area, at the far end of what would have been Ford's seventy-five-mile
city, where they helped lay the foundation for America's space
program. By the 1960s, decades of government effort had been
expended there, careers had been made and wounded, and billions
of taxpayer dollars had been spent.

Much had changed. The river valley around the old Shoals is
still lovely to look at, still dotted with historic small towns, still home
to hospitable, hardworking, resilient people. But instead of sharecropper shacks, there are highway interchanges, research parks, strip
malls, and, in Huntsville, a sleek international airport. Aerospace
and defense industries, auto parts makers, chemical manufacturers,
biotechnology firms, and telecommunications centers spread over
the old cotton and corn farms.

It's nice, but it's no utopia. In important ways, it's a lot like high-tech areas in other parts of the country—the Research Triangle in North Carolina, for instance, or the suburbs around San Francisco. The highways are green and enjoyable but hard to tell from suburban roads in any other part of the country. There is plenty of development but not an extraordinary amount by national standards. While all that government investment helped the Tennessee Valley outpace most of the South economically through the 1960s, Alabama's statewide median income still languishes near the bottom of American states. And while the area up north around the Shoals is a little more prosperous than the southern part of the state, it's been out-developed by many other areas of the nation.

Nor was the Tennessee Valley spared the problems that can accompany growth. Once the dams were built (thirty-one of them at final count), the TVA in the latter half of the twentieth century started building coal and nuclear power plants, with the attendant air pollution and waste disposal issues. It developed its waterfront land along all that new lakeshore, and further encouraged industrial and residential investment.

Critics in the 1980s began questioning the TVA's shift from idealistic community-builder to modern agent of regional development. With the economic changes came others, harder to pin down with figures but apparent to many longtime residents: The feeling of the place was changing. The old Tri-Cities around Wilson Dam were gradually morphing from distinctively southern agricultural and small-industry market towns into destinations for professionals, retirees, and tourists, their old brick downtowns and historic homes often charmingly restored, their essential characters gradually changed. Guntersville, one of the old cotton towns on the river, was buried by water behind one of the TVA dams and rebuilt on higher ground. Now it's known as Alabama's Lake City, a popular vacation spot and home to a major bass fishing tournament. Things change.

In response to the Lilienthal-fueled myth of the TVA, scholars have more recently questioned the praise heaped on it in the 1940s and 1950s. The Great Lakes of the South provided great recreation for boaters and fishermen but also inundated archaeological sites and drowned homes, farms, businesses, and entire towns like Guntersville. There has been economic development but at the cost of thousands of families uprooted and displaced, none with a choice, many unwillingly. Some fifty thousand people were affected by land condemnations during the early TVA years. Many were tenant farmers and sharecroppers who didn't own land and were forced to move without much money to start over. The owners of the land they worked often did their best to help, and government caseworkers sometimes worked heroically to find them public support, but in the end thousands of poor people were forced to give up their old ways of life for new lives on higher ground and new jobs as day laborers.

And later historians have raised questions about just how much the TVA, with all its resources and projects, actually affected the economy of the region. Changes in the valley might have been accelerated by the TVA, but similar changes—mass electrification and increased industrialization, the reduction of tenant and sharecropper farming—were taking place at the same time across the nation, without the TVA.

For instance, Harcourt Morgan had run dozens of agricultural programs, employed hundreds of workers, and spent millions of dollars trying to steer farmers off of cotton and corn and toward more diversified crops and less soil-destructive techniques. However, his many successes were dwarfed by larger forces at play. Just as the nitrate factories, subject of so much attention and debate in the 1920s, became more or less irrelevant by the 1940s thanks to technical advances in making nitrogen fertilizers, so technology was helping change American farming. Everywhere, not just in the Tennessee Valley, farms were being electrified and mechanized, moving from relatively small family-run operations to big industrial agriculture outfits that benefited from larger-scale, ever-bigger machines, more sophisticated irrigation setups, and extensive use of new fertilizers, pesticides, and herbicides. Between 1934 and 1974 more than 70 percent of farms disappeared in the state of Tennessee, while the value of total farm production rose 33 percent (in constant dollars). More crops were being produced by a third the number of farmers. Technological change created what one historian called "a cruel but effective winnowing process," removing small farmers who couldn't afford to invest in the ever-more-expensive land, machines, and supplies they needed, while only the biggest and most efficient operations survived. Tenant farmers and sharecroppers were the first to go under, followed by many small family farms. The social effects were tremendous. And we're just beginning to come to grips with the longer-term effects of industrial agriculture on the biosphere, soil quality, and sustainability.

The TVA played a significant role in part of this evolution (especially through its highly successful fertilizer research effort, which was critical in developing many of today's most important and widely used formulations). But while it pushed the process somewhat, it was only a small part of a bigger national trend.

It's the same story with cheap power. Tennessee Valley residents paid less for electricity, thanks to the TVA, farms electrified, and more people bought freezers and refrigerators and vacuum cleaners. Per capita use of electricity soared twentyfold in the region between 1933 and 1960. Just as Ford had helped turn the automobile from a rich man's luxury to a common man's everyday ride, Lilienthal had helped turn electricity into a widely used necessity of life. But similar trends in mass electrification and increasing consumption were taking place across the country, and almost as fast. They were spurred in part by a program to build more big hydroelectric dams on major rivers, increasing the amount of electricity available, and in part by other New Deal programs to support rural electrification and public utilities.

It all makes the effects of Ford's bid and the TVA hard to parse from the greater factors at play at the same time across America: the general increase in power use, the shift from rural to urban to suburban, the move from heavy industrial production to tech and service industries, the postwar rise in incomes and uptick in leisure activities.

But certainly the TVA sped these changes, made them bigger than they otherwise would have been. Didn't it? Scholars who study the issue have not found a definitive answer. In an extensive economic study in the 1980s, William U. Chandler compared the development of Tennessee (which benefited greatly from the TVA) to that of neighboring Georgia (which did not) and found that per capita increases in income were about the same in both states; that rural electrification was no faster in the TVA region than outside it; and that growth in manufacturing jobs might actually have been slower where the TVA held sway. He concluded, "No persuasive evidence supports the notion that TVA significantly improved the economy of the Tennessee Valley." The reason? "Creating an entity that does not answer to the marketplace, to an electorate, or even to elected representatives cannot be expected to work well." That said, a number of other analyses have been more favorable to the TVA, showing above-average increases in industrial jobs and per-capita income in the TVA region compared to the rest of the country.

Much depends on the timing of the study. In the early years through the 1930s, the influx of TVA money and expertise might have pushed the Tennessee Valley along faster than its neighbors, giving Lilienthal the happy statistics he was so good at sharing. But then World War II pushed the nation as a whole in the same direction, spurring industrial development, creating jobs, and kicking off the economic boom of the 1950s and 1960s.

Whatever the answer, a few things seem certain: The region benefited but not as dramatically as George Norris and FDR might have hoped—and the rest of the nation quickly caught up.

No one (as far as this author knows) has done an in-depth study of a related question: If Henry Ford's bid had been accepted, would his seventy-five-mile city had done more good than the government did with the TVA?

The question is important, because it gets to the heart of a choice that animated much of the discussion about Muscle Shoals in the 1920s, and much of the battle between Ford and Norris. Which is better for the nation: private development or public development? Should corporations run the show, or should the government?

There are too many hypotheticals in Ford's case, too many "maybes" to form a definite answer. My own thoughts run this way: If Ford had built his Detroit of the South, it would have been trumpeted around the world. Ford and his crack communications team would have released a flood of positive media, raising Ford's image as a civic planner without equal. He would have dealt with the government from a position of strength in asking for public funds for more dams with favorable terms for his own interests. He would have made a lot of electricity (most of which he would have soaked up for his own industries), controlled floods (though not as effectively as the TVA), and made some cheap fertilizer (at least for a few years, until he realized that those old nitrate plants were money losers). He would basically have turned the valley into one long, loosely integrated automobile plant, and quashed his competitors.

Liebold's power within the company might well have grown, and with it a strengthening of the pro-German, anti-Semitic views he shared with Ford. While his bid for the Shoals was active, one of his biggest fans in Germany, Adolf Hitler, wrote in *Mein Kampf*, "It is Jews who govern the stock exchange forces of the American Union. Every year makes them more and more the controlling masters of the producers in a nation of one hundred and twenty millions; only a single great man, Ford, to their fury, still maintains full independence." Soon after pulling out of the project Ford opened car manufacturing plants in Berlin and Cologne, and there is evidence he was in secret discussions with German firms to develop synthetic oil and gasoline to fuel them. Other commercial ties between Ford and the Nazi regime have been described in several books. The Ford Motor Company might not have been the only US firm working with the Nazis, but it was an important one.

It's easy to imagine a world where Henry Ford is more respected across the nation and the world, his industrial empire more powerful, his ties with Germany stronger, his pro-Nazi sentiments more widely shared. Would he have run against FDR? It's a scenario that lends itself to frightening alternative histories.

More to the point, if Ford's bid for the Shoals had been approved, there would have been less time spent on ceramics workshops and planting kudzu, and more devoted to building auto parts factories and creating micro-farms. His ribbon city might well have flourished for a few decades. Ford would indeed have been a Caesar of the South.

But then the world would have changed. Ford's dream of factory workers taking time off to happily plow and plant a few acres and sell their produce at a local market has not come true to any great extent anywhere in the world, not because of Ford pulling out, but because it makes scant economic sense. The growth of the suburbs, the benefits and pleasures of home ownership in quiet neighborhoods outside the city, became popular not because of Ford, but because of federally backed mortgage programs, highway building, and the G.I. Bill after World War II. What would Ford's utopian industrial empire look like today? You have only to look at today's Detroit and the towns of the Rust Belt to see what happens when a region dedicates itself to a single industry. When technologies change and consumer spending evolves, the old industries either adapt or go under. The same would likely have happened to Ford's dream city on the Tennessee. Today, had they been built, its 1920s- and 1930s-style factories and small farms for workers would look like relics of another age. And it's likely that something much like today's TVA-fueled region around the Shoals would have risen in its place.

Perhaps the problem is framing private versus public economic development as an either/or choice. If Muscle Shoals shows anything, it shows that development happens from the push and pull between the two—Norris's deep study and Washburn's business daring, FDR's New Deal and Ford's emphasis on serving the needs of workers and consumers.

The tension between public and private that we still see playing out in Washington, DC, is both necessary and energizing. We need both. And when the two sides respect and learn from each other, the results can be electric.

EPILOGUE

THIS BOOK HAS focused on the period from just before World War I to the start of World War II. But almost everyone and everything involved had a longer story. Here's what happened to some of the major players:

Frank Washburn, the man who first envisioned a great dam across the Tennessee, designed and built Nitrate Plant #2, and founded American Cyanamid, died of pneumonia in 1922, just as his firm was figuring out how to do battle with Henry Ford for control of the Shoals.

Tireless Tennessee Valley booster "Colonel" J. W. Worthington continued working as a lobbyist after Ford pulled his bid. And although he strove as always to stay in the background—"He moved quietly and mysteriously," wrote a Birmingham newspaper—he occasionally made news. In 1930 Senator George Norris backed a congressional investigation to look into power and fertilizer company efforts to keep the Shoals in private hands. Worthington's name kept coming up during the hearings. He was working several sides of the issue, helping the fertilizer folks, advising the power folks, and even assisting with speeches by an Alabama senator who sat on the investigating panel. Evidence surfaced that Worthington had given a $1,000 bribe to a newspaper editor to favor his clients. When Worthington was called to testify, he destroyed or hid all relevant documents, pleaded illness, took a train to Detroit, and checked into a hospital, staying there until the hearings were over. It ruined his reputation, and he never again achieved the prominence he had in the 1920s. Still, he was something of a model for all later super-lobbyists. He died in 1942 at age eighty-six.

Ernest Liebold, Henry Ford's quietly efficient right hand, also went into a decline. When Ford gave up both the presidency and his dream of an industrial empire in Alabama, Liebold's power in the company began to wane. In the mid-1930s something in his adding-machine mind sprang loose. Without a word of explanation, he resigned his board positions at two Detroit banks, got in a car, and took off. The police, alerted to his disappearance by Ford officials, found Liebold registered under a false name in a hotel room in Traverse City. He seemed exhausted; it's possible he suffered a nervous breakdown. But he pulled himself together, returned to Detroit, and went back to work. In 1938, Hitler's government awarded him the Order of Merit of the German Eagle, first class (Ford received an even higher Nazi honor the same year). But Liebold never regained his boss's trust or his former power within the company. He was fired in 1944 and died in 1956.

Thomas Edison, after pulling his support from Ford's bid in the early 1920s, began spending more of his time at his winter home in Fort Myers, Florida, where he and Ford were next-door neighbors. Edison took advantage of the benign climate to grow more than one thousand varieties of plants, many of which he used in his unsuccessful research into substitutes for rubber. The two old camping buddies remained close friends; late in life, when Edison was confined to a wheelchair, Ford bought himself one to keep at his Florida home so they could race. As Edison lay dying of complications of diabetes in 1931, a set of test tubes was kept open near his bed to catch his last breath. One was sent to Ford and is now on display at the Henry Ford Museum in Dearborn.

George Norris ended up a hero. While fighting the Ford bid he had been demonized in the South, but after 1932 he became a favorite of people in the valley, who called him "Uncle George" and displayed his picture on the walls of houses, stores, and restaurants. FDR called him "a prophet," and he was lauded by writers as "far ahead of his time" and a man who "captured the future before others even saw it." Norris wanted to expand his integrated TVA model—power, flood control, navigation, recreation—to other river systems, but the money and political will was not there. He was eighty-one years old when he made a last run for the Senate during World War II, and Nebraska voted him out. So he retired to his modest home in McCook, Nebraska, and started writing his memoirs, summarizing his service in a sentence: "I have done my best to repudiate wrong and evil in government affairs." John F. Kennedy honored him among eight senators in his 1956 book *Profiles in Courage,* and the US Postal Service issued a stamp in 1961 showing him with the Norris Dam in the background and the phrase "Gentle Knight of Progressive Ideals" across the bottom. Norris died in 1944.

David Lilienthal, riding high on the success of the TVA, was named head of the new Atomic Energy Commission in 1946. For four years he was in charge of advising the government about the growth of the nation's nuclear arsenal and the possibilities of using atomic power to make electricity. He brought to the job the same mix of hard work and public relations skill that had made him so successful in the Tennessee Valley. But he was seen as a little too soft for the Cold War era—he was in favor of setting up an international group to oversee nuclear arms, was against the development of the hydrogen bomb, and warned of the dangers of nuclear waste—and resigned his AEC position in 1950. He went to work in the private sector, hoping to make more money, but his consulting ventures never quite worked out as he'd hoped. He died in 1981, at age eighty-one.

After ending his bid for Muscle Shoals, Henry Ford's ambition seemed to ebb. He shut down his assembly line for the Model T, the car that had changed America. It had made him rich, it had made him famous, it been in continuous production for eighteen years and was still selling. But the market had changed so much, with so many new models from so many competitors, that even Ford had to admit that it was time to change.

He let his son, Edsel, run more and more of the company. Ford still had a hundred things going, but now he put more of his effort into Greenfield Village, his outdoor-museum–cum–theme park in Dearborn, where he installed historic buildings shipped in from around America. He reconstructed a New England village clustered around a pond with a gristmill, installed a brick railroad station with steam locomotives, relocated the farmhouse where he'd been raised and the garage where he'd built his first Quadricycle, and built a replica of Edison's Menlo Park laboratory. He arranged concerts of old-time fiddle music. It was a place to show families what America used to be back in the good old days, before modernization and changing morals started to ruin everything. This became Ford's new utopia, part open-air schoolroom, part Disneyland, part personal trip down memory lane. He opened the park to the public in 1933. It remains a major tourist attraction.

And he slowly fell back into his own peculiarities. His big stone house on the Rouge River was often close to empty, just Henry and Clara and a few servants knocking around. He obsessed more than ever about big money forces plotting against him. As one of his top lieutenants recalled, "In later years he had suspicion amounting to hallucination that bankers and General Motors were out to ruin him."

In 1943 his son and heir, Edsel, not yet fifty years old, died of cancer. Henry, now close to eighty, stepped back in to take the reins at the Ford Motor Company. But he wasn't the man he had once been. He had been suffering from heart problems and his mental state was erratic. After a couple of years he was convinced to turn over the company's management to his eldest grandson, Henry Ford II.

In 1947, the Rouge flooded and knocked out the small power plant that Ford had installed to electrify his house. A few days later he suffered a cerebral hemorrhage. In the end, the man who had dreamed of creating a futuristic all-electric city "died as he had entered the world eighty-three years earlier," wrote biographers Peter Collier and David Horowitz, "by the light of an oil lamp and a few candles."

SOURCE NOTES

I HAVE NOTHING against footnotes. In many books, they're essential. I once spent a couple of years running a university press, and I work with stacks of academic books in my research. While reading these books, mostly published by university or small specialty publishers, and in articles that appear in scholarly journals, I appreciate the careful references and small-type footers that note the sources of every quote and assertion. That is the right thing for those books and journals; it's just not the right thing for the books I write.

I write about STEM topics (science, technology, engineering, and mathematics), which can be challenging material for general readers without much science background. My job is to open those worlds, accurately and compellingly, to people who might not otherwise enter them. The challenge I face is that the primary material of scientific communication—the scholarly journal articles and books with all those footnotes—are written in what might as well be a foreign language for general readers. It is the language of science, with its unfamiliar specialized terms, data-heavy presentation, and dryly objective tone. I translate that material into language that will engage readers who otherwise would be put off from important ideas only because they're cloaked in statistics, long and unfamiliar words, graphs, and charts.

I want readers to race through my books without getting bogged down. So in place of footnotes I offer these brief, chapter-by-chapter Source Notes, which allow interested readers to dive more deeply, if they want, into the material I used. This is an abbreviated list of the most important books, archives, journal articles, and other media from which I gathered information. While it's no substitute for complete footnoting, it does offer signposts for readers who want to explore. The "author (date)" notes point readers to complete citations in the more extensive Bibliography that follows.

GENERAL NOTES

In addition to the individual books and articles in the Bibliography, I relied heavily on contemporary news stories. The newspapers of the 1920s and 1930s were very different from today's ever-smaller, often understaffed local papers. In those days there were journalists working all over; it seems as if every small city and town had a vibrant daily paper, and sometimes two or three, offering lots of locally written news and opinion with detail and color. I relied on stories from a dozen Alabama papers as well as big-city dailies in New York, Chicago, Washington, DC, and elsewhere. Thanks to digitization, many of these long-ago stories are quickly accessible and searchable online; my favorite (pay) service is newspapers.com, and there are others available through your local library or online.

In addition, I spent a week at the Benson Ford Research Center in Dearborn, Michigan, going through the archive of Ford company papers. These are abbreviated as BFRC.

INTRODUCTION

The opening scene of Ford and Edison arriving in Florence is drawn entirely from contemporary news reports in local and national papers.

CHAPTER 1

The history and geography of the Tennessee River was drawn from Callahan (1980), Downs (2014), Lilienthal (1944), McDonald (1997), Whitman (1939), Winn (2014), Inskeep (2015), Davidson (1992), and the descriptions by James Agee in Ashdown (2005). The journal of John Donelson, outlining his nightmare float down the Tennessee, can be found online at https://tsla.tnsosfiles.com/digital/teva/transcripts/33635.pdf. Biographical material on the tireless Tennessee River booster John W. Worthington is from Almon (1975), Downs (2014), Johnson (1980), Newman (1994), McDonald (1997), and Sheffield (1985); more can be found in contemporary news reports, the files of the BFRC, and the John Warren Worthington papers at the University of Alabama Special Collections. My Washburn information came from BFRC files, contemporary news reports, obituaries, and Washburn (1910).

CHAPTER 2

The larger history of nitrogen fertilizers can be found in Hager (2008), McClung (1923), Haynes (1954), and Clarke (1977). The rushed lead-up to and construction of the dam and nitrogen plants at Muscle Shoals, including the National Defense Act of 1916 and the study of Charles Parsons, are from Pritchett (1943), West (1925), Clarke (1977), Haynes (1954), Downs (2014), Wik (1962), Garrett (1968), McDonald (1997, 2014), Tennessee Valley Authority (1983), and two different Johnsons (1980 and 2016). More on the war years can be found in Schaffer (1984). For this chapter in particular I also relied heavily on local and national newspaper stories of the day, and in-person visits to the sites of the nitrate plants and workers' villages.

CHAPTER 3

Much of the basic Henry Ford material throughout this book, including the history of the Ford Motor Company, is from Benson (1923), Collier and Horowitz (2002), Guinn (2019), Lacey (1986), Lewis (1987), Miller (1922), Newton (1987), Nevins and Hill (1957), Watts (2006), and Wik (1972), with many additional personal details from Ford's own books (1922, 1926). This I supplemented with contemporary newspaper reports, archival material from BFRC, and the memories and stories of his employees found in Marquis (2007), Sorenson (2006), and the BFRC's trove of oral histories of Ford Motor Company employees and management. Nevins and Hill (1957) are particularly good on the Mount Clemens trial, and important additional details about the *Chicago Tribune* libel suit were drawn from contemporary news and magazine articles. Sources for the shutdown of the wartime Muscle Shoals project are the same as those listed for Chapter 2, supplemented with contemporary news coverage of the issue in Congress.

CHAPTER 4

In addition to the Ford material listed for Chapter 3, I added scores of contemporary newspaper and magazine articles to build this chapter. Ford's anti-Semitism has been the subject of many books; I used Ribuffo (1980), Nevins and Hill (1957), Lacey (1986), Wallace (2003), Woest (2012), and Baldwin (2001). Wherever possible, I relied on Ford's own words, as printed in his memoir (Ford [2017]), in the pages of the *Dearborn Independent*, and quoted in many newspaper articles of the day. His anti-Semitism was entwined with his views on the degeneration of America, and particularly what he saw as the decline and eventual downfall of its major cities. During his early Muscle Shoals period (1921–22) Ford often made off-the-cuff anti-Semitic remarks to reporters. Many of the big-city daily newspapers would not report these ethnic slurs, but smaller regional papers were less shy and apparently more supportive.

CHAPTER 5

Most Ford biographers hardly mention his initial Muscle Shoals visit and first bid in 1921, although Wik (1972), Sheridan (1986), and Watts (2006) give it some attention. I pulled together details primarily from contemporaneous newspaper coverage. More about Secretary of War Weeks and General Lansing Beach are found in government documents and reports from the later hearings, in Johnson (1980), and in articles about and histories of the engineering of the Shoals projects, particularly Milton (1925), Hubbard (1961), Downs (2014), and Pritchett (1943). Guinn (2019) offers details on the camping trip with Harding, as do numerous news articles of the day. The Worthington burglary and scandal were gleefully covered by newspapers both north and south, and the suspected ties of the anti-Ford movement to Treasury Secretary Mellon and his aluminum investments were bandied about in the political magazines and newspaper opinion pieces; today's social media conspiracy theories have nothing on the yellow press of the 1920s.

CHAPTER 6

Ford's personal secretary and personal banker Ernest Liebold was, to me, a fascinating character. He receives attention in just about every Ford biography, especially in Collier and Horowitz (2002), and his pro-German, anti-Semitic sentiments are described in more detail in Woest (2012), Baldwin (2001), and Wallace (2003). Marquis (2007) offers an unflattering contemporary description by a coworker who dealt with Liebold every day, and there is a Liebold oral history at BFRC that offers additional insights. Despite the fact that Liebold was reputed to be ferociously diligent and meticulous, detailed records of his work with Ford—years of correspondence, memos, and office files, all his communications with the boss—are unavailable at the Ford archives at BFRC; presumably these documents have been lost, destroyed, or sequestered. The Liebold-Worthington correspondence in the Muscle Shoals files at BFRC, on which I relied, is only partial; Worthington occasionally refers to Liebold replies or other communications that are missing. There are hints that Liebold relied heavily on the telephone for communication with his many informants, which leaves no written record. The material on the Ford-Weeks positioning leading up to Ford's visit to the Shoals in December 1921 is from contemporary news reports.

CHAPTER 7

The facts I've chosen about Thomas Edison's life and his pre-1921 relationship with Ford come mainly from the Edison biographies: Baldwin (1995), Israel (1998), Morris (2019), Newton (1987), and Vanderbilt (1971). Vanderbilt is especially good on the first, fateful meeting of Edison and Ford in Detroit, and more can be found in Lacey (1986). Details on Edison's camping trips with Ford are from Guinn (2019) and news accounts. The quote about Ford and Edison being freaks of a feather is from Benson (1923). On the Ford-Edison publicity trip to Muscle Shoals in late 1921, I relied mainly on scores of local newspaper stories, supplemented with material from Sheridan (1986), Hubbard (1961), and a local oral history of the barbecue as told by the host, Ed O'Neal, himself. There is also a telling cartoon of that event that ran in the Birmingham paper at the time, showing Ford chopping wood, Edison keeping warm near a fire, a chorus of fawning locals, a line of Black waiters hoisting trays of steaming food and making comments like, "If ah had dat man's money, ah nevuh would work no more," and a vamp or two in slinky dresses. More on the Ford-Edison idea for using "energy dollars" can be found in Foster (1923) and Hammes (2006); it was the subject as well of contemporary (and generally critical) articles and editorials, especially in the financial press.

CHAPTER 8

During early 1922, the Ford bid for the Shoals and his tangle with Weeks became one of the biggest news stories in the nation. Most of this chapter was constructed from the numerous news accounts of the day, along with government reports accessed at the National Archives, and the Worthington correspondence and Muscle Shoals material at BFRC. In addition I used material from Pritchett (1943), Haynes (1954), Hubbard (1961), Downs (2014), Wik (1955, 1972), and Watts (2006).

CHAPTER 9

While the Ford for President boomlet is mentioned in all the Ford biographies listed for Chapter 3, it has rarely been treated in any depth. The exception is Wik (1972), who analyzes Ford's political appeal. Guinn (2019), Lewis (1987), and Nevins and Hill (1957) also give it some attention. Marquis (2007), who worked closely with Ford for years at a high level, makes observations on Ford's political aspirations. A closer sense of the atmosphere and enthusiasm around his possible run comes from the many magazine and newspaper articles that appeared about it through 1923 and most of 1924.

CHAPTER 10

Most of the material describing the real estate frenzy around Muscle Shoals is from contemporary news articles, many from the small papers in the area. The story of the Johnson sisters is told in correspondence in the BFRC's Muscle Shoals files. Norris (1992) was appalled at the greed and shadowy methods of the real estate companies; more can be found in Downs (2014), Wik (1972), Hubbard (1961), McDonald (1997), and Tennessee Valley Authority (1983).

CHAPTER 11

Congressional political maneuvering around the Ford bid in 1922 spurred a great deal of news coverage, and I used it, along with material from the Norris files at the National Archives, the Muscle Shoals files in the BFRC, and the congressional hearings transcripts of the Kahn and Norris committees to create the narrative in this chapter. Additional material came from Hubbard (1958, 1959, 1961), Johnson (1980), and Wik (1972). More on Norris's life is found in his autobiography, Norris (1992), as well as Zucker (1996), Budig and Walton (2013), and Villard (1936).

CHAPTER 12

Ford would talk to the press about bits and pieces of his idea for a seventy-five-mile city along the Tennessee (see for instance Crowther, 1923), but his full vision was best laid out in two magazine articles by McClung (both 1922). More on Ford's interest in water power and electricity as a driver of city design can be found in Tobey (1996), Hubbard (1961), and Lewis (1987). Additional context on the idea of small utopian garden cities, including Mumford's, Wright's, and Ford's nostalgia for the past in planning the future, can be found in Molella and Kargon (2003), Graham (2016), Kargon and Molella (2008), and Krieger (2019). Rosenbaum (1993) details Frank Lloyd Wright's long interest in Muscle Shoals; a Wright house still stands in Florence.

CHAPTER 13

The ongoing fight in Congress was tracked by Worthington in his long correspondence with Liebold, which I found in the BFRC Muscle Shoals files; I also used many contemporary news accounts as well as government documents from the National Archives. The plan for Ford City was laid out in a series of large display ads that ran in papers nationwide. The sources for the Ford for President movement are listed under the sources for Chapter 9. As Ford's observant and later outspoken former top executive Samuel Marquis acidly noted, "If our government were an absolute monarchy, a one-man affair, Henry Ford would be the logical man for the throne."

CHAPTER 14

Most of the source material for the end days of Warren G. Harding and the advent of Calvin Coolidge is taken from Shlaes (2013) and contemporary news accounts; see also Wik (1972). Fred Black's oral history is at BFRC. The funeral appearance by Ford and Edison is from Guinn (2019). Ford's political ambitions are sourced from the materials listed for Chapter 9. "So are your flivvers, Mr. Ford" is from Woest (2012). I relied on congressional testimony and contemporary press coverage to trace the circumstances of Ford's controversial meeting with Coolidge; the interpretation of these events is my own.

CHAPTER 15

The journalist James Martin Miller was another of those background 1920s figures who caught my interest. It took a good deal of time to track down information about his life and career, much of it found here and there in scattered news pieces of the day, and some of it in Miller's own words in his books and articles. Records at BFRC offer additional details. Miller's two sessions of testimony before Norris's committee were published verbatim and are available through congressional publications. The interpretation of these events is my own. Miller's life would make an interesting minor biography.

CHAPTER 16

Downs (2014), Pritchett (1943), McGraw (1971), Johnson (1980), Tennessee Valley Authority (1983), Lane (1925), and Johnson (2016) relate various aspects of the Muscle Shoals scene after Ford pulled out. This I supplemented with archival materials from BFRC and contemporary news coverage.

CHAPTER 17

The description of what life was like in the Tennessee River valley in the years when TVA was starting is drawn from Agee (1933, 1985, 2013), Daws (1981), McDonald (1997, 2014), Downs (2014), Rinks (2014), Ezzell (2018), and Chandler (1984). Details on the visit of FDR and Norris to the area, and the effects of the New Deal, are found in contemporary news articles as well as Kargon (2008), Downs (2014), McDonald (1997), Freeman (2014), Sheridan (2014), and Makima (2014). The birth of the TVA is told in McGraw (1971), Callahan (1980), Lilienthal (1944), and Morgan (1974).

CHAPTER 18

The early days of the TVA have been described at length in a number of books; I relied on Callahan (1980), Chandler (1984), Downs (2014), Hargrove and Conklin (1983), Hargrove and Wills (1994), Lilienthal (1944), McCarthy and Voigtlander (1983), McGraw (1971), Morgan (1974), Pritchett (1943), Selznick (1966), and Whitman (1939). Relocating the valley population was the focus of Daws (1981) and McDonald (1982). Arthur Morgan's experimental town of Norris makes an appearance in many of these books: See also Kargon (2008), Hicks (2001), Schaffer (1986), and Graham (2016). Agee (1935) offers an eyewitness account. As usual, I used a variety of contemporary articles from magazines and local newspapers. See also the work of local historian Clemons (2018) and Schaffer (1986).

CHAPTER 19

Many of the basic TVA sources listed for Chapter 18 also include information on Lilienthal's work to establish the yardstick for electrical production costs, and mention his skirmishes with Willkie. Tobey (1996), Hargrove (1987, 1994), Callahan (1980), and McGraw (1970, 1971) make it a major focus; Whitman (1939) offers more local color. All of these sources provide snapshots of Lilienthal during his TVA years, but perhaps the best way to understand his combination of high-mindedness, public service, and PR ability is by reading his own words, especially Lilienthal (1944). Lewis (2018) offers a complete Willkie biography.

CHAPTER 20

The Morgan-Lilienthal power struggle is a theme that echoes through all the histories of the TVA listed for Chapters 18 and 19. Particular attention is paid in Hargrove (1994), McGraw (1970), Chandler (1984), Colignon (1997), Downs (2014), and Davis (1989). It is interesting to read the first-person accounts of the two principals in close order, with Morgan bitter long after the fight was over (1974) and Lilienthal soaring in victory (1944). Most of the major histories also offer summary analyses of the long-term effects of the TVA.

EPILOGUE

The later-life material for each of the major characters comes from the major sources for them (listed under Source Notes for various chapters; Washburn and Worthington in Chapter 1; Liebold, Chapter 6; Edison, Chapter 7; Norris, Chapter 11; and Ford, Chapter 3). I also depended on contemporary news articles and obituaries to fill in the details of their later lives.

SOURCES

Agee, James. "T.V.A." *Fortune* 8 (1933): 81–97.

Agee, James. "TVA: Work in the Valley." *Fortune* 11 (1935): 93–98.

Agee, James. *Cotton Tenants: Three Families.* New York: Melville House, 2013.

Allen, Frederick Lewis. *Only Yesterday: An Informal History of the 1920s.* New York: Perennial Library, 1931.

Almon, Clopper. "J. W. Worthington and His Role in the Development of Muscle Shoals and the Tennessee River." *J. Muscle Shoals History* III (1975): 49–63.

Alvarado, Rudolph, and Sonya Alvarado. *Drawing Conclusions on Henry Ford.* Ann Arbor: University of Michigan Press, 2001.

Ashdown, Paul, ed. *James Agee: Selected Journalism.* Knoxville: University of Tennessee Press, 2005.

Baldwin, Neil. *Edison: Inventing the Century.* New York: Hyperion, 1995.

Baldwin, Neil. *Henry Ford and the Jews: The Mass Production of Hate.* New York: PublicAffairs, 2001.

Bates, J. Leonard. "The Teapot Dome Scandal and the Election of 1924." *The American Historical Review* 60, no. 2 (1955): 303–22.

Benson, Allan L. *The New Henry Ford.* New York: Funk & Wagnalls, 1923.

Bradford, Jesse C. "A History of the City of Muscle Shoals." *J. Muscle Shoals History* XIX (2014): 183–90.

Bryan, Ford R. *Henry's Lieutenants.* Detroit: Wayne State University Press, 1993.

Budig, Gene A., and Don Walton. *George Norris, Going Home.* Lincoln: University of Nebraska Press, 2013.

Callahan, North. *TVA: Bridge over Troubled Waters.* New York: A. S. Barnes & Co., 1980.

Chandler, William U. *The Myth of TVA: Conservation and Development in the Tennessee Valley, 1933–1983.* Cambridge, MA: Ballinger Publishing, 1984.

Clarke, Margaret Jackson. *The Federal Government and the Fixed-Nitrogen Industry, 1915–1926* (PhD thesis). Corvallis: Oregon State University Press, 1977.

Clemons, L. C. (Bill). *TVA: The Great Experiment.* Personal Collection. Florence, AL: self-published, 2018.

Coffey, Brian F. "Fertilizers to the Front: HAER and US Nitrate Plant No. 2." *J. Soc. for Industrial Archaeology* 23, no. 1 (1997): 25–42.

Colignon, Richard A. *Power Plays: Critical Events in the Institutionalization of the Tennessee Valley Authority.* Albany: State University of New York Press, 1997.

Collier, Peter, and David Horowitz. *The Fords: An American Epic.* San Francisco: Encounter Books, 2002.

Crowther, Samuel. "Muscle Shoals." *McClure's Magazine* 54, no. 11 (1923): 31–38

Dakin, Edwin. "Henry Ford—Man or Superman?" *The Nation* 118, no. 3064 (1924): 336–38.

Davidson, Donald. *The Tennessee, Vol. 1: The Old River, Frontier to Secession.* Nashville: J. S. Sanders, 1992.

Davidson, Donald. *The Tennessee, Vol. 2: The New River, Civil War to TVA.* Nashville: J. S. Sanders, 1992.

Davis, Kenneth S. "Crisis Behind the TVA." Invention & Technology 5, no. 1 (1989): 8–16.

Daws, Laura Beth. *The Greater Good: Media, Family Removal, and TVA Dam Construction in North Alabama.* Tuscaloosa: University of Alabama Press, 1981.

Dennis, Bobby. "Industrial Growth in Northwest Alabama Since 1933." *J. Muscle Shoals History* VII (1979): 143–49.

Downs, Matthew L. *Transforming the South: Federal Development in the Tennessee Valley, 1915–1960.* Baton Rouge: Louisiana State University Press, 2014.

Ekbladh, David. "'Mr TVA': Grass-Roots Development, David Lilienthal, and the Rise and Fall of the Tennessee Valley Authority as a Symbol for U.S. Overseas Development, 1933–1973." *Diplomatic History* 26, no. 3 (2002): 335–74.

Engineering Association of the South, Nashville Section. *America's Gibraltar: Muscle Shoals.* Nashville: Muscle Shoals Association, 1916.

Ford, Henry. *Today and Tomorrow.* Cambridge, MA: Productivity Press, 1926.

Ford, Henry (with Samuel Crowther). *My Life and Work.* Garden City: Doubleday, 1922.

Foster, William Trufant. "Edison-Ford Commodity Money." *Proc. Acad. Political Science in the City of New York* 10, no. 2 (1923): 57–75.

Freeman, Lee. "Facts and Folklore About FDR's Visits to Muscle Shoals." *J. Muscle Shoals History* XIX (2014): 30–50.

Garrett, Jill K. *A History of Florence, Alabama.* Columbia, TN: J. K. Garrett, 1968.

Graham, Wade. *Dream Cities: Seven Urban Ideas That Shape the World.* New York: HarperCollins, 2016.

Grandin, Greg. *Fordlandia: The Rise and Fall of Henry Ford's Forgotten Jungle City.* New York: Metropolitan Books, 2009.

Greenwood, Ernest. "The Myth of Muscle Shoals." *The Independent,* Feb. 28, 1925: 230–32.

Guinn, Jeff. *The Vagabonds: The Story of Henry Ford and Thomas Edison's Ten-Year Road Trip.* New York: Simon & Schuster, 2019.

Hager, Thomas. *The Alchemy of Air.* New York: Crown Publishing, 2008.

Hammes, David L., and Douglas T. Wills. "Thomas Edison's Monetary Option." *J. Hist. of Economic Thought* 28, no. 3 (2006): 1–4.

Hargrove, Erwin C. "David Lilienthal and the Tennessee Valley Authority." In Doig, Jameson W., and Erwin C. Hargrove, eds. *Leadership and Innovation: A Biographical Perspective on Entrepreneurs in Government*. Baltimore: Johns Hopkins University Press, 1987: 25–60.

Hargrove, Erwin C. *Prisoners of Myth: The Leadership of the Tennessee Valley Authority, 1993–1990*. Knoxville: University of Tennessee Press, 1994.

Hargrove, Erwin C., and Paul K. Conklin, eds. *TVA: Fifty Years of Grass-Roots Bureaucracy*. Urbana: University of Illinois Press, 1983.

Haynes, William. *The American Chemical Industry II: The World War I Period, 1912–1922*. New York: D. Van Nostrand Co., 1954.

Hicks, George L. *Experimental Americans: Celo and Utopian Community in the Twentieth Century*. Urbana: University of Illinois Press, 2001.

Hubbard, Preston J. "The Story of Muscle Shoals." *Current History*, May 1958: 265–69.

Hubbard, Preston J. "The Muscle Shoals Controversy, 1920–1932." *Tennessee Historical Quarterly* 18 (1959): 195–212.

Hubbard, Preston J. *Origins of the TVA: The Muscle Shoals Controversy, 1920–1932*. New York: Norton, 1961.

Inskeep, Steve. *Jacksonland*. New York: Penguin Press, 2015.

Israel, Paul. *Edison: A Life of Invention*. New York: Wiley & Sons, 1998.

Johnson, Evans C. *Oscar W. Underwood: A Political Biography*. Tuscaloosa: University of Alabama Press, 1980.

Johnson, Timothy. "Nitrogen Nation: The Legacy of World War I and the Politics of Chemical Agriculture in the United States, 1916–1933." *Agricultural History* 90, no. 2, (2016): 209–229.

Kargon, Robert H., and Arthur P. Molella. *Invented Edens: Techno-Cities of the Twentieth Century*. Cambridge, MA: MIT Press, 2008.

King, Judson. *The Conservation Fight: From Theodore Roosevelt to the Tennessee Valley Authority*. Washington, DC: Public Affairs Press, 1959.

Kitchens, Carl T. "The Role of Publicly Provided Electricity in Economic Development: The Experience of the Tennessee Valley Authority, 1929–1955." *J. Economic Theory* 74, no. 2 (2014): 389–419.

Krieger, Alex. *City on a Hill: Urban Idealism in America from the Puritans to the Present*. Cambridge, MA: Harvard University Press, 2019.

Lane, Alfred P. "Muscle Shoals—Bonanza or White Elephant?" *Scientific American* May 1925: 293–95

Lacey, Robert. *Ford: The Men and the Machine*. New York: Little Brown & Co., 1986.

Lewis, David L. *The Public Image of Henry Ford*. Detroit: Wayne State University Press, 1987.

Lewis, David Levering. *The Improbable Wendell Willkie*. New York: Liveright Publishing, 2018.

Lilienthal, David E. TVA: *Democracy on the March*. New York: Harper & Brothers, 1944.

Lilienthal, David E. "The Regulation of Public Utility Holding Companies." *Columbia Law Review* 29, no. 4 (1929): 404–440.

Makima, Mary Shaw. "My Firsthand View of Roosevelt's Visit." *J. Muscle Shoals History* XIX (2014): 52–55.

Marquis, Samuel S. *Henry Ford: An Interpretation*. Detroit: Wayne State University Press, 2007.

McCarthy, D. M., and Clyde W. Voigtlander, eds. *The First Fifty Years: Changed Land, Changed Lives*. Knoxville: Tennessee Valley Authority, 1983.

McClung, Littell. "The Seventy-Five Mile City." *Scientific American* 127, no. 3 (1922): 156–57.

McClung, Littell. "What Can Henry Ford Do with Muscle Shoals?" *Illustrated World* 37, no. 2 (1922): 184–91.

McClung, Littell. "Taking Nitrogen from the Air." *Scientific American* 128, no. 5 (1923): 298–99.

McClung, Littell. "Building the World's Largest Monolith." *Scientific American* 129, no. 1 (1923): 8–9.

McDonald, Michael J. *TVA and the Dispossessed*. Knoxville: University of Tennessee Press, 1982.

McDonald, William L. *A Walk Through the Past: People and Places of Florence and Lauderdale County, Alabama*. Killen, AL: Heart of Dixie Publishing, 1997.

McDonald, William L. "Life in Muscle Shoals During the Depression." *J. Muscle Shoals History* XIX (2014): 152–57.

McGraw, Thomas K. *Morgan vs. Lilienthal: The Feud Within the TVA*. Chicago: Loyola University Press, 1970.

McGraw, Thomas K. *TVA and the Power Fight, 1933–1939*. New York: J. B. Lippincott Co., 1971

Miller, James Martin. *The Amazing Story of Henry Ford: The Ideal American and the World's Most Famous Private Citizen*. Chicago: M. A. Donohue & Co., 1922.

Miller, Nathan. *New World Coming: The 1920s and the Making of Modern America*. New York: Da Capo Press, 2003.

Milton, George F. "The South and Muscle Shoals." *The Independent*, Jan. 19, 1924: 39–40.

Milton, George F. "The Ruhr of America." The Independent, June 6, 1925: 631–33.

Molella, Arthur, and Robert Kargon. "Environmental Planning for National Regeneration: Techno-Cities in New Deal America and Nazi Germany." In Molella, Arthur, and Joyce Bedi. *Inventing for the Environment*. Cambridge, MA: MIT Press, 2003: 107–29.

Morgan, Arthur E. *The Making of the TVA*. Buffalo: Prometheus Books, 1974.

Morris, Edmund. *Edison*. New York: Random House, 2019.

Newton, James. *Uncommon Friends: Life with Thomas Edison, Henry Ford, Harvey Firestone, Alexis Carre, and Charles Lindbergh*. New York: Harcourt, 1987.

Nevins, Allan, and Frank Ernest Hill. *Ford: Expansion and Challenge*. New York: Charles Scribner's Sons, 1957.

Norris, George W. *Fighting Liberal: The Autobiography of George W. Norris* (2nd. ed.). Lincoln: University of Nebraska Press, 1992.

Pinci, A. R. "Woodrow Wilson's Ford Boom." *Forum* LXXVIII (1927): 181–90

Pritchett, C. Herman. *The Tennessee Valley Authority: A Study in Public Administration*. Chapel Hill: University of North Carolina Press, 1943.

Ribuffo, Leo P. "Henry Ford and 'The International Jew.'" *American Jewish History* 69 (1980): 437–77.

Rinks, Barry. "The Effects of the Great Depression on Lauderdale County." *J. Muscle Shoals History* XIX (2014): 126–51.

Rosenbaum, Alvin. *Usonia: Frank Lloyd Wright's Design for America*. Washington, DC: The Preservation Press, 1993.

Schaffer, Daniel. "The Moral Materialism of War: Muscle Shoals, Alabama, 1917–1918." Knoxville: Tennessee Valley Authority Office of Natural Resources and Economic Development Cultural Resources Program, 1984.

Schaffer, Daniel. "Ideal and Reality in 1930s Regional Planning: The Case of the Tennessee Valley Authority." *Planning Perspectives* 1, no. 1 (1986): 27–44.

Selznick, Philip. *TVA and the Grass Roots: A Study in the Sociology of Formal Organization*. New York: Harper & Row, 1966.

Sheffield: City on the Bluff, 1885–1985. Sheffield, AL: Friends of Sheffield Public Library, 1985.

Sheridan, Richard. "Thomas Alva Edison's Visit to Muscle Shoals." *J. Muscle Shoals History* XI (1986): 127–33.

Sheridan, Richard C. "Visits to the Muscle Shoals Area by Future, Current, and Former Presidents." *J. Muscle Shoals History* XIX (2014): 3–26.

Shlaes, Amity. *Coolidge*. New York: Harper Perennial, 2013.

Silverstein, Ken. "Ford and the Fuehrer." *The Nation* 270, no. 3 (2000): 11–13.

Sorensen, Charles E. *My Forty Years with Ford*. Detroit: Wayne State University Press, 2006.

Strows, W. H. "Muscle Shoals and Permanent Agriculture." *Outlook* 130, no. 17 (1922): 698–99.

Tennessee Valley Authority. *Fiftieth Anniversary of TVA*. Muscle Shoals AL: National Fertilizer Development Center, 1983.

Tobey, Ronald C. *Technology as Freedom: The New Deal and the Electrical Modernization of the American Home*. Berkeley: University of California Press, 1996.

Vanderbilt, Byron M. *Thomas Edison, Chemist*. Washington, DC: American Chemical Society, 1971.

SOURCES

Villard, Oswald Garrison. "Pillars of Government: George W. Norris." *Forum and Century* 45, no. 4 (1936): 249–53.

Wallace, Max. *The American Axis: Henry Ford, Charles Lindbergh, and the Rise of the Third Reich*. New York: St. Martin's Press, 2003.

Washburn, Frank. "The Power Resources of the South." *Annals of the American Academy of Political and Social Science* 35, no. 1 (1910): 81–98.

Watts, Steven. *The People's Tycoon: Henry Ford and the American Century*. New York: Vintage Books, 2006.

Webbink, P. "Status of the Muscle Shoals Project." *Editorial Research Reports v. 4*. Washington, DC: CQ Press, 1928.

West, William Benjamin. "America's Greatest Dam." *Scientific American* 124, no. 19 (1921): 364–65.

West, William Benjamin. *America's Greatest Dam, Muscle Shoals, Alabama*. New York: Frank E. Cooper, 1925.

West, William Benjamin. "Muscle Shoals Active at Last." *Scientific American* 149, no. 4 (1933): 149–51.

Whitman, Willson. *God's Valley: People and Power Along the Tennessee River*. New York: Viking Press, 1939.

Wik, Reynold M. "Henry Ford and the Agricultural Depression of 1920–1923." *Agricultural History* 29, no. 1 (1955): 15–22.

Wik, Reynold M. "Henry Ford's Science and Technology for Rural America." *Technology and Culture* 3 (1962): 247–58.

Wik, Reynold M. *Henry Ford and Grass-roots America*. Ann Arbor: University of Michigan Press, 1972.

Wiltse, A. J., and R. R. Humphries. ed. *Florence Alabama: The Power City at Wilson Dam, Muscle Shoals*. Florence, AL: Humphries & Wiltse, 1925.

Winn, Nicholas. "Muscle Shoals—The Problem and the Development." *J. Muscle Shoals History* XIX (2014): 191–96.

Woest, Victoria Saker. *Henry Ford's War on Jews and the Legal Battle Against Hate Speech*. Stanford: Stanford University Press, 2012.

Zucker, Norman L. *George W. Norris: Gentle Knight of American Democracy*. Urbana: University of Illinois Press, 1966.

ACKNOWLEDGMENTS

Sincere thanks to the people of the Shoals region who helped with the research for this book. I was lucky enough to be introduced to a group of local historians who showed me around and shared pieces of history that have not yet appeared in print; special thanks here to Shoals-area residents Joel Mize, Nancy Gonce, Bill Clemmons, and Richard Sheridan. Thanks as well to the staff at the excellent Florence-Lauderdale Public Library, who helped me as I spent days combing through the local newspaper microfilms and historical files. Joyce Fedeczko at the IFDC library at the Shoals provided help, as did the staff at The Henry Ford, both the Ford Museum and Greenfield Village. The archivists at the Benson Ford Research Center in Dearborn, where the Ford papers are accessed, were knowledgeable, efficient, and very helpful.

As always, I owe thanks to my agent, Nat Sobel, and the staff at Sobel-Weber. Nat and I have been working together for thirty years, and I hope we do it for thirty more.

Jamison Stoltz, the editor of this book (as well as *Ten Drugs*, my last one), is great to work with: enthusiastic, constructive, insightful, endlessly patient, and always essential. Many thanks to him and the fine Abrams Press team he works with.

Finally, special thanks to two good friends who helped at every stage of this project: Amit Roy, former head of the International Fertilizer Development Center (which grew out of the fertilizer research program of the TVA and is headquartered on the old TVA site near the Shoals), and Taylor Pursell, a fertilizer innovator and leading businessman whose family has been prominent in Alabama for generations. These two men first brought me out to the Shoals, opened up the area and its rich history, and opened my eyes to the history of agriculture around the world. They hosted me during visits, introduced me to people and places, informed me about local doings, and fed me some of the best barbecue I've ever had. They were vital in making this book happen; I owe them both a deep debt of gratitude.

INDEX

African Americans, 17–18, 39–40
Agriculture Committee, 150, 154–65, 178–80, 203–4
Alabama economy, 220–22, 259–65
Alabama Power, 27–28, 97–98, 99, 101–2, 154–55, 159, 179, 189, 209–14, 215, 245–46
aluminum, 89–90, 92, 102, 253
American Cyanamid, 23–24, 34–37, 44, 61–62, 267
America's Gibraltar, Muscle Shoals booklet, 29–30
anti-Semitism, 72–74, 96, 98, 110, 114, 123, 133, 134, 136–37, 263–64
assembly lines, 50–51, *51*, 67, 68–69
Associated Press interview, 168–69
automobiles, 175–76. *See also* Model T

banking, 97–98, 114–15, 123
Battle of New Orleans, 14–15
Battle of Shiloh, 18
Beach, Lansing, 78–80, *80*, 81, 83–84
Benz, Carl, 106
Black, Hugo, 153
bolshevism, 62, 74, 212
Bosch, Carl, 33
Bryson, Bill, 48

camping trips, 85–86, *86*, 108–9, 136, 186–87
Cannon, Joseph, 153
Chandler, William U., 262
Chicago real estate firm, 146–48
Chicago Tribune, 54–58, 71, 88–89, 133
Civil War, 6, 17–19
Clinch River, 233–34
coal, 19–21, 69, 100, 154–55
Coffee, John, 17
Collier, Peter, 108
Collier's, 183–84, 204–6
Commager, Henry Steele, 257–58
Commonwealth & Southern Corporation (C&S), 244–49
Congress, 4, 5, 204, 246

congressional hearings, 126–28, 149–50, 155–65, 196–203, 214–15
conservation, 88
Coolidge, Calvin, 186–93, 196, 198–206, 211–15
cotton, 17–18, 60, 99, 219–20
Couzens, James, 134, 183
Creek War, 14–15
C&S. *See* Commonwealth & Southern Corporation
Cumberland Trace, 12
currency, 114–16, 136, 161–62
cyanamide, 23–24, 34–37, 205–6, 267

Daimler, Gottlieb, 106–7
dams, 21–24, 27–30. *See also* Muscle Shoals bid; Tennessee Valley Authority
  American Cyanamid and, 34–37, 38
  construction of, 38–41, 229–36
  Norris Dam, *233*, 234–35
  power companies and building of, 215–16
  Wilson Dam, 38–41, *43*, 205, 210, *210*, 215, 223, 246–48
Davis, John W., 211
Dearborn Independent, 72–74, 100, 136, 184, 188, 197
Detroit Edison, 50, 107
Donelson, John, 12–14
Duke, James, 97–98

economy
  in Alabama, 220–22, 259–65
  Civil War and, 18–19
  contraction of, 58–61
  cotton and, 17, 60, 219–20
  farming and, 17, 60, 122, 219–21
  Great Depression and, 217–18, 220–25
  growth of, 38–45
  Harding administration and, 138
  industrialization and, 19–20
  New Deal and, 221–25, 239
  poverty and, 19, 220–21
  in Roaring Twenties, 65–67
  World War I and, 38–45, 58–61

Edison, Thomas, 1–5, *2*, *21*, *86*, *112*
  background on, 107–8, 119
  as congressional witness, 160–63
  electricity and, 20–22, 92, 173
  on fertilizer, 118–19, 160–61
  in final years, 268–69
  Ford, H., and, 53–54, 85, 100, 103–4,
    105–20, 132, 160–63, 183, 186, 268–69
  Model T and, 108
  on real estate speculation, 146
  Reese and, 131
Edison Illuminating Company, 107
Edmundson, E. A., 202
electricity. *See also specific topics*
  Edison and, 20–22, 92, 173
  "Ford City" and, 167–76, 181–82
  government and, 24–27, 34–38, 58,
    229–39, 241–49, 256–58
  hydropower and, 20–24, 27–30, 34, 37–39,
    92–93, 113, 167–68
  Norris on control of, 209–18
  rates, 241–43, 247–49, 251, 261
  TVA and, 241–49, 251
  "energy dollars," 114–16, 136, 161–62

Farm Bloc, 150, 178–82
Farm Bureau, 117
farming, 3, 5, 49–50, 99–100, 113, 117,
  126–27
  Agriculture Committee and, 150, 154–65,
    178–80, 203–4
  of cotton, 17–18, 60, 219–20
  economy and, 17, 60, 122, 219–21
  in "Ford City," 170–72
  Fordson tractor for, 70–71, *71*
  sharecropping and, 219, 239, 261
  TVA and, 235–38, 243–44, 260–61
Federal Water Power Act, 83, 127, 164, 178
fertilizer, 6, 7, 205–6, 211, 213
  for cotton, 17, 219–20
  Edison on, 118–19, 160–61
  Muscle Shoals bid and, 82–83, 90,
    99–100, 118–19, 125, 127–28, 149–50,
    156–63
  TVA and, 235–38
"Fertilizer Trust," 125
Firestone, Harvey, 85, *86*, 108–9, 136, 186
Fitzgerald, F. Scott, 66
floods, 179, 233
Florence, Alabama, 1–5, 17, 143, 205, 221,
  223, 258

Florence Times, 143
Ford, Clara, 1–2, 109, 162, 183–84, 192, 270
Ford, Edsel, 133, 270–71
Ford, Henry, 1–5, *2*, *48*, *66*, *86*, *112*, *137*,
    263–65. *See also* Muscle Shoals bid
  aluminum and, 89–90, 92, 102
  on American "decline," 73–75
  as anti-Semitic, 72–74, 96, 98, 110, 114,
    123, 133, 134, 136–37
  background on, 49–53, 65–69
  Coolidge and, 186–93, 196, 198–206
  Dearborn Independent and, 72–74, 100,
    136, 184, 188, 197
  Edison and, 53–54, 85, 100, 103–4,
    105–20, 132, 160–63, 183, 186, 268–69
  "energy dollars" and, 114–16, 136, 161–62
  in final years, 267, 270–71
  gas engine and, 106–7
  Harding and, 85–86, 103, 137–39
  Highland Park factory and, 67–70
  letters supporting, 125–26
  libel trial and, 47–48, 54–58, 65
  Liebold and, 94–98, 121, 128, 136, 146,
    148, 182–84, 190, 196–200, 203–5,
    268
  Model T and, 47–49, 50–52, *51*, *66*,
    66–69, 107–8, 135
  My Life and Work by, 136
  Norris and, 150, 164–65, 178–80, 195–205,
    209
  "Peace Ship" and, 53–55, *54*
  for president, 131–38, 177, 182–84, 187–93
  public relations and, 52, 55, 71–72,
    99–104, 167–76
  River Rouge factory and, 67–71, 70, 135,
    167–68
  on speculation, 146–48, 181
  World War I and, 52–55
The Ford Age (film), 184
"Ford and The Land of Opportunity" political
  cartoon, *93*
Ford Archives, 7–8, 124–25, 138–39
"Ford City," 7–8, 167–76, 181–82, 204–5
"Ford Day," 126
Fordson tractor, 70–71, *71*

gas engine, 106–7
General Chemical Company of Long Island,
  36, 41, 44
Germany, 31–36, 40–41, 45, 73, 95–96, 106,
  263–64, 268

gold, 113–15
Gorgas plant, 154–55, 159, 188–89, 197
Grant, Ulysses S., 18
Great Depression, 217–18, 220–25
Guinn, Jeff, 134
Guntersville, Alabama, 259, 260

Haber, Fritz, 33
Haber-Bosch system, 33–37, 61–62, 205–6
Haber plant. *See* Nitrate Plant #1
"The Hand of Politics" (*Nashville Tennessean*), 129
Handy, W. C., 6
Harding, Warren G., 61–63, 65, 77–78, 86, 122, 127
    death of, 185–86
    Ford, H., and, 85–86, 103, 137–39
    presidency of, 136, 137–39
Hearst, Randolph, 211–12
Heflin, J. Thomas, 162, 203
Helltown, 39
Hendrix, Tom, 15–16
Hetch Hetchy Reservoir, 156
Highland Park factory, 67–70
Hoover, Herbert, 89, 102–3, 123–24, 215, 221
Hoovervilles, 221
Horowitz, David, 108
House Military Affairs Committee, 127–28, 149
housing, 39, 110, 173–74, 221
Howell & Graves, 144–46
hydropower, 20–24, 27–30, 34, 37–39, 92–93, 113, 167–68. *See also* dams; Muscle Shoals bid; Tennessee Valley Authority

Illustrated World, 169
immigration, 73–74
Indian Removal Act, 1830, 15
industrial chemistry, 33–37, 41, 44, 118–19
industrialization, 19–20, 49–51, 92, 264–65
iron ore, 19–20

Jackson, Andrew, 14–17
jazz, 65
Jews, 72–74, 96, 98, 110, 114, 123, 133, 134, 136–37, 263–64
Jim Crow, 40
jobs, 3, 38–41, 59–60, 67–68
    in "Ford City," 170–74, 181–82
    TVA and, 238–39

Johnson, Ellen, 146–48
J. P. Morgan, 98

Kahn, Julius, 154–55
Knoxville, Tennessee, 235, 238
kudzu, 239
Kuhn, Loeb & Company, 98

labor unions, 67–68
Ladd, Edwin, 163, 164
land condemnation, 260
League of Nations, 60–61
Liebold, Ernest
    as anti-Semitic, 96, 98, 263–64
    in final years, 268
    Ford, H., and, 94–98, 121, 128, 136, 146, 148, 182–84, 190, 196–200, 203–5, 268
"Light Thrown on a Dark Subject" (*Puck*), 25
Lilienthal, David, 226–28, 242–49, 251–57, 261–63, 269–70
lobbying, 24–25, 28–29, 37, 88–89, 125–26, 267–68
Lusitania, 31

Maybach, Wilhelm, 106
Mayo, William B., 94, 100, 122, 126, 128, 149–50, 155, 188, 190
McClung, Littell, 169–70
McClure's Magazine, 135
McCormick, Robert R., 54–56
McGraw, Thomas, 242, 249
Mellon, Andrew, 89–90
Miller, James Martin, 196–203
Model T, 47–49, 50–52, *51*, 66, 66–69, 107–8, 135
Morgan, Arthur E., 225–28, 229–35, *236*, 241–43, 251–56, 254
Morgan, Harcourt, 226–28, 235–38, *236*, 252–53, 260
Mount Clemens courtroom, 47–48, 54–58, 65
Mumford, Lewis, 174–75
Muscle Shoals, 2–4, 263–65
    as "Alabama Ghost," 214–18
    Civil War and, 17–19
    construction in, 39–45, *42–43*
    exploration of, 12–15
    growth of, 38–45
    Jackson and, 14–17
    Native Americans from, 12–16

Muscle Shoals (cont.)
  Norris and, 223–28
  post-World War I, 58–62
  real estate, 143–48, 145
  Roosevelt, F., and, 222–23
  settlement of, 12–18
  Tennessee River region and, 6–7,
    11–15, 18
  TVA and, 225–39, 241
  World War I and, 31–33, 40–41, 44–45,
    58–60
Muscle Shoals bid
  by Alabama Power, 209–14
  aluminum and, 89–90
  congressional hearings on, 126–28,
    149–50, 155–65, 196–203, 214–15
  Coolidge and, 186–93, 196, 198–206,
    211–15
  Edison and, 103–4, 109–20, 118
  fertilizer and, 82–83, 90, 99–100, 118–19,
    125, 127–28, 149–50, 156–63
  Ford's first interest in, 80–90, 91–94
  Ford's last meeting over, 186–93
  Ford's planned utopia "Ford City" and,
    167–76, 181–82, 204–5
  Ford's surrender of, 204–6
  after Ford's surrender, 209–18
  Liebold and, 97–98, 128, 182, 190,
    196–200
  Miller and, 196–203
  negotiations and, 82–90, 99–104, 122–28,
    137–39, 149–50, 155–65
  Norris, and, 150, 154–65, 178–80,
    195–205, 209–18, 223
  by other private parties, 158–59
  politics behind, 97–104, 137–39, 149–50,
    155–65, 177–84, 187–93, 195–205
  pro-Ford letters for, 125–26
  public relations, Ford, and, 167–76
  setbacks and roadblocks, 86–90, 121–30,
    149–50, 154–65, 177–84, 195–205
  unraveling of, 154–65, 195–205
  Weeks, Ford, and, 62–63, 77–80,
    82–84, 86–87, 91, 98–103, 122–28, 124,
    149–50, 188–90
  Worthington and, 81–82, 88–89, 97–100,
    122, 127, 149, 155, 157–58, 163–64,
    179–81, 203–4
Muscle Shoals bills, 223–25
Muscle Shoals Hydro-Electric Company,
  23–24, 27. See also Muscle Shoals bid

Muscle Shoals Intelligence Bureau, 144
music, 6–7, 65
My Life and Work (Ford, H.), 136

Nashville Tennessean, 129
Natchez Trace, 12
National Archives, Washington, D. C., 8
National Defense Act, 1916, 32–35, 55
Native Americans, 12–16, 29
Nazis, 263–64
Newberry, Truman H., 133–34
New Deal, 221–25, 239, 244–46, 261–62,
  265
New York Herald, 54, 182
New York Times, 202
nitrate, 32–37, 58, 61–62, 213, 236–37. See
  also cyanamide
Nitrate News, 39
Nitrate Plant #1 (Haber plant), 38, 41, 44, 58,
  61–63, 82–83, 127, 158
Nitrate Plant #2, 38, 41, 44–45, 58–59, 59,
  61–63, 82–83, 127, 267
Norris (town), 234–35
Norris, George, 4, 143, 152, 224, 267, 269
  Agriculture Committee and, 150, 154–65,
    178–80, 203–4
  background on, 150–54
  Ford, H., and, 150, 164–65, 178–80,
    195–205, 209
  Muscle Shoals and TVA, 223–28, 241
  Muscle Shoals bid and, 150, 154–65,
    178–80, 195–205, 209–18, 223
  politics and, 152–54, 178–80, 195–205,
    209, 215–18
Norris Dam, 233, 234–35

O'Neal, Ed, 117

Parsons, Charles, 35–37, 158
"Peace Ship," 53–55, 54
Pinchot, Gifford, 88
politics
  Ford for president and, 131–38, 177,
    182–84, 187–93
  Great Depression and, 221–22
  Muscle Shoals bid and, 97–104, 137–39,
    149–50, 155–65, 177–84, 187–93,
    195–205
  Norris and, 152–54, 178–80, 195–205,
    209, 215–18
  post-World War I, 60–62

Populists, 152
poverty, 19, 220–21
private railcar, 1–2
Progressivism, 152
Prohibition, 134
Prohibition Party, 132, 187
public relations, 52, 55, 71–72, 99–104,
    109–10, 122, 124–25, 167–76, 256–57
Puck, 25

Quadricycle, 104

racial segregation, 39, 40
racism, 40, 74. *See also* anti-Semitism
railroads, 18, 19–20, 134
REA. *See* Rural Electrification
    Administration
real estate, 110, 143–48, *145*, 181, 220–21,
    230–31
Reese, Bert, 131
renewable energy, 3
Revolutionary War, 12
River Rouge factory, 67–71, *70*, 135, 167–68
Roaring Twenties, 4–5, 65–67, 217
Roosevelt, Franklin D., 221–26, *224*, 239,
    241–48, 251–55, 258, 261–63, 265, 269
Roosevelt, Theodore, 31, 88, 152
Rural Electrification Administration (REA),
    244

Scientific American, 169–70
secession, 17–18
settlers, 12–18
"The Seventy-Five Mile City" (McClung),
    169–70
sharecropping, 219, 239, 261
Sheffield Standard, 112
"Ship of Fools" (*New York Herald*), 54
slavery, 17–18
smallpox, 13
socialism, 62
Spanish Influenza, 60, 65
speculation, 16–17, 143–48, *145*, 181,
    220–21
steam engine, 20–21, 49–50, 92
steel, 69

Tecumseh, William, 18
Te-lah-nay, 15–16
Tennessee Federation of Women's Clubs,
    126

Tennessee River Improvement Association
    (TRIA), 27–30, 82, 89
Tennessee River region, 6–7, 11–15, 18,
    22–23, 256–65
Tennessee Valley Act, *224*
Tennessee Valley Authority (TVA)
    C&S and, 244–49
    dam building by, 229–35, 236
    farming and, 235–38, 243–44, 260–61
    jobs and, 238–39
    Lilienthal and, 226–28, 242–49, 251–57,
        261–63
    Morgan, A. E., and, 225–28, 229–35, *236*,
        241–43, 251–56, *254*
    Morgan, H., and, 226–28, 235–38, *236*,
        252–53, 260
    overview of, 225–28, 259–65
Tesla, Nikola, 26, 92
tourism, 256
Trail of Tears, 15–16
TRIA. *See* Tennessee River Improvement
    Association
TVA. *See* Tennessee Valley Authority
TVA (Lilienthal), 256–57

Underwood, Oscar, 27–29, *28*, 37, 81, 150,
    157, 204, 210–15
urban development, 4, 38–45, *42–43*, 65–67
urban migration, 65–67, 74–75
utopia, 2–4, 7–8, 167–76, 181–82, 204–5

Wall Street, 5, 98, 123, 217
Wall Street Journal, 179
War of 1812, 14–15
war preparedness, 31–37, 55
Washburn, Frank, 22–23
    American Cyanamid and, 23–24, 34–37,
        61–62, 267
    Muscle Shoals Hydro-Electric Company
        and, 23–24, 27
    TRIA and, 27–30
Weeks, John W., 62–63, 77–80, 82–84,
    86–87, 91, 98–103, 122–28, *124*,
    149–50, 188–90
"Weeks *vs.* Ford" cartoon, *87*
Westinghouse, George, 26, 92, 107, 173
Whitman, Willson, 217
Willkie, Wendell, 244–49
Wilson, Woodrow, 31–32, 38, 60–61, 131–32
Wilson Dam, 38–41, *43*, 205, 210, *210*, 215,
    223, 246–48

World War I
  economy and, 38–45, 58–61
  Ford, H., and, 52–55
  Muscle Shoals and, 31–33, 40–41, 44–45,
    58–60
World War II, 258, 262, 264
Worthington, John W., 19–24, 34–37, 111,
    112
  in final years, 267–68

Ford, H., Muscle Shoals bid, and, 81–82,
    88–89, 97–100, 122, 127, 149, 155,
    157–58, 163–64, 179–81, 203–4
  lobbying by, 24–25, 28–29, 37, 88–89,
    267–68
  TRIA and, 27–30, 82, 89
Wright, Frank Lloyd, 175

Youth's Companion, 84